A Quick Index to Twenty Essential Questions

BUILDING TYPE BASICS FOR

elementary and secondary schools

BUILDING TYPE BASICS FOR

elementary and secondary schools

Stephen A. Kliment, Series Founder and Editor

BRADFORD PERKINS
Perkins Eastman Architects PC

JOHN WILEY & SONS, INC.

New York, Chichester, Weinheim, Brisbane, Singapore, Toronto

Interior design and layout: Thumb Print and Figaro.

Library of Congress Cataloging-in-Publication Data

Perkins, L. Bradford
    Elementary and secondary schools / by L. Bradford Perkins, Jr.
        p. cm.
    Includes biographical references and index.
    ISBN: 0-471-32700-X (alk. paper)
        1. Elementary school buildings—United States—Design and construction. 2. High school buildings—United States—Design and construction. 3. Elementary school buildings—United States—Planning. 4. High school buildings—United States—Planning.
    I. Title.
    LB3218.A1 P47 2000
    373.16—dc21

                                                                        00-020591

For Lawrence Bradford Perkins Sr. FAIA
and Dwight Heald Perkins FAIA,
who led the way for 80 years.

CONTENTS

CONTENTS

CONTENTS

CONTENTS

PREFACE

STEPHEN A. KLIMENT, *Series Founder and Editor*

This book on schools is one of the first in Wiley's "Building Type Basics" series on principal building types. It is not a coffee-table book lavish with color photography but meager in usable content. Rather, it contains the kind of instant information architects, consultants, and their clients need in their various kinds of work, where, inevitably, time is scarce. As architectural practice becomes more generalized and firms pursue and accept design commissions for a widening range of building types, the books in this series offer a convenient hands-on resource providing basic information on the initial design phases of a project, and answers to the questions design professionals routinely encounter in these crucial early stages. Members of selection committees will also find in the series essential information about building types, that can be helpful in screening architects and engineers.

After a period of neglect, resulting in part from declining enrollments in many school districts, national attention has shifted back toward the state of our educational system, and of our school buildings in particular. Bradford Perkins, senior partner of Perkins Eastman Architects and author of this volume, points out: "The reasons for this shift go far beyond the last decade's rapid growth in the school-age population. There is a growing rediscovery of the fact that the quality of the physical environment has a major role to play in the future of our children's education."

It should be obvious that a 16-year-old boy or girl crowded with 39 other boys and girls into a 900 sq ft classroom designed for 28, with peeling plaster, a meager 20 footcandles of light on the desktops, and no connections to the Internet, is going to need the intellectual stamina of an Einstein and a teacher equal to a Socrates if he or she is to learn. In New York City in 1999, 59 percent of the schoolchildren were trying to learn in overcrowded schools; in the Borough of Queens, the figure was 76 percent. A recent General Accounting Office (GAO) study estimated that one in three public schools needed extensive repair or replacement, and that $112 billion would be needed to bring them up to present standards.

Yet the sorry condition of so many of the nation's schools is just one challenge in the education of our youngsters. Another is the growth and movement of the U.S. population. Much of the growth is from a record-high level of immigration. Population movement can be attributed, in large part, to the continuing economic and climatic attractions of the Sun Belt. Both conditions lead to overcrowded schools.

Moreover, there has been an overall influx of students as the children and grandchildren of the baby-boomer generation come of age. They are spurring a demand for school space as they advance in a long-term surge, from prekindergarten through high school.

Yet it is not just the demand for what are known as "classroom seats" that is changing the landscape of school construction. Another challenge, equally difficult for school boards, school planners, and designers to address, is the changing character of the school itself. Schools are experimenting with— indeed, implementing—learning techniques that demand types of new types of physical environments. Preeminent here are the educator's efforts to capitalize on the wealth of learning content provided by the Internet. Special education and other focused programs are also big considerations.

A related development is the contemporary school building's growing role in the community. Taxpayers want their money's worth, and schools are being asked to serve the larger community with continuing education, social events, and sports and entertainment for young and old.

A far-reaching emerging trend is toward larger classrooms. Over the past few decades children have been taught on a discipline-by-discipline model—separate periods for science, mathematics, language, sociology, history, and so forth. Typically, lectures on these subjects were structured around a textbook. Now, points out Perkins Eastman partner Aaron Schwarz, there is evidence of a shift toward multidisciplinary learning and multisource instruction. Increasingly, learning is centered on projects. Teams of students attack a problem using a multidisciplinary approach and any number of resources. This change in methodology should influence the design of schools.

"Classrooms can no longer be thought of in the traditional sense as having an instructor at the front of the room at the blackboard with students at desks and chairs or tablet armchairs in regimented rows," says Schwarz. "Ideally, the classroom needs total flexibility. But that is hard to achieve while still bringing utilities—power, data, or gas and water to lab benches, etc.—to student locations. Infrared technology has not yet replaced hard wiring. Perhaps future classrooms will need to be much larger, to allow for traditional instructional areas surrounded by clusters of project areas all in one room."

So if multidisciplinary, multisource instruction is a good thing, then perhaps we may well see fewer single purpose rooms such as the biology lab or computer lab. Instead, the general classroom will be outfitted so as to afford student teams all of these resources immediately at hand. Indeed, the discrete computer lab is already beginning to vanish, because students need less instruction in simple computer skills and teachers prefer to have computers in the primary classrooms.

Multidisciplinary, multisource instruction may mean that teachers will move from class to class while students more or less stay put. In other words, Schwarz points out, students studying a multifaceted project in a classroom, with all resources at hand, will have specialist teachers visit the classroom to teach the various disciplines involved. Closest to this concept are the cluster-teaching methodologies used in middle schools. "In kindergarten," he says, "this model has been used for years, by creating activity centers within the classroom and with art and music teachers visiting the classroom. Oddly enough, most state standards require larger classroom sizes for kindergarten than for upper grades. This is clearly inversely proportional to the size of the student. It is deemed necessary for the multidisciplinary, multiresource instruction traditionally used at lower grade levels."

Not many decades ago, open-plan schools or "classrooms without walls" were popular. This trend ended for the most part, and many open-plan schools were reconfigured, with hard walls dividing hitherto open class areas. The open plan was flawed, perhaps, but it may also have failed because teaching methodologies had not yet caught up with the physical model.

Other emerging trends in elementary and secondary education to consider in school design include:

- Lifelong learning—adults will go back to school to update and expand what they learned there on their first trip through.
- Dauntingly large high schools will be broken up into more intimate units, along the lines of "houses" in colleges and boarding schools.
- School hours will be extended, to realize 24-hour benefit from a costly facility.
- Security will become a key design factor, in an effort to thwart threats to students, teachers, and administrators.
- The trend toward more stringent promotion and graduation standards will intensify school utilization.
- To lure good teachers, as shortages affect certain regions of the country, school plants and teaching technology must be made more attractive.
- As voucher programs and other policy changes spur schools to compete for top students, the quality of their environments will be raised to entice students and parents.
- With energy crises always on the horizon and "green" issues drawing sizable groups of citizens to their cause, schools will integrate sustainable design to accommodate those concerns.
- Flexibility will be built into the schools to allow for changes in curricula and teaching technology.
- High-profile philanthropists, such as William Gates III and Barnes & Noble's Leonard Riggio, are giving large sums to support public school systems, mainly in inner-city districts. This support seems to be aimed chiefly at providing state-of-the art learning equipment, Internet access, training, and teacher salaries, but will inevitably serve to enhance the impact of freshly conceived physical facilities.

The volumes in this series are tightly organized for ease of use. The heart of this volume is a set of twenty questions most frequently asked about a building type in the early phases of design. These twenty questions, indexed on the end-papers of the volume, are answered throughout the text, supplemented by essential diagrams, drawings, and illustrations.

This volume on schools consists of a rather long first chapter ("Predesign") on the predesign phase for facilities ranging from early childhood through high school. It includes introductory material on such special types as vocational schools, boarding schools, and schools for physically and mentally disabled students.

Following Chapter 1 are chapters that correspond to the remaining twenty questions. These chapters cover circulation; the unique features of school design, including design process and design trends; site planning issues; codes; energy and environmental challenges; structural, mechanical, and electrical systems; information technology; materials; acoustics and lighting; interiors; wayfinding; renovation and retrofit; matters of operation and maintenance; and issues of costs and financing.

I hope, this book serves you well—as guide, reference, and inspiration.

ACKNOWLEDGMENTS

This book includes major contributions from many individuals and firms.

CHAPTER 1 includes sections by my Perkins Eastman colleagues: Aaron Schwarz, Alan Schlossberg, Armand Quadrini, Scott Hillje, and Joanne Violanti, as well as advice from H. Evan Powderly of the Byram Hills School District and Blair Perkins Grumman.

CHAPTER 2 includes sections by Aaron Schwarz and Jennifer Beattie of Perkins Eastman Architects.

CHAPTER 4 includes sections by Aaron Schwarz.

CHAPTER 6 has extensive input from Marvin Mass of Cosentini Associates, Norman Kurtz of Flack & Kurtz Consulting Engineers LLP, and David L. Grumman of Grumman/Butkus Associates, Ltd.

CHAPTER 8 includes extensive advice from Norman Kurtz and David L. Grumman.

CHAPTER 9 includes extensive input from Lenny Zimmerman of Flack & Kurtz.

CHAPTER 11 is largely the work of Jennifer Sisak of Perkins Eastman.

CHAPTERS 12 AND 13 are largely the work of Jennifer Beattie, with the advice of Fred Shen of Shen, Milsom, Wilke.

CHAPTERS 14 AND 15 are largely the work of Jennifer Sisak.

CHAPTERS 16 AND 18 include extensive input from Armand Quadrini, Scott Hillje, Charles Williams, and Fred Petraglia of Perkins Eastman.

Michael LaForte provided extensive graphic design assistance.

Finally, the overall book owes a great deal to my research assistant, Jessica Sheridan, and two young teachers: my nephew, Caleb Perkins, and my daughter, Judith.

BUILDING TYPE BASICS FOR

elementary and secondary schools

CHAPTER 1
PREDESIGN

INTRODUCTION

The design of schools continues to be a major challenge for the design professions. There are more than 80,000 public schools in the United States in more than 15,000 districts. Public school construction starts exceeded $17 billion in 1998, and the American Institute of Architects (AIA) reports that this work generates the profession's single major source of fee income. The General Accounting Office estimated in 1996 that it will take $112 billion to return existing facilities to good overall condition and bring them into compliance with federal mandates. Moreover, it estimated that one-third of the nation's schools require extensive repair or replacement, and 60 percent have at least one major building component in need of major repair.

The backlog of renovations and repairs is only part of the future challenge. After a decline that generally ended in the 1980s, school enrollment is projected to rise steadily until at least 2007, when enrollment may level off. Such growth, of course, is not evenly distributed across the more than 16,000 public school districts and private institutions. Some states will continue to experience rapid growth. Florida, for example, had to accommodate an average increase of 58,000 children per year during the 1990s. Yet at least 20 states are expected to experience declines after the year 2000.

Even in communities with stabilizing enrollment, the need for school construction is still likely to be an issue. Part of the need is caused by building age and obsolescence, but a large part also derives from the evolving nature of K-12 education. As of the year 2000, many schools must accommodate a broader curriculum, reduced class sizes, and more special programs, such as preschool, special education, and English as a second language, as well as new technology. All of these developments have generated the need for significant additions to and reconfigurations of existing facilities.

Continuing demand for additions and reconfigurations is inevitable, because schools must continue to evolve as education evolves. Schools constitute one of the building types whose built environment has a direct impact on the quality of the functions they accommodate—in this case, teaching, learning, and related activities. Thus, for as long as educating our young is a central issue in society, the planning, design, construction, and operation of schools will be an essential and challenging task.

THE LEARNING PROCESS

Probably the most important issue that school designers (and their clients) must understand is how the physical environment relates to and can support the learning process. As a child grows, he or she typically learns in different ways, and the physical environment of the school should reflect this characteristic. This book is based on a strong conviction that the physical environment has a direct impact on the educational process. A well-designed environment can help stimulate and support teaching, whereas a poorly designed school can inhibit learning. Unfortunately, although some experienced design professionals understand the interrelationship, there has been too little written on this topic directly for the design professions.

DEVELOPMENTAL GUIDEPOSTS FOR CHILDREN AND ADOLESCENTS

	Physical	Emotional
Early Childhood (ages 3–5)	• Body growth slows, more adult proportions develop. • At 6, neural development 90% complete. • From 4 to 8 years, lymphoid development increases from 40% to 90%. • Most children farsighted. • Muscle development begins at 4 years, but larger muscles dominate.	• Tend to fear imaginary or anticipated dangers. • Crying and tantrums diminish, anger can be expressed in words (often by threatening or yelling). • Anger directed at cause of frustration, retained for longer periods of time, but 4-year-olds begin to seek ways to hide it from others. • Channeling anger and frustration is important.
Middle Childhood (ages 6–9)	• Apparent difference between growth rate of girls and boys (girls closer to end growth states, boys taller and heavier). • Nearsightedness may begin to develop at 8 years. • 6-year-olds use whole bodies for activities and large muscles are more developed, 7-year-olds more cautious and show ease with fine motor skills, 8-year-olds develop fine motor skills and increased attention spans. • Nervous habits begin to appear at age 7.	• 6-year-olds begin to assert independence and demonstrate confidence. • 6-year-olds fear the supernatural. • 7-year-olds are more stable, narcissistic, polite, responsive, empathetic, less aggressive and can draw connections between cause and effect. • 8-year-olds demonstrate greater independence, vacillate between moods, and begin to sense how others feel toward them. • 7- and 8-year-olds discover some of their limitations and may hesitate to try new tasks, but 8-year-olds seek to create an external image of competence and confidence.
Late Childhood (ages 9–11)	• More resistance to disease. • Steady increases in body measurements: height and weight (girls more than boys), and muscle growth. • Have fine motor skills. • May feel uncomfortable with scrutiny. • Many girls begin showing signs of puberty.	• Fear exclusion from peers. • Prone to outbursts but try to control them. • 10-year-olds mild tempered, seek reassurance from others, anger comes and goes quickly. • 10-year-olds most afraid of heights and dark. • 11-year-olds fear school, friends, for parents' welfare, strange animals, threatening world events; are more easily angered, often resulting in physical violence, but can control outbursts more appropriately.
Early Adolescence (ages 12–14)	• Enter pubescence, puberty, and postpubescence. • Activated primary and secondary sex characteristics.	• Emotions vacillate, responses are inconsistent. • 12-year-olds may develop a derogatory sense of humor to control emotions. • 13-year-olds withdraw from others, tending toward secrecy and sullenness. • 14-year-olds use derogatory humor as defense and primary form of communication.
Late Adolescence (ages 15–18)	• Height and weight stabilize. • Girls generally physically mature by 18, boys by 19.	• Feel restrained or controlled by adults. • Have insecure self-image, may fear inadequacy. • Focus attention on opposite sex or close peers. • Feel challenged to find comfortable self-image.

Social

- Begin to understand concept of taking turns and tend to imitate adults.
- 4-year-olds prefer to spend time playing and cooperating with others and can pick up social cues from surroundings.
- 5-year-olds prefer to play with others.
- May create imaginary playmates if deprived of contact with other children, but most will outgrow these playmates by age 5.

- Family influence decreases, peers are more important, teachers become authority figures.
- 6-year-olds have many internal conflicts, resulting in capriciousness.
- 6-year-olds choose playmates on qualities of age and size (not gender or ethnicity), and 7-year-olds are more aware of social status or ethnicity differences among themselves.
- 7-year-olds are self-critical and often disassociate themselves from frustrations.
- 7-year-olds are well mannered unless bored, and 8-year-olds are more developed socially.
- 7-year-olds are more conscious of position among peers; boys and girls play separately.
- 8-year-olds prefer company and approval of peers, and exhibit more self-control and modesty.

- Socialize in exclusive groups with own sex (boys' groups gravitate toward bravado and competition, and girls' are well structured and more concerned with maturity).
- Develop important individual friendships, which are often fluid.
- Ties to family less important than ties to peers; adult shortcomings looked at critically, often leading to conflicts.

- Motivated by desire to fit in with peers, which prevents individual expression but emboldens adolescents to assert independence from home.
- Peer groups are exclusive and develop from single-sex to coed.
- Intensely drawn to a best friend, believing that only this other person understands.

- Independence asserted, power struggles with parents, most concerned about social life.
- If uncomfortable with adulthood, may withdraw to former behaviors.

Linguistic

- Age 3: 600 to 1,000 words, simple sentences.
- Age 4: 1,100 to 1,600 words, good syntax, plurals used, fluency improves, 4-, 5-, and 6-word sentences, 3- to 4-syllable phrases.
- Age 5: 1,500 words, nearly perfect syntax, fluency with multisyllabic words, 5- to 6-word complete compound or complex sentences.

▲ *A successful teaching environment still begins with the relationship of a good teacher with his or her students.*

There has, of course, been a great deal of research on how children learn, and one of the most common references is Benjamin S. Bloom's *Taxonomy of Educational Objectives* (1956). Although there is continuing debate about some aspects of this taxonomy, it provides useful background for programming any school. Information drawn from this important work is included in the table on pages 2–3. Bloom's work has been fundamental in planning the educational programming for each age group. It has also helped to move school planning away from the rigid standard classrooms that

dominated school design earlier in the century. Rooms and furniture scaled to the children, more flexible classroom configurations, and many other physical changes have been adopted to reflect the changes that have been incorporated in educational programming.

More recently other theories have also stimulated changes in school design. One of the most influential is Howard Gardner's theory of multiple intelligences. Within this theory, intelligence is defined as the ability to solve real-world problems or to do something valued within one's culture. Gardner originally identified seven distinct types of intelligence, or styles of learning, which are outlined on the facing table, but he has recently expanded his list with two more.

In Gardner's theory, all seven (or nine) forms of intelligence are equally valuable and viable. Most school curricula, however, favor certain styles of learning over others. In the United States a bias toward verbal/linguistic and logical/ mathematical intelligences has influenced the planning, design, and equipping of American schools. Yet if a student's strength is artistic, the classroom and teaching can be adapted to make art the door to learning.

SEVEN INTELLIGENCES

Type	Likes To	Develops Related Skills	Learns Best By
Linguistic Intelligence "The Word Player"	Read Write Tell stories	Memorizing names, places, dates, and trivia	Saying, hearing, and seeing words
Logical/Mathematical Intellegence "The Questioner"	Do experiments Figure things out Work with numbers Ask questions Explore patterns and relationships	Math Reasoning Logic Problem solving	Categorizing Classifying Working with abstract patterns/relationships
Spatial Intelligence "The Visualizer"	Draw, build, design, and create things Daydream Look at pictures/slides Watch movies Play with machines	Imagining things Sensing changes Reading maps, charts	Visualizing Dreaming Using the mind's eye Working with colors/pictures
Musical Intelligence "The Music Lover"	Sing, hum tunes Listen to music Play an instrument Respond to music	Picking up sounds Remembering melodies Noticing pitches/rhythms Keeping time	Rhythm Melody Music
Bodily/Kinesthetic Intelligence "The Mover"	Move around Touch and talk Use body language	Physical activities (sports/dance/acting) Crafts	Touching Moving Interacting with space Processing knowledge through bodily sensations
Interpersonal Intelligence "The Socializer"	Have lots of friends Talk to people Join groups	Understanding people Leading others Organizing Communicating Manipulating Mediating conflicts	Sharing Comparing Relating Cooperating Interviewing
Intrapersonal Intelligence "The Individual"	Work alone Pursue own interests	Understanding self Focusing inward on feelings/dreams Following instincts Pursuing interests/goals Being original	Working alone Individualized projects Self-paced instruction Having own space

This theory does not mean teaching every lesson in seven (or nine) different ways. Instead, it suggests personalization. Gardner uses the image of a room with a number of doors. The room represents the subject being taught, and the doors symbolize alternative ways for a student to enter the room and access the topic. In outline, this theory suggests structuring the learning process so that the following occur:

- Students enter through the door related to their dominant intelligence. Each access point consists of lessons, learning centers, activities, etc.

- Students also study the topic from the other points of access after having acquired a basic understanding using their dominant intelligence.

- Students work cooperatively with others who may have come to the topic through a different door. This clarifies ideas and reinforces the subject learned.

- Students synthesize the knowledge they have collected about a topic.

- Students teach what they have learned to others and apply what they have learned to other topics.

Many teachers, as well as a growing number of schools, are using this approach. The August 1997 issue of *School Planning & Management* described a renovation program at the Saltonstall School in Salem, Massachusetts. The goal of the renovation was "to create an incubator for innovative programs in elementary education statewide." One of the decisions was to incorporate Gardner's theory, which meant the following:

- A focus on technology, inasmuch as "good multimedia programs present material verbally, spatially, musically,

and logically." Instead of having one electrical outlet on a wall, the classrooms were wired to support computers, VCRs, a listening center, an overhead projector, and other such equipment.

- The renovation priorities were ranked by their impact on learning. Money was shifted from a number of typical building renovation priorities to technology and other teaching aids. For example, a decision was made to add sinks in each classroom for art and science projects. This innovation cost $1,000 per sink but eliminated travel to a special room and increased the number of activities that supported students with high spatial and kinesthetic intelligence.

- Multipurpose spaces were created to permit flexible teaching areas. Even the auditorium has no fixed seating.

- Balconies off classrooms were used as teaching areas for weather and science topics.

- A "flow room" was created to provide a place where a student can focus on a topic of particular interest. "Flow" is designed to foster a focused state of attention. Flow is connected to the multiple intelligences theory in that students are more likely to have flow experiences in activities they find interesting, leading them to invest time and effort in difficult tasks—an important learning skill.

Whether Gardner's multiple intelligences theory or other theories are applied to school design, it is clear that the physical environment should reinforce the educational program. No fixed classroom environment will do the job properly. Training materials for teachers also

▶ The classroom has evolved from the rigid seating plan illustrated in the 1915 predecessor to this book, Modern School. (Courtesy of HMFH Architects.)

▶ The more flexible settings favored today all too often have to be created within minimally renovated versions of the 1915 example above. East Boston Early Education Center, East Boston, Massachusetts. HMFH Architects, Inc.

reinforce the relationship of the classroom's physical environment to the learning process. For example, the materials used by the national program Teach for America make the following recommendations:

- An open, stimulating environment is one that invites students to explore and participate, [and] makes it easy for students and the teacher to carry out learning activities (e.g., students should be able to see the chalkboard, students can easily access learning materials, teacher can circulate easily among the students, etc.).

- Organize students [if you use assigned seating] into heterogeneous groups for cooperative learning, or design seating arrangements to minimize unnecessary talking or maximize collaboration between students.

- Many students need personal space to feel that they belong to the classroom and that they can keep their personal belongings safe.

- Because most people work best in a variety of different settings, you may want to create different opportunities for students to sit up straight, stand, lean, lounge, etc. Some teachers use beanbags or carpets to provide alternative spaces for students.

- Learning centers are areas in a classroom where small groups of students can . . . focus on specific skills or content areas.

- Visual displays are an important aspect of a classroom environment that supports student learning [and offer] a great opportunity to focus your students on their academic goals and reinforce the material that you are teaching.

The Teach for America guidelines reflect a shift in thinking about the learning process. In his book *In School*, Ken Dryden concluded, "This past decade, the focus of education has shifted back to the classroom . . . . People have come to realize again that a school works in the classroom—or it doesn't work at all; that education may be about teaching and teachers, but really it is about learning and kids; and that education reform may be for *all* kids, but really it is for the majority of kids in every class who are doing just adequately or worse."

SCHOOL PROGRAMMING AND PLANNING GUIDELINES

Over the years, most state departments of education, as well as many organizations, have developed standards to guide the planning, design, and construction of school facilities. These standards vary, reflecting the learning process and curricula for different age groups as well as for children with special needs. It is not possible to cover every variation in these planning standards; rather, this chapter introduces representative program guidelines for the eight most common types of school:

- Kindergarten and Preschool

- Elementary School

- Middle (or Junior High) School

- High School

- Special Needs Schools (for children who are physically or emotionally disabled, blind, deaf, etc.)

- Vocational School

- Selective Academic and Magnet Schools

- Boarding Schools

This book does not make many distinctions between public and private schools. Although many private and parochial schools are not subject to the same regulations as public schools, most are trying to accomplish the same mission. Therefore, it is assumed here that the guidelines developed for public education are relevant to most other schools as well.

Kindergarten and Other Early Childhood Programs

Introduction

Kindergarten typically is a child's first introduction to school or a transition from another preschool program: nursery school, Head Start, certain forms of day care, or any of the many other types of early childhood programs. In most school systems children enter this program at age 5 or 6, but a growing number of states are mandating early childhood programs for younger ages.

Kindergarten generally is defined as a form of preschool education in which children are taught through creative play, social contacts, and natural expression. The concept was originated in Germany in 1837 by Fredrich Froebel; kindergarten, "child's garden," was based on the idea that children's play was significant. Froebel employed games, songs, and stories to address the needs of

◀ The entire school environment should play a role in the learning process. Margaret Shadick Cyert Center for Early Education, Carnegie Mellon University, Pittsburgh, Pennsylvania. Perkins Eastman Architects.

children (at that time generally ages 3 to 7). The kindergarten served as a transitional stage from home to school, often a child's first formal learning experience. In 1861, American educator Elizabeth Palmer Peabody opened the first kindergartens in the United States, in Boston. By the 1920s kindergartens were included in public schools in most parts of the United States.

Historically, a child's first day at kindergarten was often his or her first

The first step of a child's education life must, above all, be an easy one. This means a kindergarten room that welcomes, encourages, becomes a friend. In design terms, it calls for spaces within the room that are large enough for a wide range of activity, varied and interesting enough to entice the child and hold his attention. The kindergarten should have a generous view of nature... and it should be made easy to enter. (Perkins 1957, pp. 42–44)

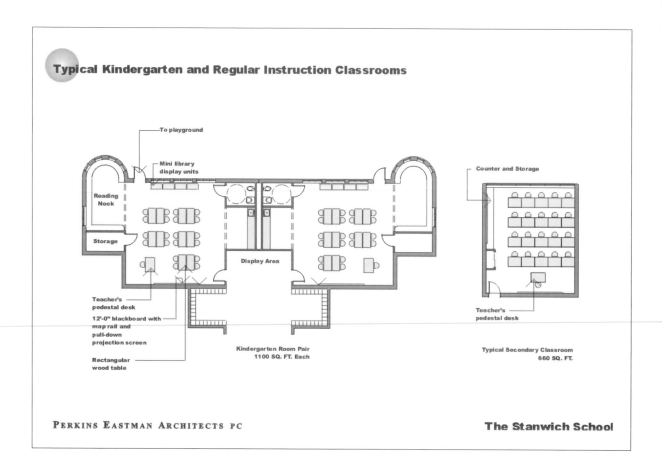

Typical Kindergarten and Regular Instruction Classrooms

To playground

Mini library
display units

Counter and Storage

Reading
Nook

Storage

Teacher's
pedestal desk

12'-0" blackboard with
map rail and
pull-down
projection screen

Rectangular
wood table

Display Area

Kindergarten Room Pair
1100 SQ. FT. Each

Teacher's
pedestal desk

Typical Secondary Classroom
660 SQ. FT.

PERKINS EASTMAN ARCHITECTS PC

The Stanwich School

▲ *Early childhood program and kindergarten spaces typically are larger, more flexible, and able to accommodate far more storage than the rooms designed for older students. The Stanwich School, Greenwich, Connecticut. Perkins Eastman Architects.*

formal learning experience away from home, but today more children have been exposed to other forms of preschool programs or child care. Thus, the issue of separation from home and parents must be considered, as well as the transition to a group social environment made up mostly of faces the child does not know. Since the early 1950s and 1960s neighborhood schools, often within a short walk of home, were replaced by central school districts and complex busing networks to collect children from many neighborhoods. In recent years many school districts began to reverse districting concepts, particularly at the

elementary school level, and focus on the creation of community-based schools. Yet there are many districts that still prefer the Princeton Plan, whereby a central school is built for each age group.

The design of schools for early childhood education has always sought comfortable, supportive, and adaptive settings conducive to a learning process derived from familiar play and hands-on activities. Specific features associated with home, as well as school, are considered in developing an appropriate transitional setting. The type, size, scale, and variety of more public and private spaces underlie appropriate design and planning.

Much like a house, containing public spaces (living room, parlor, foyer, family room) and more private spaces (kitchen, upstairs bedrooms, bathrooms, etc.), a school should create spaces for comfortable retreat, and quiet, reflective play, as well as for small and large group activities. Today the typical age of children in kindergarten programs ranges from 4 to 6 years.

In 1991, as part of a *Newsweek* search for the "10 Best Schools in the World," the early childhood programs developed in Reggio Emilia, Italy, were identified as exemplary. This system, which has become one of the most popular international models, is particularly relevant to the subject of this book. In Italy as a whole, preschool programs have been operating for about 25 years, since the enactment of legislation requiring a free education to be accesible to children ages 3 to 6. This law was followed in 1971 by additional legislation establishing infant/toddler programs.

In the community of Reggio Emilia, with some 130,000 inhabitants, results have generated international interest in early childhood education programs. The Reggio approach is built on the creation of conditions for learning that encourage a child's construction of "his or her own powers of thinking through the synthesis of all the expressive, communicative and cognitive langauges" (Edwards et al., 1993).

What makes the Reggio philosophy so appealing to architects and designers, as well as educators, is its reliance on the physical environment as a significant contributor to appropriate conditions for learning. The Reggio schools continue to refine the use of every aspect of the environment to stimulate curiosity and support creative learning. The following are key principles of the Reggio Emilia approach:

- *Environment as third teacher*—a belief that the environment should play an equal role to that of the teacher. The environment must not only be flexible and adaptable to changing teaching styles, but to individual instructors as well. The environment should at once be stimulating, surprising, comfortable, and familiar. It should allow for small and large group projects as well as intimate spaces for one or two children to explore learning. Classrooms should reflect the students' lives and include display space for projects, artwork, and objects of nature. Common space should be available for art classes and dramatic play and for the gathering of children from different classes in group activities.

- *Emergent curriculum/adaptive environment*—builds on the interests of children. Topics for study are captured from the talk of the children, through community or family events, and from known interests (e.g., puddles, shadows, dinosaurs, etc.). Teachers devise specific projects, provide needed materials, and offer possibilities for parent/community support and involvement. The environment should support the spontaneous development of projects and the needs of planned projects, as well as the demands of changing curricula and educational practices.

- *Multiple forms of representation/ exploration*—graphic arts are integrated as tools for cognitive, linguistic, and social development.

◀ *Like a third teacher, the classroom environment should be stimulating, surprising, and comfortable. Margaret Shadick Cyert Center for Early Education, Pittsburgh, Pennsylvania. Perkins Eastman Architects.*

▶ *Collaborative small- and large-group work is an important part of the early childhood learning process. Margaret Shadick Cyert Center for Early Education, Pittsburgh, Pennsylvania. Perkins Eastman Architects.*

The presentation of concepts and hypotheses in multiple forms of representation, such as print, art, construction, drama, music, puppetry, and shadow and light play, is essential. The environment should be able to provide impromptu settings as well as the specific equipment, space, or furnishings needed.

- *Collaborative small and large group work*—considered valuable and necessary to advance cognitive development. Children are encouraged to dialogue, critique, compare, negotiate, hypothesize, and problem solve through group activities. Multiple perspectives promote both a sense of group membership and the uniqueness of self.

- *Curriculum child centered/teacher framed*—the teacher's role is complex. Teachers are learners alongside the children. They are resources and guides, lending their expertise to the children. They carefully listen, observe, and document the children's work and the growth of their classroom community. Teachers are committed to reflection about their own teaching and learning just as they stimulate thinking and promote peer collaboration among the children.

In the United States the primary source of standards—other than state or local regulatory departments—is the National Association for the Education of Young Children (NAEYC) in Washington, D.C. NAEYC issues the most widely used accreditation standards for programs for children ages 0 to 8 years, which are often higher than state licensing standards. Among the general goals that all early

childhood and kindergarten programs should strive to achieve are the following:

- Create a visually rich, fun, and surprising environment.

- Provide spaces and surfaces for display of children's work.

- Provide a variety of settings for work-in-progress.

- Introduce a variety of social settings for small and large groups.

- Make strong connections between the indoors and the outdoors; above all, use daylighting as much as possible.

- Connect spaces to promote communication, orientation, and flexible programming and staffing.

- Build in flexibility of space to accommodate evolving teaching practices.

- Create a distinctive, pleasing entrance.

▲ Not all learning takes place in the classroom. Tenderloin Community School, San Francisco, California. (Photograph by Ethan Kaplan, courtesy of Esto Photographics.)

- Pay special attention to the scale and height of typical elements such as windows, doors, doorknobs/pulls, sinks, toilets, counters, furnishings, mirrors, steps, shelving/storage, light switches, towel dispensers, and other accessories.

Access to kindergarten programs typically is through the public elementary school system but there are many other options, such as child-care centers, day schools, and private elementary schools. Minimum space standards for early childhood education and kindergarten programs have historically been determined by state regulation, often by the Department of Public Welfare for child-care centers and day schools or by the Department of Education for programs that are components of the public schools. Most minimum space standards are based on a square-foot allowance per child, but these standards can vary from state to state.

Criteria for high-quality early childhood programs.

The physical environment

- The indoor and outdoor environments are safe, clean, attractive, and spacious. There is enough usable space indoors so children are not crowded. There is a *minimum* of 35 sq ft of usable playroom floor space indoors per child and a *minimum* of 75 sq ft of play space outdoors per child. Program staff have access to the designated space and sufficient time to prepare the environment before children arrive.
- Activity areas are defined clearly by spatial arrangement. Space is arranged so that children can work individually, together in small groups, or in a large group. Space is arranged to provide clear pathways for children to move from one area to another and to minimize distractions.
- The space for children (three years and older) is arranged to facilitate a variety of small group/or individual activities including block building, sociodramatic play, art, music, science, math, manipulatives, and quiet reading and writing. Other activities such as sand play and woodworking are also available on occasion. Carpeted spaces as well as hard surfaces, such as wood floors and ample crawling/toddling areas are provided for infants and young toddlers. Sturdy furniture is provided so nonwalkers can pull themselves up or balance themselves while walking. School-age children are provided separate space arranged to facilitate a variety of age-appropriate activities and permit sustained work on projects.
- Age-appropriate materials and equipment of sufficient quantity, variety, and durability are readily accessible to children and arranged on low, open shelves to promote independent use by children. Materials are rotated and adapted to maintain children's interest.
- Individual spaces for children to store their personal belongings are provided.
- Private areas are available indoors and outdoors so that children can have occasional solitude.
- The environment includes soft elements such as rugs, cushions, or rocking chairs.
- Sound-absorbing materials are used to minimize noise.

- Outdoor areas include a variety of surfaces, such as soil, sand, grass, hills, flat sections, and hard areas for wheel toys. The outdoor area includes shade, open space, digging space, and a variety of equipment for riding, climbing, balancing, and individual play. The outdoor area is protected by fences or by natural barriers from access to streets or other dangers.

- The work environment for staff, including classrooms and staff rooms, is comfortable, well organized, and in good repair. The environment includes a place for adults to take a break or work away from children, an adult-size bathroom, a secure place for staff to store their personal belongings, and an administrative area that is separated from the children's areas for planning or preparing materials.

For projects involving renovation, state guidelines rarely acknowledge the difficulties inherent in adapting older buildings. It is very important to review local building codes for new and renovated projects. Common amendments/issues that should be given special attention include the following:

- Number of exits and travel distance restrictions

- Special emergency lighting requirements

- Number of floors and/or maximum distance above grade

- Types of special locking permitted

- Separations from other uses, if in a mixed-use building/complex.

Typical space guidelines are as follows:

- 35 to 50 usable sq ft/child for indoor activity/classroom space

- 75 to 100 sq ft/child for outdoor activity space

  (This area does not typically include staff workspace, administrative offices, storage areas, toilet areas, etc.)

The required space standards often fall short of those recommended by social and behavioral research, in both quantity and arrangement of space. Research also indicates that facilities with too little space (less than 35 usable sq ft of space per child) may lead to more aggressive/destructive behavior, fewer friendly contacts, and less solitary learning and play. Conversely, too much space (more than 50 usable sq ft of space per child) can result in reduced attention spans, more supervision required by staff, and an increase in aimless, random behavior. Thus, some current experts recommend the following:

RECOMMENDED MINIMUM SPACE REQUIREMENTS

Direct activity/classroom space	42 sq ft/child
Staff support/storage space	38 sq ft/child
Observation space (often used by parents or staff)	9 sq ft/child
Subtotal assignable space	89 sq ft/child
Nonassignable space, "multiplier"*	20 sq ft/child
Total facility space/ child	109 sq ft/child
Outdoor activity space	75–200 sq ft/child

*The multiplier is applied to the program area to account for circulation, wall thickness, miscellaneous support spaces, and so forth, but may not include adequate space for mechanical/electrical equipment depending on the system selected. Source: *Campus Child Care News* 11(1) (January 1996).

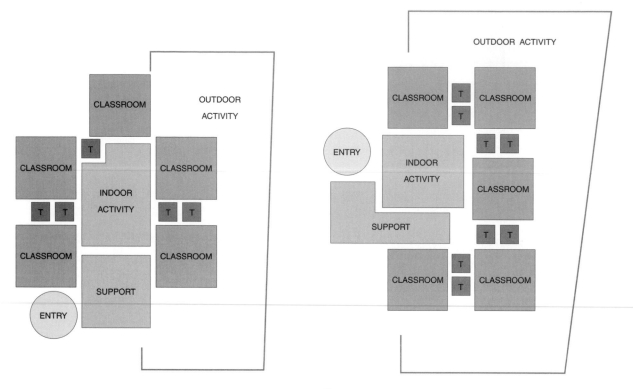

▲ Plan organization:
Cluster model; organized around open play space
Focus is to the interior.

▲ Plan organization:
Cluster model; organized around common services and corridor
Focus is to the outdoors.

Outdoor activities

The amount of recommended space for outdoor activity/play can vary significantly. It is best to provide at least the minimum required space, rather than no outside space at all. Compensation for lack of outdoor space with additional indoor activity space, in equal proportion to the outdoor requirement, is acceptable. Given the constraints of building sites, particularly in urban or inner-city locations, outdoor space may not be possible. In such situations, designers must find inventive solutions for access to

fresh air and sunlight. Any outdoor space, however small, can be important, providing release to the children, and offering a broad range of educational opportunities, even if not satisfying requirements for an outdoor area.

Sample program

As mentioned earlier, state guidelines for the design and planning of early childhood education and kindergarten facilities provide little insight into the space needs of specific facilities and their design. Following is a sample facility program,

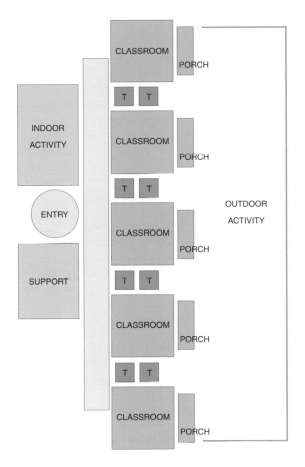

▲ Plan organization:
Linear model; organized along an interior spine.
Focus to the outdoors and covered porches at each classroom.

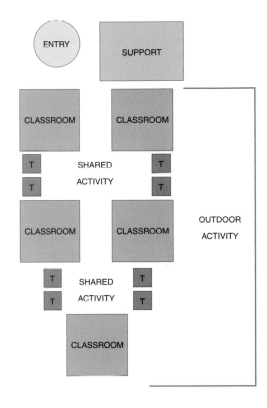

▲ Plan organization:
Hybrid linear; organized along a complex spine
made up of a series of activity/play spaces.

assumed for 100 children, and a list of typical spaces and design issues for consideration (Early Childhood Regional Magnet School Proposal, developed for the Connecticut communities of New Britain, Farmington, Newington, Plainville, and Southhampton in collaboration with the Capital Region Education Council, the School of Education of Central Connecticut State University, and local education and regional human service agencies). With facilities of significantly larger size than shown in this example, consideration should be given to creating smaller clusters of classrooms organized around shared activities that can be arranged to create a sense of multiple neighborhoods or houses.

SPACES IN SAMPLE FACILITY PROGRAM*	
Program Space	**Area (Sq ft)**
Entry area	200
Program assistant/reception	120
Administrative assistant's office	120
Director's office	160
Administration copy/supply room	100
Staff workroom/break area/toilet	350
Meeting/parent conference room	200
Quiet room/first aid	100
Kindergarten classrooms (5 @ 800 sq ft each)	4,000
(classroom area includes storage, cubbies, kitchen, etc.)	
Classroom bathrooms (5 @ 80 sq ft each)	400
Central activity/dining area	1500
Central activity storage	200
Art studio (with kiln)	500
Art studio storage	60
Kitchen/food storage	600
General facility storage	200
Subtotal usable space	8,810
Multiplier for circulation, mechanical area, etc. @ 1.2	1,760
Total Facility Program	**10,570 sq ft**
(average @ ±106 sq ft/child)	

*Kindergarten program for 100 children

Typical planning/program standards and alternatives

Parking and drop-off

- Review of applicable local zoning regulations regarding parking, often based on ratio of spaces to children/staff.

- Adequate drop-off/pickup space at the beginning and end of each day for buses and parents who drive their own children. Consider a long curb pickup lane or short-term loading/unloading spaces at the entrance.

- Adequate lighting at parking and drop-off areas is critical for safety and security.

Entrance

- Welcoming, spacious area with adequate seating and places for informal visiting.

- Large enough to accommodate small groups of children and adults.

- Well heated/cooled.

- Often the place where children exhibit the signs of anxiety over separation from parents.

- Display areas for bulletins/flyers and artwork/children's projects at both adults' and children's eye level.
- Close to administrative area to provide security and accommodate parent-teacher/administrator meetings.

Administrative space

- Located near entrance for easy access by families and for view of main entrance.
- Administrative offices as required; director's office with adequate space for small meeting table.
- Staff mailboxes.
- Small meeting room.
- Space for records storage/supplies.
- Space for a small quiet room/first aid room.
- Staff workroom/break area with bathroom.

Corridors/transition spaces

- Viewed as extensions of activity space.
- Avoid long, straight hallways; provide nooks and alcoves for sitting, play, and display.
- Provide space for wall/ceiling-hung projects, display cases for various art objects.
- Open corridor spaces with interior glass windows looking into adjacent classroom/activity spaces; take advantage of borrowed natural light.
- Avoid designing corridors so they have no other use but circulation.
- Use carpeting or other acoustic materials to reduce noise.

Classrooms

- A good class size is approximately 20 children per classroom.
- Select materials/finishes to help reduce noise (think in terms of 20 children at active play).
- Create areas for distinct activities (e.g., group meetings, quiet individual concentration, laboratory/semiactive spaces, workshop/studio spaces for art, drama, blocks, games, etc.). These areas are best created through the use of movcable furnishings, shelves, bookcases, and so forth, to promote flexibility and the individual character of each classroom. Rectangular spaces are typically easier to configure than square or oddly shaped areas.
- Provide a soft living-room-like area for visiting/relaxing.
- Design space to meet both children's and adults' physical needs. Be sure to provide seating, tables, workspace, and storage suited to both.
- Provide space for cubbies/lockers either between classrooms or within classrooms; allow for adult assistance.
- Provide for display of plants/objects.
- Take advantage of areas below windows for quiet seating nooks or play areas.
- Provide a play area specifically suited to wet or messy activities.
- Include a kitchenette, to serve a group of classrooms or the entire school area, with counters and cabinets at heights for both children and adults; include locking cabinets.
- Provide sinks for both children and adults within the classrooms and near the wet play area.

- If possible, lower sills of windows to within 18 to 24 in. above the floor, to conform to a child's scale.
- Provide ample daylight, with good shade/blind control for nap and quiet activity time.
- Provide flexible lighting levels to accommodate various activity moods.
- Provide bulletin/display boards for children and adults.
- Install an individual temperature control for each classroom.
- Install a child-accessible drinking fountain (can be incorporated with a low sink).
- Provide a toilet room directly adjacent to the classroom; consider special child-accessible fixtures.
- Install hands-free faucets to promote hand washing and general hygiene.
- Provide areas/closets for storage of supplies, games, nap mats/blankets, etc.
- Provide a quiet room/area, possibly shared by adjacent classrooms for disruptive children or for individual play.
- Balance the need for small, quiet spaces with openness to permit adequate supervision of staff-child interaction.

Art studio

- Ample natural light, with good shade/blind control.
- Bulletin boards/display boards/display shelving for children and adults.
- Separate kiln room if ceramics work is part of the program.
- Large library-like tables to support individual and group work.

- Ample storage for art supplies.
- Sensible finishes for easy cleanup after art activities.
- Extra-deep sinks for both children and adults within the art studio.
- Locking storage cabinets adjacent to sink and counter areas.
- A bathroom for children either in the art studio or nearby.

Observation/consultation space
(Optional—used for staff teaching/parent consultation.)

- Observation space positioned to observe child-child and child-teacher interaction, often within the classroom. (Such spaces are typically provided in early childhood or day-care facilities, usually not in pre-K or kindergarten).
- Isolate acoustically to allow for discussion of classroom behavior.
- Consider one-way mirrored glass to conceal identity of observers, particularly when parents are included in group.
- May be a space shared by classrooms; useful as quiet activity room if also accessible from classroom.
- Separate lighting control from classroom to support one-way viewing.
- Entry/exit should be possible without view from observed area.

Kitchen/pantry

- Position for easy/secure delivery access; adjacent to dining area.
- If possible, allow for view from dining area with interior windows to promote child-staff interaction and learning.

◀ Art studio with ceramics program. Margaret Shadick Cyert Center for Early Education, Pittsburgh, Pennsylvania. Perkins Eastman Architects.

▶ In some early childhood and kindergarten facilities observation/ consultation space may be a program element. Margaret Shadick Cyert Center for Early Education, Pittsburgh, Pennsylvania. Perkins Eastman Architects

- Arrange space to allow for display cooking; try to maintain free sight lines through the kitchen space.
- Provide adequate ventilation.

Communication systems

- Each classroom/area should have a phone and intercom communication.
- Consider locating data outlets within the classrooms to allow for computers/access to the Internet, as well as internal e-mail communication from classroom to classroom.
- Each classroom should have a computer work area.
- Provide multiple electrical outlets in classroom/activity areas for a range of equipment. Consider specifying child-proof outlets.
- Provide data outlets at administrative/staff work areas.

Handicapped accessibility

- Design for full accessibility for children and staff; consider automatic entry doors at the main entrance.
- Consider accessibility issues influenced by a child's scale (see the following section on toilet facilities).
- Provide ramps at any stairs or platform areas.
- Consider accessibility at classroom kitchen sink areas for both adults and children.
- Consider clearances in furnished areas, particularly classrooms and dining areas, for appropriate wheelchair maneuvering space.

Toilet facilities

- Include some child-size toilets, but plan for transition to full-size/adult toilets.

- A preschool bathroom should be directly accessible from the classroom and should be easily supervised by the teacher.
- Provide a minimum of one toilet and sink per classroom.
- Consider hands-free flush/faucet systems to encourage use and promote general hygiene.
- Provide a separate facility for staff and visitors.
- Adapt at least one toilet fixture for accessibility; *do not* use a typical 17 in. high fixture; provide lowered grab bars at a standard 15 in. high fixture.
- Provide locked storage cabinets for cleaning supplies, etc.

Outdoor space

- Direct outdoor access from each classroom is best, or it may be from a central point in the facility.
- Consider sheltering devices against sun, wind, rain, etc.
- Develop different play zones for active group play, quiet individual play, etc.
- Provide bathrooms close to the outdoor play area.
- Use natural land formations/terrain for exploring; trees, rocks, small hills for running, climbing, sliding, etc.
- Allow for good visibility to all areas of the outdoor play space.
- Provide secure boundaries with fencing; try to buffer/soften the appearance of the fencing with plantings.
- Vary surfaces for play—asphalt, concrete, grass, sand, or synthetic recycled interlocking resilient matting

◀ Safe outdoor play areas are an essential program element. Berkley Community School, Berkley, Massachusetts. Earl R. Flansburgh + Associates, Inc. (Photograph by Wheeler Photographics.)

beneath climbing/swinging equipment; *avoid gravel!*

- Provide varied outdoor lighting conditions; use shade structures.
- Provide storage space for all outdoor play equipment, if possible accessible from both outside and inside the facility.

Indoor activity spaces

Design of the classroom—scale, variety, and flexibility of space. A well-designed classroom environment is safe for children, supports their emotional well-being, stimulates their senses, and challenges their skills. Subdividing the classroom into well-defined "activity pockets," identifies physical spaces that are each functionally limited to one activity, but not completely closed off from the rest of the classroom or instructor supervision. Observation of preschool children at play suggests that there is a tendency for them to cluster

into small groups of less than five, with a mean of about two children. If activity areas are sized for two to five children and an instructor, they should range between 40 and 60 sq ft each. In addition, space should be provided either within the classroom or in a nearby area to allow for an entire class to meet as a single group. The following are simple suggestions for creating activity pockets:

- Care should be taken to allow as much flexibility and adaptability of small activity areas as possible.
- U-shaped or L-shaped low walls can be used to delineate activity areas. The number of activity areas created with permanent walls should be limited, as they can also restrict flexibility.
- Area rugs or other floor finish changes can be used to delineate areas.
- Bookshelves, low bookcases, or other storage and display cabinets can be used to define edges.

▶ Storage, small project areas, extensive display areas, varied floor surfaces, and other features are important design elements. Whiting Athletic Complex, Whiting, Indiana. Fanning/ Howey Associates.

- Other furnishings can also be used to define edges, such as the back of a sofa, the edges of reading chairs or comfortable seating, and display systems.
- Existing columns can be used to define edges or corners.
- Ceiling- and floor-level changes can align with centers' boundaries; it is important to consider accessibility to raised platform areas.
- Bay windows, with built-in benches and the addition of other defining elements such as an area rug or low bookcase, can be used for a small activity area.
- Canopies, curtains, latticework, or fabric can be hung from the ceiling to create an area.

- Color, lighting, other material changes can be used to further enhance the articulation of pockets.

For activity areas to function, they must contain all of the resources required to support the intended activity. All supplies, work surfaces, materials, storage, audiovisual equipment, and required power souces should be provided. Seating and furnishings should adapt to the needs of the activity as well as the size of the group. Finally, there should be an activity area in each classroom that comfortably supports the play of one child as a place for refuge or solitary activity.

Personalization, display, and storage. Providing inventive and creative ways to display the work and projects of the children is essential to support "habitation"

◀ Display wall/system
common activity corridor.
Margaret Shadick Cyert
Center for Early Education,
Pittsburgh, Pennsylvania.
Perkins Eastman Architects.

of their space. Every part of the
architecture should be thought of as
potential display space; walls, ceilings,
floors, and furnishings throughout the
facility should be used. Care should be
taken to provide a variety of display spaces
for two-dimensional flat work and three-
dimensional pottery, mobiles, sculpture,
and small crafts. The display area should be
flexible and allow for quick and easy
change. A display space should be designed
for viewing by both adults and children.
Appropriate lighting should emphasize the
displays and should be adjustable in both
position and intensity. The following are

suggestions for display spaces:

- Picture rails or shelves along walls.
  Particular attention should be given
  to corridor areas, where walls may
  become repetitive.

- Closed display cases arranged for
  viewing from one side or from all
  sides.

- Open, adjustable shelving.

- Metal gridwork or other mesh
  materials attached to walls or ceilings
  to hang artwork/projects.

- Windowsills or areas in front of
  windows where natural light and the

interplay of light and shadow can enhance the objects viewed.

- Other flexible display systems that can be moved or reconfigured to create different desired effects.

Color, pattern, and light. The use of varied colors and textures can be very desirable. A range of textures friendly to a child's skin and body adds another aspect to a child's experience with the physical environment. A number of textures can be considered: wood, ceramic tile, various plaster surfaces, metal or wire screens, fabric, rubber, various metal surfaces, safety mirror and glass.

Colors can be vibrant or subdued, but there is no need to limit environments designed for children to the ubiquitous primary colors. Research has suggested that bright red hues create excitement, and deep purples and greens are stabilizing and soothing. Yellow, as well as being restful, is the first color that can be perceived by small infants. There are, however, many facilities designed with little or very simple color to provide the most neutral backdrop possible. James Greenman, a nationally respected expert on the design of early childhood settings, advocates this approach because, he believes, the environment should not compete with the artwork and projects of the children. Moreover, it does not overstimulate the children. A neutral background allows the environment to be personalized and animated by its inhabitants. In essence, the space is regarded as an active representation of the children's work and learning process.

Light, both natural and artificial, must be carefully planned. Varied lighting not only adds to the interest of the environment, but also provides options for creating moods, supporting different activities, and learning. Daylighting may be a significant part of the education curriculum. Through observation of the sun, children can begin to understand the passage of time, the changing of the seasons, and the movement of the planet. Daylight should be allowed to enter the building from different orientations and locations. Large windows, skylights, and outdoor sundials all help to connect sunlight with the children's daily lives.

The Elementary School

Elementary schools typically are defined as including grades 1 through 5 or, sometimes, grade 6. The program criteria set here for grades 1 through 5 can also be used for grade 6, if included in the elementary program. Elementary schools often also include prekindergarten and kindergarten.

Major program elements

The program elements of an elementary school can be categorized in three major areas:

1. *Classrooms:* general purpose classrooms, special education classrooms

2. *Specialized program areas:* music room, science room, art room, computer lab, gymnasium, cafeteria, auditorium, library

3. *Administrative and resource areas:* general office, principal's office, guidance office, nurse's office, faculty room, teachers' resource room, specialized resource areas for remediation

It is these three areas that determine the net square footage needed for an

◄ Many new elementary schools have to be built on tight urban sites. Agassiz Elementary School, Cambridge, Massachusetts. HMFH Architects.

◄ Crow Island School in Winnetka, Illinois, is considered by many as the first modern elementary school. It became the model for the large postwar school building boom. Perkins, Wheeler & Will with Eliel & Eero Saarinen.

elementary school. However, the amount of square footage dedicated to each of these categories can vary greatly from building to building. The number of classrooms is dependent on class size, the applicable standards, and the enrollment projections for each grade level. The amount of square footage dedicated to specialized program areas is somewhat discretionary and depends on how many special programs will be offered. The number of such programs depends, in turn, on the operating budget, the size of the student body, and other factors. However, many school spaces are designed with shared functions, such as one single space used for gymnasium, auditorium, and cafeteria. The special program areas should not be considered in computing the student capacity of an elementary school. In elementary schools, classroom space determines school capacity. Administration and resource areas are programmed on a school-by-school basis and are dependent on staffing, operating budgets, and other factors. Typical space standards for each of these categories are discussed in the following paragraphs.

Net-to-gross calculations.

Final programs in most schools will vary because of differences in curriculum, class

TYPICAL SCHOOL SIZES	
School	GSF/ Student
Elementary	108
Middle	156
High	175

Source: Learning by Design '99. "Planning a School," 1999.

size, the efficiency of the plan, and many other factors. The AIA has compiled a schedule of typical school sizes by gross sq ft per student for national use, as shown in the table above.

Gross square feet (GSF) or gross building area, is the entire area of the plan of the school building, including interior and exterior walls, corridors, stairwells, mechanical rooms, and so on. Net sq ft (NSF) refers to the net usable area of specific program elements. For example, if we refer to a 1,000 NSF flexible laboratory space, we mean a space that has 1,000 sq ft of actual useable space within its four walls.

The GSF area per student will vary depending on the number of students in the design population. As the student population decreases, the GSF-per-student factor typically increases. Conversely, an increase in the number of students allows for greater economy and a smaller GSF per

TYPICAL MINIMUM CLASSROOM SIZES, ELEMENTARY SCHOOLS	
State	**Requirements**
New York	The minimum standard for an elementary classroom is 770 NSF, based on 27 students.
California	Grades 1 through 12 require not less than 960 NSF, or an equivalent space that provides not less than 30 sq ft per student.
Virginia	Requires 975 sq ft for first grade and 800 sq ft for grades 2 through 5.
Florida	Recommends 25 students per classroom for grades 1 through 3, at a range of 36 to 40 NSF per student, and 28 students per classroom for grades 4 through 6, at a range of 30 to 34 NSF per student.

SIZE REQUIREMENTS FOR SPECIAL EDUCATION CLASSROOMS	
State	**Requirements**
New York	A 770 NSF classroom is sized for a maximum pupil capacity of 12 students, whereas a classroom size of 450 NSF accommodates a maximum capacity of 6 students.
Virginia	Self-contained classrooms for 10 students are sized at 750 sq ft.
Florida	Self-contained special education classrooms are sized for 10 students at a range of 90 to 100 NSF per student.

student. It is also important to note that these GSF numbers are for new construction only. Additions to existing schools tend to be less efficient; furthermore, the planning of the original school probably did not consider current teaching methodologies and technology, requirements of the Americans with Disabilities Act (ADA), and other infrastructure needs.

Classrooms

For general-purpose classrooms, it is typical to size rooms for approximately 28 students. Note that most schools attempt to keep the number of students per classroom lower than this, usually 22 to 24 students. Nonetheless, unless otherwise established, it is prudent to design for 28 to make up for population growth, unbalanced section sizes, and similar contingencies. Classroom sizes typically range from 750 to 1,000 NSF. Many states have minimum standards for classroom size. Examples are given in the table at the bottom of page 28. The larger the classroom the better. Elementary-age students need to sit either at individual tables and chairs or at group tables. Project areas within the classroom are also needed, which may include areas for

science, computer clusters, and other equipment-intensive spaces. In addition, adequate space must be allowed for classroom materials and student storage. Storage should be sized for coats as well as the popularly used backpacks. Most elementary schools do not have lockers in corridors, so storage areas must be accommodated within the classroom. Special education classrooms typically are sized to be the same or half the size of general classrooms so as to allow flexibility in the use of space over time. However, the capacity of these rooms is considerably lower (see the table above).

Specialized program areas

The quantity of specialized program areas is determined by the offerings at the school and varies from school to school. In some cases multiple functions can be accommodated in a single space, such as a cafeteria/auditorium or a science/art room. Basic sizes for each of these spaces are shown in the following lists:

Music room	850–1,000 sq ft
Science room	1,000–1,400 sq ft
Art room	1,000–1,400 sq ft
Computer lab	1,000–1,400 sq ft
Gymnasium	36 ft x 52 ft–45 ft x 70 ft[1]

[1] The smaller dimensions are the minimum in New York, the larger the minimum in Virginia. Note that locker rooms typically are not provided at the elementary level.

Auditorium	School capacity x 50% x 7sq ft[1]
Library	900–1,200 sq ft[2]
Dining Room	School capacity x 50% x 12 sq ft[3]
Kitchen	Depends on food program and equipment
Gymnatorium	Full gym plus stage; combined gym and auditorium standards

Administrative and resource areas

Requirements for administrative and resource areas are as follows:

Administration

Work area	600 sq ft[4]
Waiting area	200 sq ft
Principal's office	250 sq ft
Guidance	150 sq ft per counselor plus waiting area, if clustered

Student health

Nurse's office	150 sq ft
Exam room	80 sq ft
Waiting area	200 sq ft
Rest area	150 sq ft
Toilet room	80 sq ft

Faculty

Faculty room	600 sq ft
Teachers' resource area	600 sq ft
Specialized resource rooms for remediation	450 sq ft

Planning principles

An elementary school can be configured any number of ways. Following are a few points that should be considered in planning a school:

- Cafeterias/kitchens need service access.

- Auditoriums need service access.

- The general office and principal's office should be located near the building's primary entrance.

- Specialized program areas are shared by all students and tend to be centralized in the building plan.

- It is best to break down the scale of large-capacity elementary schools by creating wings, pods, or other identifiable program areas.

- Fire stairs are the primary means for vertical transportation in almost all schools. Therefore, these stairs should be designed wider than may be necessary by code and should provide for at least two classes using the stairs simultaneously, moving in opposite directions (5 to 7 ft stair width is common). Because stairs are the predominant means of vertical circulation, most schools should not be planned at more than two to three stories. Typically, elevators are provided only to serve people with disabilities and staff members, and for moving materials. Elevator cab sizes are too small to keep a class together while moving through the building.

- Typically, the younger grades are kept at the ground-floor level. In some

[1]Based on seating half of the school's capacity. [2]Virginia minimum is 750 sq ft plus 2 sq ft times total enrollment, in addition to stack space. [3]Based on two lunch sessions. [4]Based on a three-person office with file area. Can also serve as faculty dining room when adjacent to student dining room.

states kindergarten and first grade classrooms must be located at grade. It is common for these classrooms to have direct access to play areas without the children having to go through school corridors.

- Many school buildings are designed with more than one pair of toilet facilities per floor so as to minimize distances from classrooms.

- Elementary schools are community facilities—cafeterias, auditoriums, and gyms are commonly used after normal school hours. Therefore, separate entrances, security, and mechanical zones should be considered.

The Middle School and Junior High School

Introduction

The first middle school emerged as a separate entity early in the twentieth century. Middle schools were established in many areas to provide a mix of vocational and secondary education for the majority of students who quit formal schooling by grade 9.

Today the middle school is still evolving for most school districts in the United States. The middle school experience is intended to provide a transition from the self-contained, nurturing environment of the elementary school to the departmental configuration of the high school. Students are introduced to departmental teaching, interdisciplinary teaching, flexible scheduling, block scheduling, collaborative learning, and flexible groupings.

In the 1970s the majority of such schools were "junior high schools," mainly including grades 7 to 9, but also grades 5 to 9, 7 to 8, and 6 to 9. They were conceived as the downward extension of secondary education organized by subjects and departments (National Middle School Association, summary 3).

Since the 1970s the middle school has become the more common structure, including grades 6 to 8, but also grades 5 to 8, 5 to 7, and 7 and 8. Middle schools are based on the developmental needs (social and academic) of young

◀ *Zebulon Middle School, Zebulon, North Carolina. The Smith Sinnet Associates.*

adolescents, organized by interdisciplinary teams, with flexible organizational structures using varied teaching approaches.

Much of the debate about middle schools centers on the point at which a child is able to adjust to the middle school environment. "Middle level education is the segment of schooling that encompasses early adolescence, the stage of life between the ages of 10 and 15" (Powderly, "A User's Guide"). Fifth graders, for example, are often "simultaneously adjusting to publicity, an increased capacity for abstract thought and social changes with peers and authority figures." Young adolescents are dealing with increased "size, concern about appearance, interest in the opposite sex, greater social consciousness and desire of independence" (National Middle School Association, summary 8). As introduced in Bloom's taxonomy at the beginning of this chapter, the following are major characteristics of the emerging adolescent:

- Becoming aware of increased physical changes

- Organizing knowledge and concepts into problem-solving strategies

- Learning new social/sex roles

- Developing friendships

- Gaining a sense of independence

- Developing a sense of morality and values

The needs of young adolescents as a group are as follows:

- Diversity (in experiencing teaching, curriculum, and scheduling)

- Self-exploration and self-definition

- Meaningful participation in school and community

- Positive social interaction with peers and adults

- Physical activity

- Competence and achievement

- Structure and clear limits

Because of variation in the amount of available space, differences in educational philosophy, and other factors, there has been a great range of responses to this age group's educational needs, in regard to both space and curriculum. Moreover, the rapid school-age growth in the 1990s has reopened the question of the proper response in hundreds of school districts. In 1993 the grade configuration was as follows:

Grades 5–8	1,223 schools	(11%)
Grades 6–8	6,155 schools	(55%)
Grades 7–8	2,412 schools	(22%)
Grades 7–9	1,425 schools	(13%)

This wide range of age groups and grade configurations complicates the ability to characterize the typical space standards and physical characteristics of a middle school. Thus, for the purposes of this text, middle schools are defined as grades 6 through 8.

Program elements

The program elements of the a middle school can be categorized into four major areas:

1. *Classrooms:* general-purpose classrooms, clusters of classrooms (the "house"—see the following section), and special education classrooms

2. *Student resource centers:* technology center, music instruction area, flexible laboratory space, art instruction room, gymnasium, cafeteria, auditorium, library, special use/club meeting rooms, video technologies, and exhibition space.

3. *Teacher support areas:* conference rooms, common faculty (team teaching) planning and workrooms, faculty dining room, and adult toilet and telephone rooms.

4. *School administration:* general offices and waiting area, principal/assistant principal's suite, guidance, nurse, custodial, and specialized resource rooms for remediation.

The preceding list comprises the elements of a middle school program. The square footage of the building and incremental sizes of basic program elements will vary greatly from locale to locale. Among the factors that will affect the final program of the middle school are enrollment projections, teaching philosophy, special interests (e.g., athletics, technology, foreign languages), climate, preferred class sizes, and financial resources.

Unfortunately, it is often the financial stability of the school district and the ability and desire of its community to invest its tax resources that shape the final program. In any event, most states concur that, at a minimum, the school district must provide the "fundamental instruction spaces" necessary to accommodate enrollment projections. Typically, fundamental instruction spaces include general classrooms, library, and gymnasium spaces.

In the case of a middle school, 156 sq ft per student is a reasonable planning number for a student population ranging from 500 to 700 students.

To deal with financial and other constraints, many school programs include large common areas that have been developed to offer flexible and multifunction opportunities within the same space. Typically, the gymnasium,

auditorium, and cafeteria are combined in some fashion (sometimes for two of these functions only). This savings in construction cost must be weighed against the appropriateness of the resultant finishes, acoustic properties, lighting, and scheduling for each of the functions proposed in the multipurpose space.

Classrooms

General-purpose classrooms typically are designed to accommodate a maximum of 28 students. The permitted maximum number of students per classroom may vary somewhat from state to state. At the middle school level, the typical average class size for both new construction and building additions ranges from 23 to 25 students. This average allows for an increase in the student population of 3 to 5 students per classroom without requiring new construction. Extra capacity within the classroom can also accommodate varying class sizes.

Flexibility in the middle school classroom is critical. As discussed in a following section, "Key Middle School Design Issues," the size, configuration, and groupings of classrooms are among the planning concepts most important to the success of the increasingly popular middle school teaming and house methodology. Demountable partitions may be used between pairs of classrooms. A demountable wall is one of the components that allow the middle school program to offer block scheduling, team teaching, flexible grouping, and an integrated curriculum. The integration of technology into the classroom is also important in tailoring the net classroom size to a specific school district.

SPACE REQUIREMENTS FOR COMMON RESOURCE CENTERS, MIDDLE SCHOOLS		
Program Element	Typically Required by Code	NSF Range
Computer center	No	850–1,200 (one per 250 students)
Music instruction	No	850–1,200 (one per 250 students)
Laboratory spaces	No	1,000–1,200 (one per 125 students)
Art instruction	No	1,000–1,200 (one per 250 students)
Gymnasium	Yes	3,500 (= one station) (one station per 250 students)
Cafeteria	Yes	School population × 50% × 10 sq ft (recommended) (provides two lunch periods total)
Kitchen	No	Depends on food program and equipment; typically equal to one-third the size of dining area
Auditorium	No	School capacity × 50% × 7 sq ft (recommended) (based on seating one half of the school population)
Library	Yes	10 sq ft per student (recommended)
Special use	No	500–750 per use
Media/video center	No	750–1,000
Exhibition/display	No	Standards developed on a school-by-school basis

General classrooms in a middle school typically range from 770 to 1,000 NSF. The minimum area requirements vary from state to state and must be confirmed by the architect. Some private schools use a smaller average size because of smaller class size and/or because they do not have to meet state Department of Education standards.

Common-use resource centers
One of the themes of middle school design is flexibility. For example, technology centers are not subject specific. The same computer lab may have to accommodate distance learning, interactive foreign language studies, language arts programs, graphic design, and similar programs. The table above provides the range of NSF appropriate for these student resource centers.

Teacher support areas
The quality of support areas is a significant factor in motivating teachers. See the table below for space requirements.

SPACE REQUIREMENTS FOR TEACHERS SUPPORT, MIDDLE SCHOOLS		
Program Element	Typically Required by Code	NSF Range
Teacher/student conference room	No	500–750 (one per 125 students/house)
Faculty workroom	No	400–650 (one per 125 students/house)
Faculty dining	No	3.5 sq ft per student (shared main kitchen)
Adult toilet room	No	Varies (one per 125 students/house)
Adult telephone	No	Varies (one per 125 students/house)

SPACE REQUIREMENTS FOR ADMINISTRATION, MIDDLE SCHOOLS		
Program Element	**Typically Required by Code**	**NSF Range**
General office		
Waiting	No	200–400
Secretary	No	75–150
Principal's office	Yes	250
Assistant principal	No	200 (requirement based on school population)
		600–800 (mail, duplications, processing, etc.)
Work area	No	200–400
Copy/file/coats	No	120 per counselor, plus waiting area if
Guidance office	Yes	clustered (one per 75 students)
Nurse's suite		100–200
Waiting	No	150
Nurse's office	Yes	100 (recommended if student population is
Nurse's assistant	No	over 500)
		80 per station (recommend 1 station /150
Examination area	Yes	students)
		150
Rest area	No	80
Toilet room	Yes	450
Specialized resource Rooms for remediation	No	
		Depends on function—may include paper
Custodial	No	supply/storage, shop area, cleaning equipment, grounds equipment, etc.

School administration

Administrative areas attract both internal and public visitors. See the table above for typical space requirements.

Key middle school design issues

As discussed earlier, the middle school experience is intended to provide a transition from the elementary school's self-contained classrooms and nurturing environment to the departmental configuration of the high school. School design has historically been based on the notion that subject-specific classrooms accommodate one teacher, perhaps an assistant, and a group of students for designated periods during the school day. This "cells and bells" approach centers on the idea that the student physically goes to the subject. The educational and planning strategy of the "subject-specific classroom" (Erb, 1996), in modified versions, has been used to develop many existing school facilities. The increasingly popular middle school educational philosophy of "teaming" has developed as an alternative to the subject-specific classroom. The teaming methodology

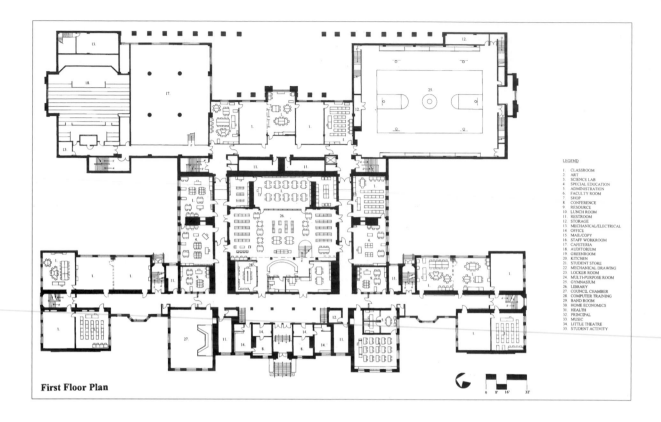

First Floor Plan

LEGEND
1. CLASSROOM
2. ART
3. SCIENCE LAB
4. SPECIAL EDUCATION
5. ADMINISTRATION
6. FACULTY ROOM
7. SHOP
8. CONFERENCE
9. RESOURCE
10. LUNCH ROOM
11. RESTROOM
12. STORAGE
13. MECHANICAL/ELECTRICAL
14. OFFICE
15. MAIL/COPY
16. STAFF WORKROOM
17. CAFETERIA
18. AUDITORIUM
19. GREENROOM
20. KITCHEN
21. STUDENT STORE
22. MECHANICAL DRAWING
23. LOCKER ROOM
24. MULTI-PURPOSE ROOM
25. GYMNASIUM
26. LIBRARY
27. COUNCIL CHAMBER
28. COMPUTER TRAINING
29. BAND ROOM
30. HOME ECONOMICS
31. HEALTH
32. PRINCIPAL
33. MUSIC
34. LITTLE THEATRE
35. STUDENT ACTIVITY

▲ *Compact middle school floor plan. Collins Middle School, Salem, Massachusetts. Earl R. Flansburgh + Associates, Inc.*

supports the notion that instructional spaces are flexible and function specific. In essence, the subject comes to the student.

Planning for the middle school level, typically grades 6, 7, and 8, has evolved in many districts to support a teaming methodology. "Teaching and learning may be improved by the design of a school building. While many factors contribute to student achievement, advocates argue that educational facilities need to be an essential part of improving education, especially as educators move toward such popular strategies as cooperative learning, group projects, or team teaching" (Lawton 1999). These teaching concepts, which foster the idea

that students may learn from one another and the environment, rather than from "the teacher standing at the front of the class," are often the basis of the current middle school concept in many districts. Cooperative learning, group projects, and team teaching are the main tools that educators use to foster the team philosophy.

Middle school teaming can be defined as an educational program that allows a subset (or house) of students in a specific grade to receive the core of their scholastic instruction from one group of teachers within a small group of flexible classrooms and support spaces. These flexible classrooms are deliberately designed to be function specific rather than subject specific. A physical example of a house includes three or four flexible classrooms, a flexible lab space, a computer/technology area, a conference area, and other support spaces.

In this concept a grade level typically is a "team." The team is composed of "houses." A common example of the teaming strategy for a grades 6 to 8 middle school is three teams (one each for sixth, seventh, and eighth grade) of two houses each. Each house in a large middle school may accommodate approximately four classrooms or 100 students. It is rare to find a middle school with exactly three grades of 200 students each. Educators suggest that this diversity in the number of students per grade and other physical discontinuities adds to the middle school experience. In its best light, the house approach offers a smaller-size environment within the whole for a core group of students and teachers to gather, chat, and grow.

The house is often the architectural building block of new middle school design. The great majority of the existing middle schools in the United States were planned and built before the teaming and house methodologies were conceived. As many school districts built new high schools, the old high school was often retrofitted to accommodate the middle school program.

Among the planning considerations for this type of school are the following:

- The relationship of the house to other houses and student resource centers is a central issue.

- Lockers are typically located in the corridor. This is part of the transition from the elementary level, where cubbies (individual open storage unit

▲ *Middle School Center, Collegiate School, New York, New York. The area doubles as a chorus rehearsal space. Helpern Architects.*

with coat hook and shelf) are often located within the classroom.

- An *enclosed* courtyard may be less desirable at the middle and high school levels, as opposed to the elementary level, where containment and supervision are handled differently. Rather than containing the school population, the design must provide students easy and safe access to the site and to athletic facilities.

- Community access should be considered in the location of principal common areas. Typically, the gymnasium and auditorium are also meeting places for parents who come to the school to see their children in athletic and performance events. Local community groups often use these spaces for their own functions. The school should be perceived as a community resource. Any opportunity to involve the community with the school is considered a benefit, and ultimately serves to increase awareness about the school and its ongoing needs and contributions to the community as a whole.

- Community use of any of the school's spaces is one of the issues that demand proper security for the school. In addition to security systems (e.g., alarms, proper lighting, detection, etc.), security also relies on the proper design and adjacency of spaces within the plan of the school. The location and configuration of entry vestibules, adjacency of main common area spaces to parking (must one walk through the entire school to get to the auditorium?), and other considerations are important in planning the school.

- The configuration of common area circulation elements should provide opportunities for students to mix and for impromptu meetings. Most new plans allow for generously proportioned stairs and landings, window openings that define a space, corridors with nodes, etc.

As with most other grade levels, middle school design should reflect several general considerations as well:

- Cafeterias, kitchens, and auditoriums need service access.

- The main administration suite should be located adjacent to the main entrance of the school. Visitors should not have to struggle to find the main office. The administration should be

aware of the comings and goings at the school.

- Specialized program areas are shared by all students and should be centralized in the building plan.

- A dedicated bus loop, separate from parent/teacher vehicular traffic, is best. Direct access for students, from the school bus into the school building, reduces the chance of injury and mishap. The plan should be configured so that once students are in the school, access to the outside common areas and athletic facilities is away from vehicular traffic.

The High School

The emergence of the dedicated high school building in the late 1800s and early 1900s occurred as a response by school districts to the ever-increasing pressure from the public to provide more, and better, education to the masses. Society was experiencing a major economic boom because of the industrial revolution, and both adults and children were hired to work in factories as cheap labor. Many parents concluded that this was no life for their children and demanded that more education be provided beyond the eighth grade.

The typical early high school consisted of classrooms, a gymnasium, a cafeteria, an auditorium, and vocational shop classrooms. The shops were intended to provide the knowledge necessary for the student to go out into the workforce and gain employment among the more skilled laborers, a idea similar to the apprenticeship concept so popular in European countries.

High schools have continued to change throughout the twentieth century. Today's high schools are still dedicated to the concept of group instruction; however, there is now greater emphasis on the importance of individual learning than in years past. Many campuses today are considered "open," allowing students to move freely on and off campus, and using flexible scheduling of classes and independent studies.

Many new courses of study are offered today, thus creating the need for more specialized rooms and often requiring larger, more flexible spaces. As a result, the square footage requirements of today's high school continue to grow beyond those of the traditional high school of the 1920s.

Space requirements

Many states have developed space standards for high school facilities to ensure equality among the many school districts within a state. New York State is among these states and requires all new construction, including additions, to meet minimum state standards, as follows:

General classroom—770 sq ft minimum is specified.
General classrooms are ever increasing in size because of the use of computers and the additional space required for new technology. This square footage is a minimum. A larger room, if affordable, is strongly recommended. The recommended size is 900 sq ft.

Views to the exterior are highly recommended and in many areas required. Adequate artificial lighting levels are critical and should be closely coordinated with the placement of blackboards, marker boards, and computers to avoid excessive glare. Flooring materials, typically vinyl composite tile or carpeting, should be easy to maintain.

Special education—varies.
Special education classroom requirements vary greatly, depending on the level of care given in these spaces and the student-teacher ratio. For classrooms that serve students who have severe mental disabilities, it is recommended that private toilet facilities, including showers and changing stations, be provided directly adjacent to or within the classrooms. A special education suite can be created, whereby one toilet facility for every two or three classrooms is adequate.

- If the student-teacher ratio is 12 to 15 students per teacher, 770 sq ft minimum is recommended.
- If the student-teacher ratio is 6 students per teacher, 450 sq ft minimum is recommended.
- If the student-teacher ratio is 8 students per teacher, 550 sq ft minimum is recommended.
- Resource rooms should be a minimum size of 300 sq ft.

Ancillary space should also be provided, equal to at least one-quarter the size of the special education classroom. This should be directly adjacent to or within the classroom. It is often recommended to locate these classrooms near the nurse/health suite.

Agricultural shop—1,500 sq ft minimum. This recommended square footage includes required storage and any computer/technology requirements. In addition, a separate classroom/instruction area should be provided at a minimum of 400 sq ft.

Art room, including storage—1,200 sq ft minimum.
One art room should be provided for every 500 students. All necessary

▶ *Typical art room illustrating the varied storage requirements. The Dalton School, New York, New York. Helpern Architects. (Photograph by Durston Sailor.)*

electrical facilities must be provided for kilns, computers, and any other special equipment. Plumbing for sinks and cleanup areas is also required. At these grade levels, art rooms are often provided for specific art concentrations such as drawing and painting, ceramics and pottery, photography, jewelry making, and so on. Each will have its own special requirements.

Business classroom—1,000 sq ft minimum.

A business classroom generally is larger than a typical classroom because of technology used today. Special attention must be given to the requirements of the school district and its planning for future technology infrastructure. Some school districts will choose to disperse computers throughout a school, enabling students to access a computer in many locations and thus eliminating the need for a specific room dedicated to business studies.

Computer classroom—1,000 sq ft minimum.

A computer classroom has requirements quite similar to those of the business classroom. Special mechanical requirements, including air-conditioning and ventilation, often make such rooms more costly than general classrooms. Views to the exterior are not necessary, but recommended. However, care must be exercised in the placement of computers to avoid excessive screen glare.

Office/secretarial practice room—840 sq ft minimum.

The requirements of an office practice classroom are similar to those of a computer classroom. The space requirement is less because the typical number of students is smaller.

Home and careers (homemaking)—1,200 sq ft minimum.

One space should be provided for every 500 students. Such classrooms often have complete residential kitchens; therefore, special attention must be given to plumbing, natural gas, and electrical requirements. A separate instruction area is often provided away from the kitchen area. Sewing may be taught in this room, or another room may have to be provided, depending on the school curriculum. If another room is needed, it is sized according to specific school needs.

Industrial arts—2,000 sq ft minimum. One space should be provided for every 500 students. An industrial arts room also requires an additional 200 sq ft minimum for storage.

Mechanical drawing/CAD—840 sq ft minimum.
Classrooms for mechanical drawing and computer-aided design (CAD) have requirements similar to those of a computer classroom. But the space requirement is less because the number of students in these rooms is typically smaller. The increased use of computers may necessitate air-conditioning these spaces.

Vocational shop—varies.
The space requirements for vocational shops vary greatly with the program requirements. Special mechanical/electrical systems may be needed for such spaces as automotive repair shops, woodworking shops, and machinist shops.

Library—varies.
The space requirements for libraries vary greatly, depending on the existing number of volumes and the anticipated growth. The number of stored periodicals and paperback books must also be considered. Some schools incorporate computer labs, teaching/gathering areas for small group instruction, and separate workspaces and private offices. Many schools provide air-conditioning in the library inasmuch as this space is increasingly used as a community resource. Because this is a multiuse space, care must be given to acoustics and lighting. Visual access to every area of the space by the librarian and staff is important to maintain ongoing supervision. To achieve this, careful placement of the reception area, book stacks, reading areas, and computer areas is critical. Visual supervision of the computer areas is especially important, because most schools now have Internet access.

Library reading room—varies.
The amount of space dedicated to reading areas within a library can be generally calculated, given that 10 percent of the school population will occupy the space at one time. For this 10 percent figure, 25 sq ft per person should be provided. The placement of reading areas of various sizes throughout the library is recommended. This arrangement will make the task of allowing adequate visual supervision from the reception area more difficult, but not impossible.

Music room—770 sq ft minimum.
A music room is often much like a general classroom; however, special attention must be given to the acoustics. The use of acoustic wall padding and/or acoustic concrete masonry units is suggested. One classroom should be provided for every 500 students.

Instruments/band—1,400 sq ft minimum.
The placement of this space and the surrounding adjacencies is critical because of the acoustic considerations. Often a separate wing or dedicated area is designated to create a music suite

▶ Music rooms require special acoustic treatment, and their location in a building should be carefully considered. Pine Ridge High School, Deland, Florida. STH Architectural Group. (Courtesy of STH.)

including music classrooms, band rooms, auditorium, choir rooms, and music practice rooms. Substantial storage is required for this space, considering the sizes and types of instruments. As a general rule, the space requirements for this area are 15 sq ft per student. One such area should be provided for every 500 students. Daylight is not necessary but recommended. Sometimes a tiered floor is desirable. Incorporating this feature will result in a space that is less flexible and will require a greater square footage per student.

Vocal/chorus—1,200 sq ft minimum. The design of this space should follow the same guidelines as a band room. Storage for this space, however, is less than that for a band room. A piano, depending on its size, may increase the required square footage. As a general rule, the space requirements for this area are 7 sq ft per student. One classroom should be provided for every 500 students. As in a band room, a tiered floor may be

included, again resulting in less flexibility and requiring a greater square footage per student.

Music practice rooms—varies. Music practice rooms vary in size, depending on whether they are used for instrument or vocal practice. Daylight is not necessary, but increased ventilation for these spaces may be appropriate. As a general rule, the space requirement for a practice room is no less than 25 sq ft total.

Gymnasium—varies. The space for a gymnasium should be no smaller than 48 ft × 66 ft. An official high school basketball court measures 50 ft × 84 ft. If a school intends to play in official tournaments, the designer of the gymnasium should plan for this court size. These decisions, however, do not take into consideration the recommended 10 to 15 ft safety zones behind each main backboard. Bleacher seating for spectator sports is often incorporated in the design of a gymnasium. The capacity of bleacher seating can be calculated by dividing the length of a bleacher row by 18 linear in. per person and multiplying by the number of rows to be provided. Careful attention must be given to acoustic and mechanical systems. Because the intended use of the space is for increased physical activity, its mechanical requirements usually surpass those of a general-use space. Lighting is critical in such a space, often requiring an increase in footcandles because of the activities performed therein. Sound systems and sports equipment, such as scoreboards, time clocks, volleyball nets, and the like, will affect the design of the space.

Larger gymnasiums are often designed to be split into two or more sections with either a folding wall or a retractable curtain. In these cases special attention must be given to exiting requirements and acoustics. Durable construction materials, discussed in chapter 11, are critical to withstand the impact of increased activities.

Special provisions must be incorporated for the protection of equipment, such as fire alarms and strobes, scoreboards, time clocks, lighting, and speakers. Wire mesh covers can be placed over these items to protect them from basketballs, volleyballs, and the like. Protection of the lighting is particularly important to prevent shattered pieces of glass from showering the floor. Shatter-proof protective safety lenses should be provided for all lighting fixtures.

One gymnasium should be provided for every 500 students. One additional gymnasium should also be provided for every 500 students, or fraction thereof, but this gymnasium may be smaller depending on the student population, school policy, and available funding. This will allow more flexibility in scheduling

◄ Most middle and high school gymnasiums must accommodate multiple practice areas as well as regulation competition spaces with spectator seating. Collins Middle School, Salem, Massachusetts. Earl R. Flansburgh + Associates, Inc. (Photograph by Wheeler Photographics.)

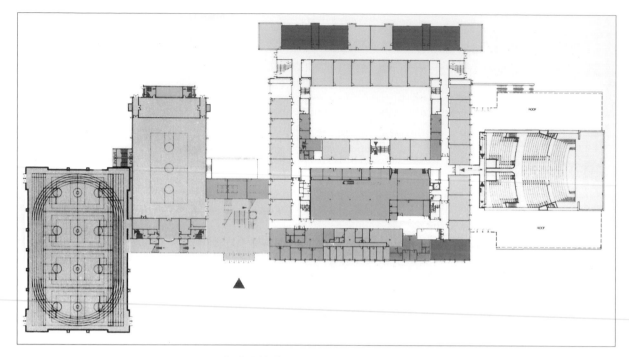

▲ Some high school athletic facilities incorporate indoor track and field areas. Andover High School, Andover, Massachusetts. Earl R. Flansburgh + Associates, Inc. ▶

◄ Swimming pools are one of the most expensive spaces, but they are often athletic resources serving the full community. Westfield High School, Westfield, Washington. Schenkel Shultz Architecture. (Photograph by Tom Galliher.)

classes and yields smaller groups that are more readily supervised.

Swimming pool—varies.
Swimming pools, sometimes referred to as natatoriums, are not as common in high schools as gymnasiums and auditoriums. Attention to mechanical and electrical requirements is critical because of the amount of moisture produced by this type of space. Separate mechanical rooms and pool equipment rooms are often required to accommodate the specialized equipment. It is important to choose material that resists moisture (see also chapter 11 on materials and chapter 8 on mechanical systems).

At minimum, a pool should be 25 yds × 7 ft lanes. The number of lanes is determined by the school district, designer, and project budget.

Locker room/showers—varies.
Locker room and shower spaces should be located in close proximity to the gymnasium and pool. Separate facilities for boys and girls are most common. This arrangement also allows for flexibility of use. For instance, a visiting team can be assigned to one of the locker rooms if it is not in use by the school. If the school district has an extensive sports program, separate visiting team facilities may be appropriate.

Adequate space must be provided to avoid tight quarters in these areas. The activity level of students before and after gym classes and sporting events is often increased. A combination of full-length and half lockers is recommended to accommodate clothing, shoes and boots, and gym gear. Lockers should be constructed of durable materials such as heavy-gauge metals or plastics. Lockers should have vents, as well as flush-mounted or recessed lock spaces to avoid sharp edges. Locker benches should be permanently mounted to the floor or wall to avoid hazards.

A gymnasium office should be provided that allows for visual supervision of these spaces. A separate office is often desirable for male and female gym instructors. These offices should also have visual access to the gymnasium areas. It is important to avoid a design that allows for visual access from the gymnasium, through the office areas, into the locker room/shower areas.

Showers can be provided as gang facilities, individual stalls, or a combination thereof. Handicapped-accessible facilities must be provided in adequate numbers to follow local codes. Schools are often used as disaster relief centers during local crises; therefore, this use should be considered in regard to its potential impact on any design.

Flooring materials should be durable and comfortable when walked on barefoot. Ceramic tile is often used; however, it is important to consider the slip resistance of selected materials. The same factors should be taken into consideration for wall materials. The designer should be aware of the ease of maintenance for products selected. Surfaces and finishes that are not easily maintained are often not maintained, which can lead to hazardous conditions.

Earth science—1,000 sq ft minimum.
Although an earth science room is similar to a general classroom, the space needed for storage is much greater. Storage for rocks, soil, microscopes, and so forth, must be provided. Students often perform experiments that must be stored for days or weeks. Space should be provided for these situations.

Biology—1,200 sq ft minimum.
A biology classroom often requires separate student work areas and a general instruction space. The designer should plan for an increased need for storage space.

Chemistry—1,200 sq ft minimum.
The instruction space in a chemistry classroom is usually more elaborate in its furnishings than the earth science and biology classrooms.

It is often desirable to provide an instruction space in which students sit at desks and learn from the teacher's instructions at the blackboard or lab table. This space is separate from the lab spaces provided for student lab work and experiments.

Natural gas or propane is provided, as well as sinks with hot and cold water. Emergency shutoffs and eye washing stations are required. Chemical storage facilities should be provided in locked cabinets or rooms. Fume hoods and special ventilation requirements are often mandated for this room. Preparation areas or rooms should be provided; their size will depend on the amount of casework provided in the main room.

Durable materials, resistant to chemical and flame damage, should be used for flooring, casework, and countertops.

Physics—1,200 sq ft minimum.
The requirements for a physics classroom are very similar to those of a biology and chemistry room. The school should develop requirements for a specific physics curriculum that can be incorporated into the final design of the room.

Study hall—varies.
As a general design aid, assume that 25 percent of the student population will be

◀ Chemistry labs may be provided with both instructional space at desks and lab benches equipped with special services and storage facilities. Nipmuc Regional Middle/High School, Upton, Massachusetts. Earl R. Flansburgh + Associates. (Photograph by Steve Rosenthal.)

out of class at a given time. Space will have to be provided for these students. Depending on the scheduling of classes, it is sometimes possible to accommodate most of the students attending study hall by using the cafeteria, auditorium, library, or unused classrooms. If a further need is anticipated beyond the use of these spaces, plan to provide 15 sq ft per student.

Cafeteria/kitchen—varies.
The size of the cafeteria/kitchen space varies greatly, depending on the student enrollment, number of scheduled lunch periods, and type of kitchen facilities required. Some school districts require full-service kitchens, whereas others may contract with a food service provider that prepares meals off-site. Whatever the specific situation, it is safe to say that 15

sq ft per person is an adequate size for the purposes of initial design work. These spaces will most likely be more expensive per square foot because of the particular equipment required. Special attention must be given to the mechanical systems, electrical systems, and fire protection of these spaces.

These facilities are often used for activities beyond the cafeteria function. Therefore, the placement of the kitchen, serving areas, and possible vending machines is critical. It is often desirable to be able to close off the kitchen after lunchtime to allow for other activities. Storage of food products, both dry goods and food requiring freezers and coolers, must be taken into consideration.

Sanitary concerns also affect the design of these facilities. Ease of maintenance

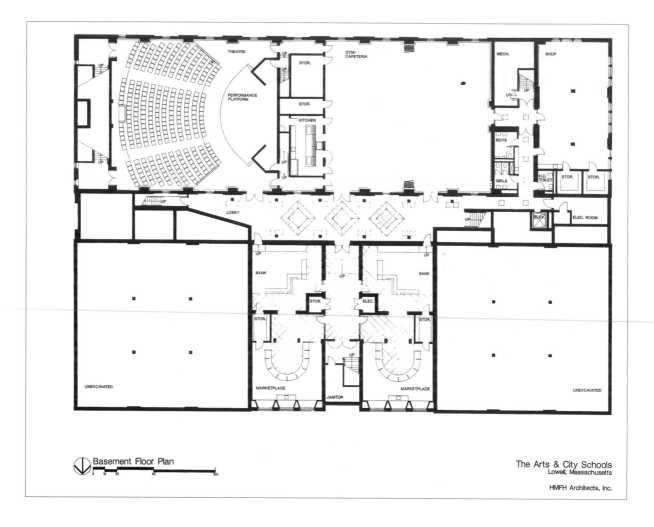

Basement Floor Plan

The Arts & City Schools
Lowell, Massachusetts

HMFH Architects, Inc.

and general cleaning of equipment is extremely important. Quarry tile floors and wall bases are often used in the kitchen/cooking area because these products are easily cleaned.

The placement of the kitchen within the school building and its relationship to the site require the consideration of several factors. Access for the delivery of products and storage facilities for garbage must be conveniently located near the service areas of the kitchen.

Auditorium (fixed seating)—varies.
As a general design rule, an auditorium with fixed seating requires 7 sq ft per person. If fixed seating is provided, the space will be dedicated to the specific use of auditorium, lecture hall, or general assembly space for large groups. This type of space will most likely have a stage. The design of a stage varies greatly, depending on the district needs. A true stage, by definition, has fly space to allow for moveable scenery, lighting, and other

◄ ▲ Assembly and performing arts spaces that can accommodate an entire grade or the full school population are important components of a high school program. Lowell Arts & City Magnet School, Lowell, Massachusetts, and Tyngsborough Junior/Senior High School, Tyngsborough, Massachusetts, HMFH Architects. ▶

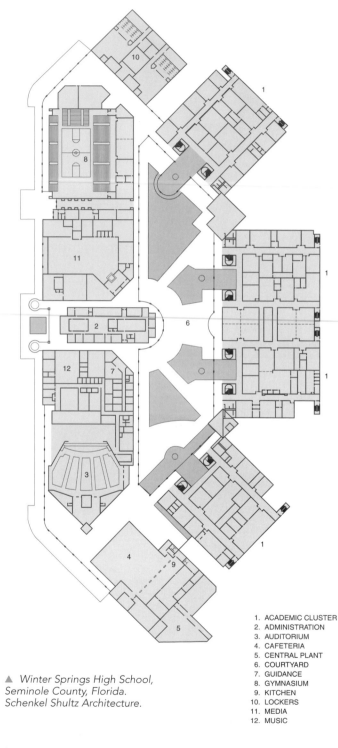

▲ *Winter Springs High School, Seminole County, Florida. Schenkel Shultz Architecture.*

1. ACADEMIC CLUSTER
2. ADMINISTRATION
3. AUDITORIUM
4. CAFETERIA
5. CENTRAL PLANT
6. COURTYARD
7. GUIDANCE
8. GYMNASIUM
9. KITCHEN
10. LOCKERS
11. MEDIA
12. MUSIC

required equipment. This type of stage most often has a curtain system, requiring equipment to control curtain movement.

Acoustics, sound equipment, and lighting equipment are critical to the design. Usually specialists are consulted by the design professional. General house lighting and special theater lighting are often provided, including a dimmer system for control.

Sloped floors with fixed seats in these spaces will enhance the viewing sight lines.

Careful attention should be given to building codes concerning fire protection, seating capacity, and seating placement, as well as aisle widths and lengths. Some auditoriums may include a balcony level, which will entail additional code analysis with respect to exiting requirements.

Depending on the amount and type of equipment included, these spaces often cost more to construct than most other spaces in a high school.

Auditorium (loose seating)—varies. A school district desiring greater flexibility may choose to have an auditorium with moveable seating. These auditoriums often have the same or similar requirements as those with fixed seats; as a general design rule, 15 sq ft per person are required. In this type of space, floors are not sloped, and folding partitions can be added to increase flexibility. Acoustical design is even more critical if the space is used for multiple purposes. To save dollars and space, a stage can be provided in a gymnasium or cafeteria to form a "gymtorium" or "cafetorium." This arrangement does accomplish the goal of cost and space savings, but it limits the activities that can be successfully accommodated in this multipurpose space.

Administration areas—varies.
Administration areas should be located adjacent to the main public entrance to enable direct visual supervision of visitors. It is important to provide a reception area for visitors to deter them from wandering through the school unattended. Security has become an ever-increasing concern in school facilities. The inclusion of metal detectors and security cameras is becoming more common. The reception area can act as a control point for the administration area and the school in general.

Private offices should be provided at 100 sq ft minimum for the principal, and vice principal(s). The principal's office is often larger to accommodate meetings with students or parents. A second means of ingress/egress for these offices is recommended for security and privacy. A conference room can be a shared facility. At a minimum, the room should be designed to accommodate 10 to 15 people at 15 sq ft per person.

In some districts, the superintendent and associated staff (business official, administrative assistants, etc.) may be located in the same area. The same space requirements apply.

Areas for copiers, facsimile machines, public announcement systems, and storage should be provided. A vault to secure examinations and petty cash is often included.

Guidance suites—varies.
The size of the guidance suite will depend on the level of service provided by the school district and the number of guidance counselors. It is recommended

that an area be provided for students to access materials such as information on colleges and other topics of interest. Separate offices for counselors, at a minimum of 100 sq ft per office, should be provided to allow for individual meetings with a student or a student and his or her parents. A conference room is also a desirable facility for somewhat larger gatherings, but may be shared with another area of the school such as the administration suite.

Nurse/health suite—varies.
The nurse/health suite is generally located near, or within, the main offices of the school. The size of this area will vary greatly depending on the total population of the building. There should be a waiting area for students and staff. A private office should be directly adjacent to the waiting area and should allow direct visual contact for supervision. This office should also have direct visual contact with a "resting room." The resting room should have cots or beds; the number included will depend on the level of service provided by the nurse, but as a general rule, there should be one bed for every 200 students.

Toilet facilities—varies.
Toilet facilities are often the least supervised areas in a school. All materials and equipment should be vandal resistant. Special toilet accessories (toilet paper holders, electric hand dryers, paper towel dispensers, sanitary napkin dispensers) should be provided where appropriate.

Wall-hung toilets will allow easier cleaning of floors. Flooring materials, such as ceramic tile or VCT (vinyl composition tile), should be easily maintainable. Ceramic tile wainscot or fully tiled walls are more easily cleaned than painted walls. Automatic flush valves have a higher initial cost and are generally more costly to repair, but they offer the advantage of not relying on the users (students, faculty, and staff) for operation. Lavatories should have supports that can reasonably withstand the force of a person leaning or sitting directly on them. Countertops with inset sinks should also be designed to accomplish this objective.

Ceiling construction assemblies should be specified to withstand the anticipated level of abuse. Metal stud and gypsum wallboard, and acoustic tile ceilings with hold-down clips, are among the common choices. Special ventilation is required.

Storage—varies.
Adequate storage facilities must be provided to accommodate the mass quantities of reading materials, paper goods, and other materials and equipment not used on a daily basis. The amount of space required varies from one school to another. As a general rule, one tenth the total gross square footage of the facility will be required. Storage areas should be placed throughout the building to allow proper access from areas that will use these facilities; storage room sizes vary according to what will be stored.

Special Schools

Today many children with disabilities are "mainstreamed" into general-population schools. These schools, which typically provide rooms for special education in addition to general classrooms, should be handicapped accessible as required by the Americans with Disabilities Act (ADA). However, there is still a need for special schools, and many have been built for both emotionally and physically disabled

students. To design these schools, the design team must study and understand these children's special characteristics. There are excellent examples of schools built for children who are blind, deaf, nonambulatory, emotionally disturbed, or with other disabilities. The following are basic points to consider when designing these schools:

- The design team must become extremely knowledgeable of the characteristics of the children's specific disability. Most special schools require unique and creative design solutions.

- Classrooms in these schools tend to have a lower student-to-teacher ratio.

- Nonambulatory children touch and view their environment and perceive space from a different height than other children. The design should not follow typical standards for mounting heights, windows, and other building elements.

- Toilet rooms should be part of or adjacent to classroom spaces to reduce distance and time without supervision.

- Travel distances to core functions should be minimized.

- Tactile surfaces are important to children who are missing other senses.

- Rooms or spaces, apart from the general classroom, should be provided for working with students one on one.

- Finishes, wall construction, and systems must be designed to withstand unusually heavy maintenance demands.

In addition, there are particular issues that should be considered in each of the more common types of special schools, as described in the following sections.

Schools for children with severe physical disabilities

United Cerebral Palsy, hospitals for severely disabled children, and other sponsors have created special schools for children with severe or multiple physical disabilities. Most such schools are designed to provide a combination of physical therapy and education that make it possible for the children to return to their families or to be adopted. The basic design considerations include the following:

1. Full wheelchair accessibility is essential.

2. Materials and systems should be selected that minimize hazards (sharp corners, exposed heating elements, hard surfaces that can hurt a child in a fall, etc.), floor surfaces should facilitate wheelchair movement, and lighting levels should be sensitive to potential visual impairment.

3. Design flexible classroom spaces keeping in mind that the children may be seated on the floor. A warm floor, low windowsills, and other special features are appropriate responses to this issue.

4. Class sizes are small, but the rooms must accommodate wheelchairs and a variety of special equipment.

5. Bathrooms should be convenient to all program areas.

6. Outdoor play areas should be designed to facilitate appropriate exercise and play in a very safe setting.

7. All educational environments are typically combined with therapy areas.

Schools for the blind and visually impaired

There are many specialized schools for the blind and visually impaired students, as well as programs in public and private

◀ The typical classroom at the Coleman School in the New York Foundling Hospital, New York City, is designed to let severely disabled students sit on the floor. It includes a mirror at eye level, low windowsills, radiant heating, and a flexible layout. Perkins Eastman Architects.

schools for children with this disability. The oldest—and most famous—is the Perkins School for the Blind in Watertown, Massachusetts. Helen Keller (who was both blind and deaf) and her teacher, Annie Sullivan (who was visually impaired), studied there before Helen entered Radcliffe, where she was graduated with honors. Many of the educational concepts for visually impaired children were developed at Perkins and have been adopted in other schools since that time. Among the most important are the following:

1. The term "visually impaired" is used because many so-called blind people have some sight. Therefore, the environment should be planned to maximize the students' independence and use of their limited sight.

2. Class sizes tend to be small and are usually set up for flexible teaching using a variety of special teaching aids, toys, and other items requiring storage.

3. Appropriate lighting is very important. Illumination should be planned to provide a high level of even light without glare or similar problems.

4. Contrasting colors and surface texture changes are typical navigational aids. Braille (for elevators and signs) is also used, but a minority of visually impaired students read braille.

5. Low furniture and sharp edges should be avoided.

6. Single-story buildings and carefully graded sites have the obvious advantage of presenting minimal challenges to this student population. Where multistory buildings are used,

elevators that call out the floor, stair handrails that are continuous along the landings, and other such details are important.

7. Most schools for visually impaired students include a number of special therapy and training areas to give students the skills to function as independently as possible when they leave the special educational setting. Many children with visual impairment must deal with other disabilities as well.

8. Life safety devices should have clear annunciator features because auditory cues are important to the visually impaired student.

Schools for the deaf

The most famous educational institution for the deaf is Gallaudet College in Washington, D.C. Like Perkins School for the Blind, it has helped develop educational guidelines for students with certain disabilities. Some of the more important facility-planning concepts and design details related to these guidelines are the following:

1. As with all good educational environments for children with any disability, class sizes are small. For example, the student:teacher:assistant ratio at the Mill Neck Manor School for Deaf Children on Long Island, New York, is 8:1:1 in a 550 sq ft classroom.

2. The teaching environment should be planned to minimize distracting background noise. Students with partial hearing need quiet. Extra attention should be given to acoustic separation between the corridors and the classrooms. Large spaces, such as

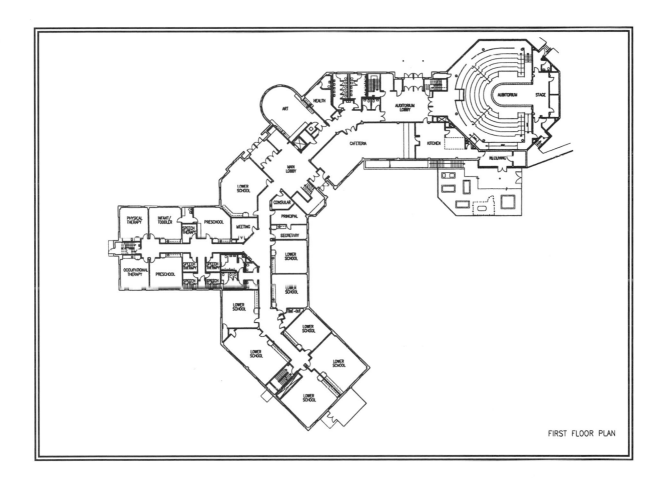

FIRST FLOOR PLAN

an auditorium, are often designed to be acoustically "dead."

3. Lighting levels should be planned to minimize glare or other visual problems because many students will rely on lip reading, computers, TV monitors, or other techniques and devices to help with their learning.

4. Technology is playing an increasing role. Text telephones, for example, have been available for some time, but many other computer-based tools are being developed and implemented.

5. Schools for the deaf also typically include extensive facilities for special therapy, physical therapy, and occupational therapy. This last area focuses on giving students the skills to live independently with their disability.

6. Life safety devices must take hearing disability into account. Flashing lights, for example, are an important part of any alarm system. A close-caption TV system often serves as the public address system. In addition,

▲ The floor plan for the Mill Neck Manor School for Deaf Children, Long Island, New York, resembles a small community's K-12 school. The differences are in the details. Buttrick White and Burtis.

the site should be planned to minimize potential student-vehicular conflict because hearing-impaired persons do not receive many audible warning signals.

Schools for emotionally disturbed children

There are many schools across the country—some started in the nineteenth century—to provide special environments for children with severe emotional or psychiatric problems. Today many such children are referred to these schools from inner-city neighborhoods and come from families in which drugs or other problems have imposed significant emotional strain

on them. As a result, the many schools developed initially for orphans or other children in need have adapted their programs to serve emotionally disturbed children. Among the key design issues are the following:

1. These facilities typically include supervised housing and mental health and therapy spaces as well as traditional school spaces.

2. The class sizes are typically small and the rooms flexible. Quiet rooms and other features may be part of the program.

3. The facilities must be robust and able to withstand heavy use.

▼ The design of the new building at the Green Chimneys School for emotionally disturbed children reflects the school's farm theme. Animals are an important part of the children's education and therapy. Perkins Eastman Architects.

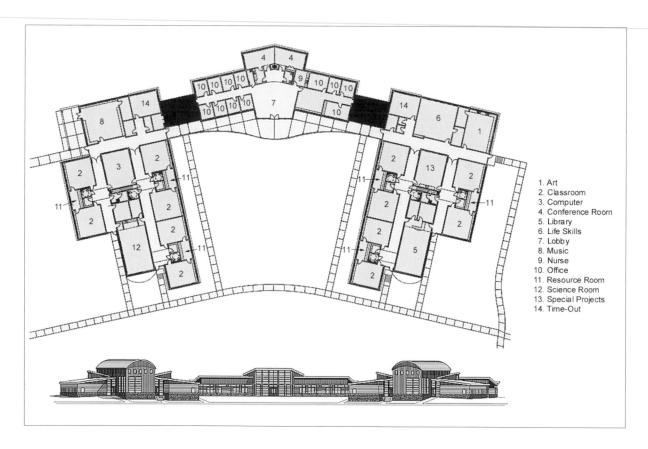

1. Art
2. Classroom
3. Computer
4. Conference Room
5. Library
6. Life Skills
7. Lobby
8. Music
9. Nurse
10. Office
11. Resource Room
12. Science Room
13. Special Projects
14. Time-Out

4. Some schools have a special character, such as a farm setting, which is integrated into the program.

5. Some areas may have to have special security features built in, but a noninstitutional character is usually a priority.

6. Outdoor activity areas may be a particularly important part of the program.

Vocational Schools

Vocational schools are most often found today in large urban school districts. In most secondary schools, vocational education is a department within the school. The old home economics and shop areas are rapidly changing in favor of more contemporary trades and occupations, many of them computer aided. Moreover, several trends have made dedicated vocational schools a less popular school type.

• The division between industrial and academic skills has eroded. Today's workplace requires more academic skill to deal with technology and more technology in academic curricula.

• Many vocational courses are now offered at community colleges and by a wide variety of for-profit providers.

• Some vocational programs—such as those providing the technical skills required in science, medicine, etc.— require interdisciplinary training.

In general, these trends mean that vocational programs should not be isolated. Instead, they should be integrated into a broader secondary school curriculum.

Vocational high schools were a common building type in earlier decades. Their numbers have diminished, but they remain an important educational resource for children who are best served by less academic and more career-specific educational programs.

Selective Academic High School and Magnet Schools

Selective academic and magnet schools have been created by public school districts for a wide variety of reasons:

• To offer specialized facilities and instruction to gifted children

• To combine a critical mass of facilities and resources so as to provide a specialized program too costly to be offered in more than one facility

• To create a school that will attract students from various neighborhoods so as to achieve better racial or geographic balance in a school system.

New York City was one of the first to establish such schools, including high schools for gifted children: Stuyvesant High School, the Bronx High School of Science, and La Guardia High School of Music and Art and Performing Arts.

Boarding Schools

There are more than 200 boarding schools in the United States today. These can be coed or single-sex schools and can have a special focus, such as specialized academic, military, or international schools. Most boarding schools serve children in their high school years, but there are also junior boarding schools for children in elementary and middle school grades. Many are more than 100 years old, located on large campuses with hundreds of acres, elaborate facilities, and distinctive atmospheres.

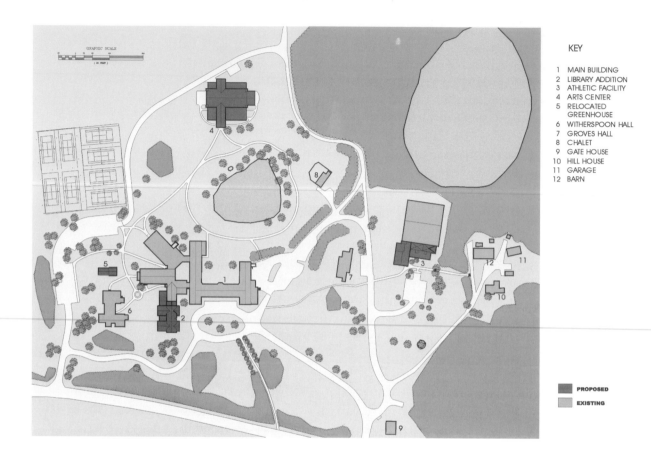

KEY

1 MAIN BUILDING
2 LIBRARY ADDITION
3 ATHLETIC FACILITY
4 ARTS CENTER
5 RELOCATED
  GREENHOUSE
6 WITHERSPOON HALL
7 GROVES HALL
8 CHALET
9 GATE HOUSE
10 HILL HOUSE
11 GARAGE
12 BARN

PROPOSED

EXISTING

▲ *Some boarding schools, such as Miss Hall's in Pittsfield, Massachusetts, by Perkins Eastman Architects, are small campuses with a few buildings, whereas others, such as Philips Andover (see page 62), resemble small college campuses.*

The planning standards and guidelines for these schools are very different from those of public schools for several reasons. Generally, the curriculum is independent and not subject to state requirements; nevertheless, a school may subscribe to a particular association that requires member schools to meet certain criteria for accreditation. In a boarding school, class size usually is smaller, the curriculum can be more diverse, and there is often a much stronger program of athletics and extracurricular activities.

Moreover, the school must provide the elements of a home.

There can be a large disparity between the facilities at different boarding schools. Some may have well-funded facilities that are comparable to those of a small college. Funding for capital projects typically is generated by the alumni through capital campaigns.

Space standards are nonexistent for boarding schools. Planning for such a facility requires detailed analysis of the mission, history, strengths, and focus of the school. Boarding schools compete with each other for students. Most fill a particular niche, which makes them attractive to their target markets. The image of the school is very important to both parents and alumni. A strong determinant in assessing programmatic need can be an evaluation of how a school's facilities compare with those of its peer institutions.

As a 24-hour community, the school must also serve as home and extended family to its students. Faculty are often encouraged to live on campus and to eat meals together with the students. The faculty can be instructors during the day, coaches in the afternoon, and monitors on weekends and evenings. There are often extensive community service programs, as well as many weekend and evening activities.

Classrooms and laboratories

Boarding schools generally have all the specialized classrooms and classroom laboratories that can be found in a public school, including science labs; music and practice rooms; art, photography, and ceramics rooms. Classrooms often reflect a smaller class size. Classes of 8 to 16 students are not uncommon, and instructors often use a seminar format. Depending on the size and niche of the school, there may be a separate building for a particular discipline, such as art or science, and additional specialized rooms for teaching unique classes. Faculty offices and lounges should be located convenient to the classrooms.

Library

The school library or media center is usually a major focal element and often very important to the image of the school. The library typically has a distinctive

appearance and is prominently located on the campus. Boarding school libraries tend to be much larger than those of public schools because the collections are often much more extensive. Seating should accommodate a significant percentage of the school population, as the library is often heavily used for evening study hall. The library should include an office for the librarian and a circulation desk, and often incorporates seminar rooms and small group study rooms. Adequate space should be wired for research via computers with Internet connections and other technology.

Academic support center

The academic support center is a unit of the school that provides tutoring to help students who need additional learning support in a particular area. It often includes a drop-in center, where students can work with limited support without having a scheduled session, as well as offices where counselors can provide one-on-one assistance. The academic support center is often incorporated adjacent to the library area so that it can share resources.

Technology center

Where provided, a technology center should include a laboratory that can accommodate a large class for group computer instruction, as well as allow independent use. Typically, a room should be arranged with students facing a large monitor or a screen operated by a liquid crystal display (LCD) projector that the instructor can manipulate. The desks or tables should be arranged in a manner that permits instructor to move about the room and provide assistance to students who require it. Some instructors prefer a flexible desk arrangement that allows desks to be reconfigured in small groupings or other arrangements. In addition, the center should house office space for the technology director and staff, as well as storage space for software and hardware. Often a second laboratory or area is also included, with several terminals for tutoring or use when a class is in session in the main lab.

College counseling

Most schools include a room or suite of rooms where a counselor can help students select colleges and prepare application materials. These areas contain a library for catalogs and reference materials, and should be outfitted with computer and video terminals. A small conference area that college representatives can use for presentations and interviews is often provided.

Study hall

Many boarding schools have a mandatory evening study hall for some or all grade levels. Study hall can be held in the library, dining room, or other classroom space. Consideration must be given to nighttime illumination of these spaces.

Athletic facilities

Athletic facilities at boarding schools are often much more extensive than those at typical public schools. Athletics are often mandatory, daily after-school activities, that engage the entire student body during the same time period. Depending on the season and the sport, students become part of an in-school team for the sport they select. There is often a diversity of programs, such as dance, tennis, fitness, karate, golf, ice hockey, horseback riding, and swimming, to accommodate the student body's population and interests. These simultaneous activities

place significant demand on sports facilities. Spring and fall sports are often played outdoors, requiring adequate land for fields and courts.

Housing

Dormitories are often arranged by grade. Most schools prefer a mix of predominately double rooms with some single rooms. Common lounge facilities should be located centrally within a building or on each floor. Toilet facilities are typically ganged. Faculty apartments are often included in a dormitory for convenience in providing supervision and counseling. Some schools wire dorm rooms for technology, others prefer to have students use the school's common computers. The latter preference is becoming more standard with the use of laptop computers and the decreasing costs of hardware. Related facilities include a laundry for linens (sometimes contracted out) as well as coin-operated laundry facilities for students to wash their clothing.

Boarding schools typically include an infirmary within one dorm or as a freestanding building. The number of beds and toilet facilities are a function of the school's population, and there is often a residence for the attending nurse.

Incorporating faculty housing on campus is an important goal of many schools. This arrangement aids in retention of faculty and creates a feeling of community and security that is important to students and their families. There typically is a large home for the head of school that is also used for receptions and special activities, freestanding homes for faculty with families, and staff apartments in the dorms or other buildings.

Other facilities

Theater.

Drama production can be a major after-school activity at many schools. Depending on the preference of the school, performances may be given in a theater with fixed seating and a formal stage or in a black box theater. Provisions should be made for adequate lobby and support areas such as scenery workshop, prop and costume storage, dressing room and toilets.

Depending on the type of theater, it is often supplemented by a large flat-floor assembly space to gather the student body in one location for morning meetings and dances (often with students from other schools). Sometimes this space is created in an old chapel or even in the dining hall.

Board room.

All boarding schools need a suitable conference room for board of directors meetings and work sessions.

Art gallery.

Most schools have a gallery or dedicated exhibition space for displaying students' work. Some schools may also have a more formal gallery for traveling exhibitions. Depending on the nature of the gallery, issues of security, climate control, and flexible lighting should be considered. The school gallery should be centrally located and convenient for visitors.

Student center.

The student center is a lounge that serves as a place for students to spend time and socialize between classes and on weekends. This space is often furnished with comfortable seating, stereo equipment, large TV, and games such as pool or board games. It should be centrally located and convenient to classrooms and dormitories.

Dining room.

Most schools have a centrally located dining room serving three meals day to students, faculty, and staff. Buffet-style serving lines are typical, rather than table service, for most meals. Many schools want the room to be able to accommodate the entire student body at one sitting. The dining room is often part of the main building and convenient to both dormitories and classrooms. Adequate space should be provided for the servery, kitchen, and support areas.

Administrative and support areas.

A boarding school usually has several administration spaces in addition to those found in a typical public school:

- *Development offices.* A school's development office often plays a large part in maintaining alumni relations and raising funds for endowment and capital projects. This department is often located in a separate building on campus.

- *Admissions suite.* The admissions suite is often prospective students and their families' first impression. It is important to have a space that is prominently located and that creates a good impression of the school.

- *Administration.* The office of the head of school and his or her support staff, the monitors' office, the switchboard, and other administrative functions that deal directly with the students on a daily basis should be centrally located and are often found in the main academic building. The business office component can be more remotely located.

▶ *Philips Academy, Andover, Massachusetts.*

Archives.

Boarding schools often maintain fairly extensive documentation for historical purposes, including transcripts, students' files, old business records, and memorabilia. Dry, heated, secure space should be provided for these collections.

Buildings and grounds

All schools require spaces to house school laundry services, staff lockers, various workshops, and storage for furniture and equipment. Garages are required to store and maintain the school's maintenance vehicles and the vans or buses used to transport students to athletic and social events.

Adequate parking should be provided for faculty, visitors, and staff. Schools often have a policy of no cars for boarders, but day students may bring vehicles on campus. Parking for major events like graduation or theater productions may often be handled with overflow lots on lawns and fields to minimize the need for paved areas.

▲ LEGO Child Care Center, Enfield, Connecticut. Center offers both developmental and custodial care for children during their Lego years—ages 5 to 12—and is separated into four areas by age group. Jeter Cook & Jepson Architects, Inc. Photo: Nick Wheeler/Wheeler Photographics.

▶ Sunderland Elementary School, Sunderland, Massachusetts. This is not only a school but a civic center large enough to accommodate town meetings. Two main roads intersect at the bell tower. Kindergarten areas are broken up into two "houses" to ease children's transition pains from home to school. Earl R. Flansburgh + Associates, Inc., architects. Photo: Wheeler Photographics.

▲ Short Pump Middle School, Richmond, Virginia. The school is made up of two pavilions, each arranged in pinwheel fashion around a support core. Building accommodates 1200 students in grades 6 to 8, and serves as a community center after school hours. Earl R. Flansburgh + Associates, Inc., architects.

▼ Celebration School, Celebration, Florida. School is high-tech, but its looks reflect the neotraditional forms and colors of nearby Celebration town center as well as the ecology of its central Florida wetlands site. Its Disney-derived Imagineering lab teaches 3D animation. William Rawn Associates and Schenkel Shultz Architecture.

▲ Broward County School Prototype, Broward County, Florida. The 88,000 sq ft elementary school, together with an 18,000 sq ft preschool and exceptional educational center, may be built in up to 12 locations. Design is flexible to meet the demands of a variety of sites. Local school enrollments have soared because of a daily influx of 1000 persons into Broward County. Schwab, Twitty & Hanser Architectural Group, Inc.

▲ Manhattan Beach Middle School, Manhattan Beach, California. Placing a 1200-student high school on the site of a former elementary school led to a multistory building with open courts and arranged in three academic "villages," one per grade. Each village has an outdoor classroom to take advantage of the balmy climate. HMC Architects.

▶ Child Guidance Center, Stamford, Connecticut. The center, located in an older residential section, houses counseling offices, meeting rooms, and administrative space. Traditional paned windows, concrete block quoins, and pitched roof respect the neighborhood and make for a nonintimidating environment. Perkins Eastman Architects PC. Photo: Martin Tornallayay Associates.

▲ *Perry Community Education Village, Perry, Ohio.*
The village comprises a K-4 school, a school for
grades 5-8, a high school, and a phys ed/community
fitness center—all located on a 162-acre site rich in
mature trees, creeks, and ravines. One ravine
separates the earlier and the later grades. Buildings
are arranged around formal courtyards and include
a 850-seat theater. Perkins & Will, associated with
Burgess & Niple Ltd., architects. Photo:
Hedrich/Blessing.

▲ North Fort Myers High School, Fort Myers, Florida. Open corridor responds to the warm, breezy climate of southwest Florida, as do covered walkways, terraces, and canopied entryways. New classroom building replaces outdated facilities by incorporating three existing structures into a new 1600-student magnet high school. Perkins & Will, architects.

▲ Troy High School, Troy, Michigan. Entrance to 2100-student, 300,000 sq ft school is marked by a tower (center). Classroom wings overlook woods. The school is a strong expression of community pride. Perkins & Will, architects. Photo: Hedrich/Blessing.

▲ Desert View Elementary School, Sunland Park, New Mexico. The school's design reflects regional influences. Simple materials, such as green-painted bar joists, pastel colored concrete block, and canvas awnings, are combined in a budget-conscious prototype school, offering protection from the arid climate. This is one of three identical schools built 400 yards apart to keep scales small. Each school houses two grades. Perkins & Will with Mimbres, Inc., associated architects. Photo: Robert Reck.

▲ Prototype School, New York, New York. One of several schools built from a site-adapted assemblage of a predesigned kit of parts. Perkins & Will, architects. Photo: Chuck Choi.

CHAPTER 2
CIRCULATION

DESIGN CONCEPTS

The organizational strategies that designers utilize for schools must take numerous factors into consideration. Adjacencies between school program elements are determined by the following major factors:

Entry sequence. How do students enter school each day, and where do they go? Do they immediately report to a homeroom, or do they first gather in a larger area such as the gym or the cafeteria? How do staff and faculty enter the building? How does the public enter the building during the school day? Is central administration the security checkpoint? How does the public enter the building for community events?

Internal circulation. During the school day, where do students have to go, and how often? Do they travel the corridors as a class, such as in elementary school, while other classes are in session? Do they travel individually at each class period, such as in the upper grades? How much time is allotted between periods, and how far are the distances? How are student lockers used and distributed in the school?

School size. How large is the school's enrollment? Is there a need to create subgroupings within the building to mitigate the anonymity created in

facilities with large enrollments? If subgrouping is a goal, what is the differentiating factor for grouping: by grade level, full-grade groupings such as "houses," by different magnet programs, or by other elements?

Teaching methodologies. What are the teaching methodologies employed? Is there a magnet or multiple magnet program? Is there a team teaching approach?

Efficiency/cost. The amount of corridor space needed to serve each room in the building is a major component in the determination of building efficiency and resultant costs. Different organizational strategies yield varying efficiencies.

Natural light. Almost all spaces in a school building can benefit from some amount of natural light. The light requirements for many rooms are established by local codes and regulations.

Site access. Many spaces, including classrooms for lower age groups, benefit from direct site access.

BUILDING CONFIGURATIONS

The number of possible building configurations for schools is almost limitless. Nonetheless, most of these various configurations can be synthesized into a few simple partis (basic spatial organizatons). Site-specific issues (such as

---

The corridor is the school's thoroughfare. But shouldn't it be a pleasant avenue, not a forbidding tunnel? Physically, the corridor is a space for people moving from room to room. Psychologically, it can be a place for refreshment of the mind, for unwinding and relaxation and for pleasant socializing. (Perkins 1957, p. 15)

---

site size, topography, orientation, natural features, etc.) and/or the designers' intent to create specific forms can mold these basic parti models into more idiosyncratic solutions. A few of the most common partis used in school design are discussed in the following paragraphs.

Centralized resources with double-loaded classroom wings. This is probably the most fundamental building form. The essence of this concept is the centralization of all shared resources, from auditorium and gymnasium to school administration. Centralization of these functions minimizes travel distances from classrooms. This concept is readily used with elementary schools, where shared facilities are typically less in quantity and sophistication than they are for the upper grades. In addition, by dividing the classrooms into at least two wings, natural subgroupings within the school emerge, which may be a desired goal in schools with large populations or wide

grade ranges. A common architectural variation on this concept pulls together the more architecturally interesting common spaces to act as a visual centerpiece, with the more neutral classroom wings as a backdrop.

Dumbbell double-loaded classroom wings. In lieu of centralizing resources, this basic concept places shared resources at either end of a double-loaded classroom corridor. This model is efficient, but suffers from long travel distances from classrooms to resources and fewer spatial opportunities for creating subgroupings within the school.

Spine with double-loaded classroom wings. In this model, double-loaded classroom wings are organized perpendicular to (or off) a "main street" corridor spine. The shared resources of the school are also located along this main street. This model begins to maximize subgroups of classrooms within the overall school. The placement of these

▶ *The centralized resource plan.*

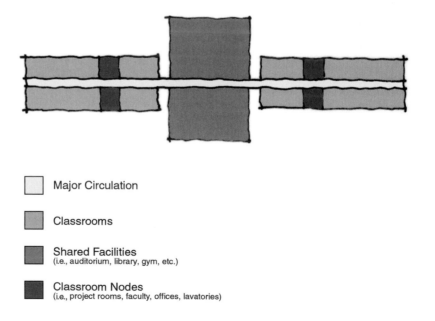

Major Circulation

Classrooms

Shared Facilities
(i.e., auditorium, library, gym, etc.)

Classroom Nodes
(i.e., project rooms, faculty, offices, lavatories)

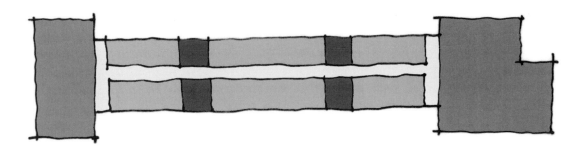

▲ *The dumbbell plan.*

building blocks along the main spine allows the designer to form outdoor spaces for quiet courtyards, project areas, play areas, and the like.

Courtyard with double-loaded classroom wings. The courtyard model is widely used in school design. Many large schools have been organized around a series of courtyards. Courtyards allow for secure open areas, which can be programmed for reading areas, science project areas, and other academic supportive functions. In courtyard design special care must to be taken to ensure that the functions surrounding the courtyard and the uses for the courtyard are compatible and do not disturb each other. In addition, local regulations should be checked for requirements concerning egress from courtyards. Sun-study analysis should also be undertaken to ensure that these open spaces remain sunny and usable. In regions of severe climate, snow removal should also be considered.

Centralized resources with single-loaded classroom wings. In this model the double-loaded classroom wing is split apart into

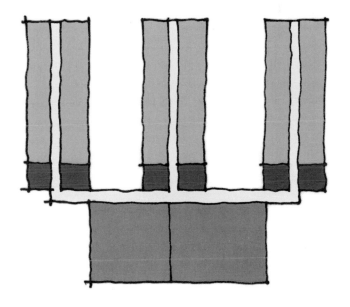

▲ *The spine plan.*

CIRCULATION

▶ *The Solomon Schechter School, Westchester, New York, is a courtyard plan. Perkins Eastman Architects.*

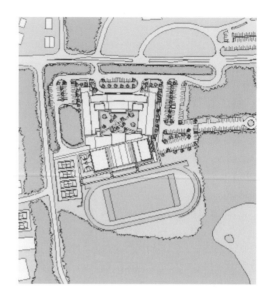

◀ *The courtyard plan.*

 Major Circulation

Classrooms

Shared Facilities
(i.e., auditorium, library, gym, etc.)

Classroom Nodes
(i.e., project rooms, faculty, offices, lavatories)

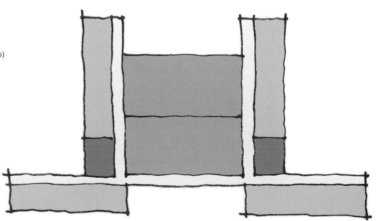

▶ *A spine with single-loaded classroom wings.*

▲ *A classroom-clustering model.*

single-loaded corridors. This configuration allows for visual differentiation of corridors and increased opportunity for subgrouping of classroom areas.

Spine with single-loaded classroom wing. In this model a "main street" separates classroom areas from shared resources. This configuration allows for visual and programmatic differentiation of the sides of the corridor.

Centralized resources with classroom clustering. In this concept a small number of classrooms are formed around central nodes. These nodes are typically programmed for functions that are shared by the surrounding classrooms. The nodes can include such program elements as faculty offices, tutorial rooms, project areas, and other essential functions such as toilet rooms and egress stairs. The classroom cluster establishes clear subgrouping of the overall school building, which enhances some teaching methodologies such as team teaching. This concept centralizes school-based shared resources, with classroom clusters located around the central resource zone.

Dumbbell with classroom clustering. This concept is differentiated from the double-loaded classroom version by the creation of secondary corridors off the main corridor, thereby reducing potential travel noise distractions and offering variation to the long central corridor.

Courtyard with classroom clustering. This model is simply a variation on a theme, based on forming a courtyard with classroom clusters and shared resource areas. Once again, major circulation is differentiated from secondary circulation feeding the classrooms. This helps to enable subgrouping and mitigates heavy traffic in front of classroom doors.

Campus plan. This model, based on college and boarding school precedents, divides the school into separate buildings that form a campus. Although this model has been used in northern climates, it is more appropriate in areas where the weather facilitates outdoor circulation.

Multigrade campuses. In some districts elementary, middle, and high school grades may share the same campus. Although separating these levels is advisable, economics may dictate their

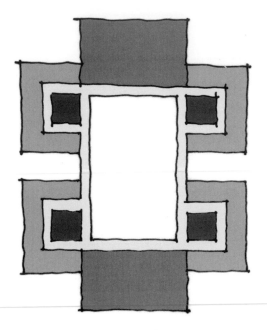

sharing some facilities such as the gym, auditorium, and so on.

Compact urban. Of necessity, some urban schools are built on small sites and are organized vertically. This is not an ideal configuration, but some of the most famous urban private and public schools have functioned within this site-imposed parti.

☐ Major Circulation

▨ Classrooms

■ Shared Facilities
(i.e., auditorium, library, gym, etc.)

■ Classroom Nodes
(i.e., project rooms, faculty, offices, lavatories)

▲ *A courtyard with classroom-clustering plan.*

CHAPTER 3

DESIGN CONCERNS AND PROCESS

This chapter focuses on four major issues in school planning, design, and construction:

- The major steps and tasks involved in planning, designing, and implementing a school building program
- The most common management problems that occur in school building programs
- Major trends
- Unique design concerns relevant to school building programs

THE PLANNING, DESIGN, AND IMPLEMENTATION PROCESS

Most design professionals consider educational facility design to be one of the more challenging project types. At times, school-building design has settled into a routine, but at its best the design of an educational facility has a dynamic relationship with the lives and activities of the children, teachers, and communities that use the school. School design is challenging and typically involves many client representatives, outside agency and public reviews, complex functional issues, rapidly changing technology, restrictive codes, and other significant design influences. Even relatively small school projects can take two to three years, and larger projects take from four to six years from initial conception to completion. The design professionals who are successful in dealing with the combination of issues involved are those who understand not only the issues but also the implementation process during which these issues are resolved.

The implementation process for most school designs can be divided into 11 steps:

1. Strategic planning
2. Identification and scoping of need
3. Selection and organization of the project team
4. Programming and predesign work—defining scope
5. Schematic design
6. Obtaining public approval and/or financing
7. Design development
8. Construction documentation
9. Selection of the construction and installation teams and purchasing
10. Construction and installation
11. Occupancy

The first part of this section discusses the design team's tasks for each of these steps. Understanding all the steps—as well as the design team's potential role in each—is an essential responsibility of any design professional.

Strategic Planning and Preliminary Definition of Need

Many educational facility projects are done within existing facilities or on existing campuses. Therefore, any project must be planned within the framework of a long-range plan. Even in new facilities, the initial building design must assume growth and change in the future.

An effective strategic plan incorporates more than site and facility issues. It must reflect the potential impact of changing approaches in education, technology, demography, funding, and other factors that will determine the future need for and use of the facility. The role of the design professional in this initial phase can be very important.

Typically, the design professionals evaluate existing conditions—from mechanical systems to interior finishes, operational issues, code compliance, and the ability of the facility to support the academic mission. Once these issues or problems are defined the design team can

develop available options and determine the potential cost and schedule for each major facility action implied by a potential development strategy. In most strategic plans, the facility's addition/expansion/modernization options are then evaluated against how well they help achieve the institution's key goals. The facility options can then be realized.

Once the strategic planning framework is set, the next step is to define the scope

▼ *Graphic outline of the major steps in a five-year facility master plan for a public school district.*

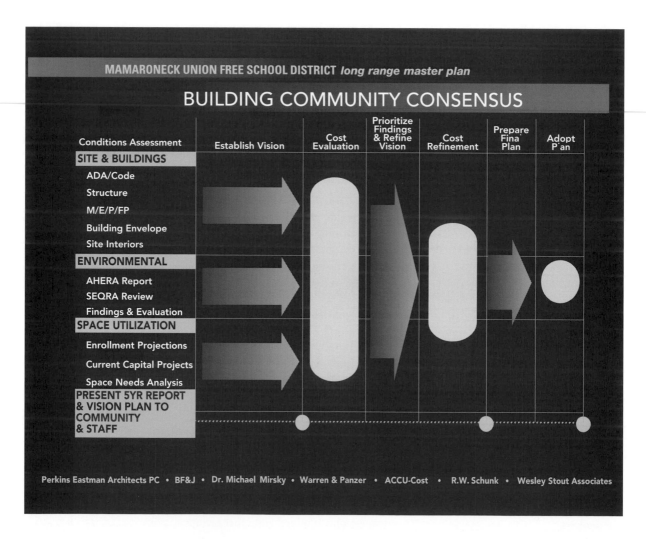

MAMARONECK UNION FREE SCHOOL DISTRICT *long range master plan*

BUILDING COMMUNITY CONSENSUS

Conditions Assessment | Establish Vision | Cost Evaluation | Prioritize Findings & Refine Vision | Cost Refinement | Prepare Final Plan | Adopt Plan

SITE & BUILDINGS
ADA/Code
Structure
M/E/P/FP
Building Envelope
Site Interiors

ENVIRONMENTAL
AHERA Report
SEQRA Review
Findings & Evaluation

SPACE UTILIZATION
Enrollment Projections
Current Capital Projects
Space Needs Analysis

PRESENT 5YR REPORT & VISION PLAN TO COMMUNITY & STAFF

Perkins Eastman Architects PC • BF&J • Dr. Michael Mirsky • Warren & Panzer • ACCU-Cost • R.W. Schunk • Wesley Stout Associates

of the specific project or projects. This preliminary definition is sometimes determined by the facility owner, but it is more efficient and productive to include the educational planners and design professionals in the process.

The primary tasks within this step include establishing an outline program and statement of project objectives, setting a realistic schedule, outlining a preliminary project budget, and defining the professional services that have to be retained. In certain cases this step also includes some preliminary test of feasibility. Most school projects must be judged by their impact on property tax, tuition, or the ability to raise the necessary funds. As a result, clients must have early confirmation that the project is financially feasible. As discussed in chapter 20, the district may retain a financial consultant at this point. All the project parameters—program, budget, schedule, and feasibility—must be reconfirmed and refined after the full team is selected, but it is important to have a realistic outline of the project before selecting the full team.

Selection and Organization of the Project Team

The design of any educational facility is a team sport. It is not uncommon for ten or more professional disciplines to be involved:

Architects

Educational planners

Equipment specialists

Interior designers

Civil engineers

Mechanical engineers

Acoustical engineers

Electrical engineers

Plumbing and fire-protection engineers

Cost consultants and/or construction managers

Telecommunications and technology consultants

Lighting designers

Landscape architects

Typically, most of the various disciplines are retained by the architect as a single cohesive team, thereby providing the school with a single source of responsibility. In addition, the following professionals may be involved:

Accountants

Financial consultants

Investment bankers

Attorneys

Bond counsel

Fund-raising consultants

Environmental consultants

Traffic consultants

Parking consultants

Other specialists involved in the financing and public approval process.

The client typically focuses on the lead professionals—usually the architects. Selection of the other members of the design team is often left to the lead firm or firms. The key issue, however, is to have a team that incorporates all the critical professional skills. Financial limits sometimes curtail the scope of the specialists' involvement, but the complexity of many educational facility projects demands that the team find a way to cover most of the specialist disciplines listed earlier.

The selection process for the lead professionals varies considerably, but a

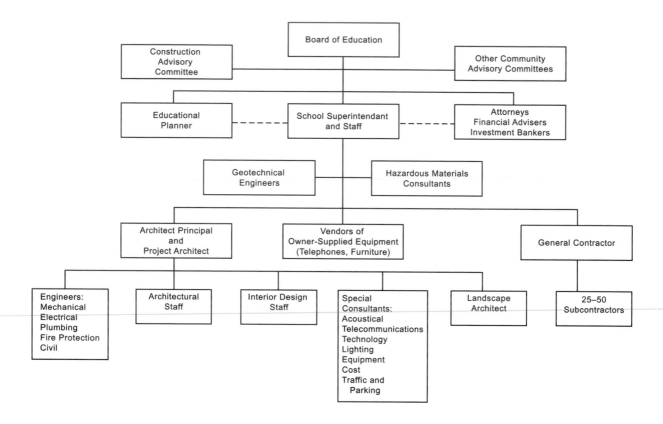

```
                          ┌─────────────────┐
                          │ Board of Education │
                          └─────────────────┘
┌──────────────┐                              ┌──────────────────┐
│ Construction │                              │ Other Community   │
│ Advisory     │                              │ Advisory          │
│ Committee    │                              │ Committees        │
└──────────────┘                              └──────────────────┘
┌──────────────┐      ┌──────────────────┐    ┌──────────────────┐
│ Educational  │      │ School Superintendant │ │ Attorneys        │
│ Planner      │      │ and Staff         │    │ Financial Advisers│
└──────────────┘      └──────────────────┘    │ Investment Bankers│
                                              └──────────────────┘
            ┌─────────────────┐  ┌──────────────────┐
            │ Geotechnical    │  │ Hazardous Materials │
            │ Engineers       │  │ Consultants       │
            └─────────────────┘  └──────────────────┘
┌──────────────┐   ┌──────────────────┐        ┌──────────────────┐
│ Architect    │   │ Vendors of        │        │ General Contractor │
│ Principal    │   │ Owner-Supplied    │        └──────────────────┘
│ and          │   │ Equipment         │
│ Project      │   │ (Telephones,      │
│ Architect    │   │ Furniture)        │
└──────────────┘   └──────────────────┘
```

Engineers: Mechanical Electrical Plumbing Fire Protection Civil

Architectural Staff

Interior Design Staff

Special Consultants: Acoustical Telecommunications Technology Lighting Equipment Cost Traffic and Parking

Landscape Architect

25–50 Subcontractors

▲ *Typical project organization for a large, new public school.*

thorough process would include the following:

1. Research is done on firms with relevant experience.

2. A written request is sent to a "long list" of firms, asking them to submit letters of interest, lists of references, and information on relevant projects. This request, sometimes known as a Request for Qualification (RFQ), includes a statement of the project objectives, an outline of the program, a schedule, and an assumed budget.

3. After a review of the submittals, four to six firms are selected for a short list and asked to make a formal presentation.

4. In some cases the short-listed firms are asked, via a request sometimes known as a Request for Proposal (RFP), to submit a written proposal summarizing the following:

• The firm's understanding of the project

• Proposed work program

• Proposed schedule

• Key personnel and subconsultant firms that will work on the project

• Proposed fees and expenses

Following the formal presentation and interviews, a contract is negotiated with the selected firm. In some cases the fee is discussed only after a team is retained, based on qualifications, and there has been a comprehensive discussion of scope, schedule, proposed specialist consultants, and other variables. In the past—and even today in some districts—the fee is set after reference to a standard fee schedule. Most experienced design teams and their clients, however, know that no two projects are the same and that the appropriate fees should be carefully calculated in each particular case. For a small, phased renovation, a fee equal to 14 percent of the project construction cost may be too little. Conversely, for a large, new high school on a flat site, a lump-sum fee equal to 6 percent may be adequate. The form of contract is typically based on one of the standard contract forms of the American Institute of Architects (AIA), but many public school districts and private schools have their own forms.

Once the lead firm is selected, the entire team must be organized. This organization must begin with the client, because only they can:

- Select the professional team

- Set the overall project goals and monitor to determine whether they are being met

- Select—from among the options prepared by the design team—the program and design solutions that best meet the objectives

- Resolve differences and problems between team members (i.e., design team and builder)

- Administer the contracts with the team members and

- Lead the relationship between the project team and the public

Most successful projects have clients who create a clear decision-making structure

and a strong team relationship with all the firms involved in the process. Some clients have even used *partnering* sessions at the beginning of a project to build the team relationships. This widely employed technique has the key members attend a one- to three-day workshop to establish a positive framework for their future working relationship. Recognizing the importance of the client's role in this relationship, the renowned Finnish-born architect Eero Saarinen liked to start a project by saying to the design team, "Let's see if we can make this guy into a great client."

Educational Specification, Programming, and Predesign

The programming phase usually begins with the preparation of the "educational specifications." These are typically prepared by an educator who knows the school system, relevant codes, and educational trends nationwide.

For the design team, one of the most challenging steps is the translation of the educational specifications into an architectural program and initial concept. In the past the client would prepare a detailed statement of its requirements or program for a project during the scoping phase. Today the increased complexity of the average project has meant that the full, detailed scope must be analyzed and defined with the assistance of the design team.

Program analysis has become a basic service provided by the architects, planners, and interior designers on educational facility projects. Among the additional particulars that the design team, with the help of specialists, must define are the number of each type of space; the

Space		SF		Occupants		Setup/furnishings	Materials		
WAMPUS ELEMENTARY SCHOOL PROGRAM WORK SHEET									
		New	Renov	Staff	Students	Setup/furnishings	Floor	Walls	Ceiling
ADMINISTRATION & LOBBY		1510	1430						
1	Reception		200	1–2	3–5	Reception desk w/computer station, desk chair, visitor seating for 4 small tables	Carpet	Paint	Tegular ACT
2	Conference Room		250	18	0	Conference table,18 chairs, pull-down screen, marker-board	Carpet	Paint	Tegular ACT
3	Principal's Office		160	1	3	Desk w/ computer station, chair, bookcase, 3 guest chairs	Carpet	Paint	Tegular ACT
4	Asst. Principal's Office		120	1	2	Desk w/ computer station, chair, bookcase, 2 guest chairs			
5	Nurse		200	1	2	Desk, task chair,chair for patient, 2 chairs for waiting, recovery bed, lockable storage cabinet, file cabinet, sink			
6	Secretarial Area		250	3	0	3 Workstations w/computers & chairs, file cabinets			
7	File Storage		200	0	0	File cabinets			
8	Supply Storage		200	0	0				
9	Remedial Room (2)		50 Ea.	1	2	Desk, 3 chairs, telephone			
10	Workroom		100			Copy machine			
11	Main Entry Lobby	710		2–3	40	Waiting benches			
	CLASSROOM WING								
12	Regular Classroom (10)	920 ea.		1–2	24				
13	Teachers' Workroom	400		4–6	0				
14	Corridor								
15	Toilet Room (2)								
16	Stair (2)								
17	Elevator								
18	Janitor's Closet								
19	Mechanical Room								
20	Computer Center	920							

▲ *Room data sheet for a high school.*

detailed functional requirements (amount of pinup and chalkboard space, desired lighting levels, etc.) and dimensions of each space; equipment requirements; mechanical, electrical, plumbing, and other services needed; and the required relationships between spaces. This important initial step is discussed in more detail in chapter 1.

The project team also has several other tasks before design can begin:

- A detailed assessment of existing conditions in the project area

- Preparation of base plans showing existing conditions in structures, a site survey, utility analyses, and soil analyses (if new construction is involved)

- An analysis of the zoning, building code, and public-approval issues that will influence the design

- Special analyses of any other issues (asbestos, audiovisual needs, structural capacity, etc.) that may affect the design, cost, schedule, or feasibility of the project

The results of the programming and related analyses are then combined into one or more preliminary concepts, an expanded statement of the project goals, and an updated project schedule and budget.

Once these project documents are available, in many cases two important parallel series of tasks, obtaining land use approvals and securing financing, begin. Public schools typically do not require zoning or other formal land-use approvals, but they usually must achieve community acceptance. Private institutions, however, typically must obtain formal land-use approvals for their proposed projects.

When required, the local land-use approval process typically starts with informal meetings with the municipal officials or planning department staff. They will help outline the steps in the process, identify any special approvals (such as zoning variances) that are required, and specify the information required at each step in the process. Most local approval processes for projects that involve more than renovation within an existing structure require a detailed site design and a schematic building design for land-use approval. On larger projects the process may also require detailed analyses of the environmental impact of increased traffic, noise, storm drainage, and other issues before local officials give their approval. It is not unusual for the land-use approval process to take one year to complete. In many cases, the design team must take the lead in this effort.

The second series of tasks that typically begins during predesign involves securing the financing for the project. Few major projects are paid for from the school system's current income. Many involve

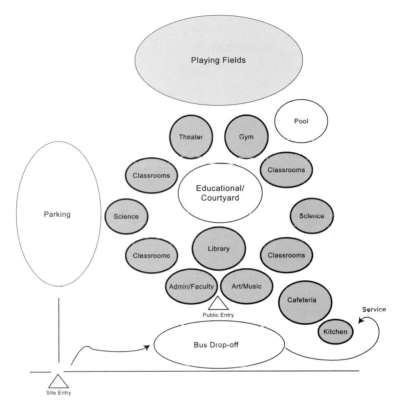

borrowing, and most larger public projects require an issue of tax-exempt bonds after a public referendum.

Fund-raising is also important for private institutions. This process can take more than a year to complete. During the financing process, the design team is often asked to assist in the required documentation, public presentations, and other steps. This involvement is covered further in chapter 20. It is usually preferable to hold the referendum after the more refined design materials are specified and cost estimates are developed during the schematic design stage, but many schools do not want to risk the fees involved without a favorable vote or fund-raising effort.

▲ Conceptual diagram for a new, private 7–12 upper school, the Solomon Schechter School, Westchester, New York. Perkins Eastman Architects.

75

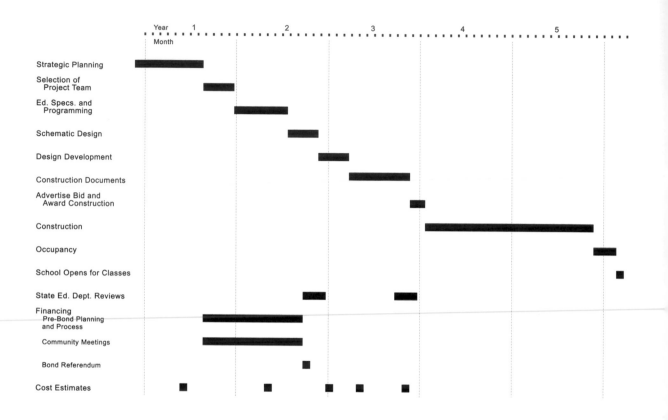

	Year	1		2		3		4		5	
	Month										

Strategic Planning

Selection of Project Team

Ed. Specs. and Programming

Schematic Design

Design Development

Construction Documents

Advertise Bid and Award Construction

Construction

Occupancy

School Opens for Classes

State Ed. Dept. Reviews

Financing
Pre-Bond Planning and Process

Community Meetings

Bond Referendum

Cost Estimates

▲ *Typical schedule for the planning, design, and implementation of a large, new school building.*

Once these predesign tasks are nearly completed, it is time to start the traditional design process.

Schematic Design
Schematic design is the first phase of the traditional design process. For most public school projects, this phase may not begin until after the school bond issue passes. During this first phase, the basic design concept is developed for all major components of the project. The standard forms of agreement for design services provide brief definitions for the schematic design phase, as well as the subsequent phases.

The standard contractual definitions of design services are based on a theoretical

process that, if it were followed, would permit the design team to move in an orderly way through the most common steps in the design, documentation, and construction of a building. This theoretical process assumes that a clear definition of the client's program exists. It also assumes that the process can progress in a linear fashion from the definition of client requirements through a series of steps—each of which results in a more complete definition of the design—until the project is sufficiently detailed to go into documentation for bidding (or negotiation) and construction.

The reality is not so orderly. Evolving program requirements, budget considerations, increased knowledge of site considerations (such as subsoil problems), and many other factors make it necessary to go back and modify previous steps. Design moves forward, but rarely in the clear, linear fashion implied by the standard two-phase description of design.

Moreover, design rarely ends with the completion of schematic design and the next phase, design development. Most design professionals agree that design choices occur at every step of the process. In other words, building design neither starts with schematic design nor ends with the completion of the design-development phase. Instead, building design is the central issue in each stage of the design team's effort, from planning and programming through the traditional design phases, contract documents, and construction. At each step in the design process, the design team faces new opportunities, new problems, and new information about the situation at hand.

Every project situation is unique. Each presents a different set of requirements and limitations; a particular set of programming, cultural, environmental,

▼ *An early schematic design plan for the Solomon Schechter School.*

technological, and aesthetic contexts to be considered; and its own set of challenges and opportunities. Design brings to the surface the major considerations inherent in the situation. It is both a problem-seeking and a problem-solving process.

Although every project has a unique combination of design influences, some of the most important are the program, the codes, the site, the constraints imposed by existing structures, the technological requirements of the systems (structural, mechanical, electrical, and etc.) to be incorporated, the cost, the schedule, and the client's particular goals. Thus, although many schools are built to house similar programs, almost every project has unique requirements.

The process by which a design team, with its consultants, converts these design influences into a specific design solution varies from firm to firm. In schematic design, however, most firms begin with a period of analysis, followed by a period of synthesis.

During the analysis stage each of the design influences is studied. Often diagrams are made of each program element, and conceptual plan alternatives are sketched. These studies in turn are analyzed to determine their potential functional, cost, code compliance, aesthetic, and other characteristics.

Thus the formal design process begins with the design team's analyses, understanding, and response to the basic project data. The combination of all of this information into a unified solution is the synthesis that is the core of schematic design.

Designers describe this synthesis in different ways. As architect Lewis Davis has noted, "Very few designers—no matter how consistent their work—can trace all influences. Some are external: technology, available materials, codes, etc. Some are internal: the designer's own education or the experience of the building just seen in Europe."

Some firms like to generate and test several alternatives before settling on a single approach. Others prefer to seek out a single strong idea around which they can organize the rest of the design.

But there is more than logic at work. Any experienced designer will note the importance of the nonrational, the nondescribable, and the poetic in the creation of a successful building design. At key points judgment, taste, intuition, and creative talent take over.

Underlying this diversity of approaches, there are some common themes and design tasks. The first is an expansion of the client's original goals statement to include clear design goals. These will help in making the inevitable decisions on trade-offs between budget and quality, appearance and energy efficiency, as well as the thousands of other major decisions in which competing priorities must be reconciled.

The next basic task is the development of a parti, or basic organization, for the project concept. As architect Edward Larrabee Barnes put it, "It is not just a case of form following function. Sometimes function follows form."

Designers also choose a design vocabulary, which includes the essential formal or aesthetic ideas that will govern the development of the design concept. Some designers develop a personal vocabulary of ideas, details, preferred materials, and so on, and refine it on each project. Others approach each project as a unique problem, selecting an appropriate vocabulary to fit the situation.

It is common for design teams to consider several conceptual solutions to a design problem. For this reason, most have developed a process for narrowing the choices to a single concept. In some cases, selection is based on a formal grading of a concept against the original project objectives. In others, it is an intuitive judgment based on experience. In most instances, designers use a combination of both.

Beyond the first conceptual steps, however, the process becomes more complex. In all but the smallest and simplest projects, the steps that follow concept development involve a team of people. Although it is true that significant projects are usually developed under the guidance of a single strong design leader, it is important to realize that not many projects have fewer than ten people involved in the decision making—architects, engineers, interior designers, specialist consultants, construction managers, public agencies, and, of course, clients. Thus, design excellence results in part from the effective management of a complex team, all of whose members contribute to the quality of the final product.

The result of all these steps is a completed schematic design. Although different projects, clients, and design teams have different definitions of the completion of this phase, there are certain commonly agreed-upon objectives and products.

1. *Objectives.* The primary objective is to arrive at a clearly designed, feasible concept and to present it in a form that achieves client understanding and acceptance. The secondary objectives are to clarify the project program, explore the most promising alternative design

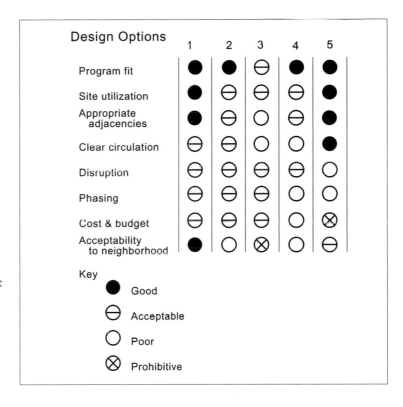

solutions, and provide a reliable basis for analyzing the cost of the project.

2. *Products.* Communicating design ideas and decisions usually involves a variety of media. Typical documentation at the end of this phase can include the following:

- A site plan
- Plans for each level, including conceptual reflected ceiling plans
- All elevations—exterior and conceptual interior elevations
- Two or more sections
- An outline specification
- A statistical summary of the design area and other characteristics in comparison to the program
- A preliminary construction cost estimate

▲ Some architects and owners use graphic tools to analyze and present design options

- Such other illustrative materials—renderings, models, or drawings—needed to present the concept adequately:

  a. *Drawings.* These are typically presented at the smallest scale that can clearly illustrate the concept (perhaps $\frac{1}{16}$ in. = 1 ft for larger buildings, and $\frac{1}{8}$ in. = 1 ft for smaller buildings and interiors).

  b. *Outline specifications.* This is a general description of the work indicating major systems and materials choices for the project, but usually providing little detailed product information.

  c. *Preliminary estimate of construction cost.* The schematic design estimate usually includes a preliminary area analysis and preliminary construction cost estimate. It is common for preliminary cost estimates made at this stage to include contingencies for further design development, market unpredictability, and changes during construction. These estimates are often developed by professional estimators or a builder selected by the client, but some design teams do their own cost estimates.

3. *Other services.* As part of the schematic design work, the design team may agree to provide energy studies; special program and design studies; life-cycle cost analyses; or other economic studies, renderings, models, brochures, or promotional materials for the client.

4. *Approvals.* The final step in schematic design is to obtain formal client approval. The importance of this step cannot be overemphasized. The schematic design presentation must be clear enough to gain both the understanding and the approval of the client. Most design teams recommend that once this has been accomplished, each item in the presentation be signed and dated by the client prior to initiation of the design development phase.

Obtaining public approval and/or financing

At this stage, and again at the end of construction documentation, the design may also be subject to review by the state's department of education or the technical arm of a city's board of education. This review usually focuses on conformance with established standards and the relevant codes. Enhancing is typically subject to voter approval of a bond issue.

Design Development

The objectives of the design development phase are different from those of schematic design. The primary purpose is to define and describe all important aspects of the project so that all that remains is the preparation at the formal construction contract documents.

As the pressures of tight schedules and the amount of fast-track construction have increased, some design firms have attempted to shorten or even eliminate this phase. However, there are strong design, technical, and economic arguments against doing so. Design development is the period in which all the issues left unresolved at the end of schematic design can be worked out, and this can be done at a large enough scale to prevent the risk of major modifications during the construction contract document phase. Working drawings and specifications are complex and intricately interrelated; changes in these documents are costly and likely to lead to coordination problems during construction.

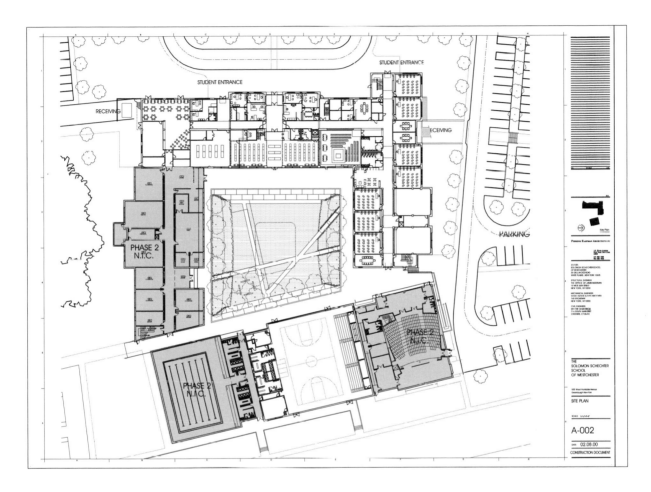

In addition, design development is the period in which the design itself achieves the refinement and coordination necessary for a really polished work. Without this step, too many important areas of design exploration are compressed into the schematic phase or left to be addressed in the working drawings.

Effective design development results in the design team's working out a clear, coordinated description of all aspects of the design. This description typically includes fully developed floor plans, interior and exterior elevations, reflected ceiling plans, wall and building sections, and key details—usually at the same scale used in the construction contract documents. It also includes the evaluation of alternative interior finishes and furnishings. In addition, the basic mechanical, electrical, plumbing, and fire-protection systems are accurately sized and defined, if not fully drawn. No major issues should be left unresolved that could require significant restudy during the development of construction contract documents phase.

▲ The Solomon Schechter floor plan at the end of schematic design.

The products of the design development phase are similar to those of schematic design—drawings and specifications that fix and describe the size and character of the project, as well as any recommended adjustments to the preliminary estimate of construction cost. It is important to bring the design development phase to a close with formal presentation to, and approval by, the client.

Construction Documentation

The design process does not really end with the completion of the design development phase; rather, the emphasis

▼ Construction documentation for the Solomon Schechter School.

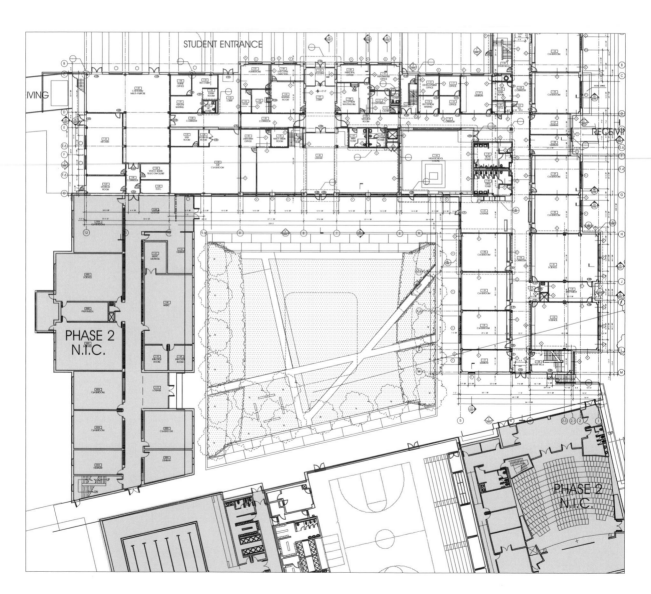

shifts to the effort necessary to have a complete, coordinated set of documents to guide the purchasing, construction, installation, and initial operations steps that follow.

The construction documents typically include drawings, specifications, contract forms, and bidding requirements. Each of these four documents plays an important role.

1. The drawings provide a graphic description of the work that is to be done.

2. The specifications outline the levels of quality and standards to be met.

3. The contract forms include the actual contract, the bond and insurance requirements, and general conditions outlining the roles, rights, and responsibilities of all parties.

4. The bidding requirements—if the project is being bid—set the procedures for this process.

The professional design organizations (such as AIA and others) have model documents for specifications, contract forms, and bidding requirements. These are good starting points, but all standard forms must be adapted to incorporate each project's unique requirements.

The largest part of this step in the process, however, is the production of a comprehensive set of drawings and technical specifications. This task often takes four to six months for the large teams on many educational facility projects. A new building or a substantial renovation of a middle school or high school can involve more than 100 sheets of drawings and several hundred pages of technical specifications. Each sheet of the drawings may involve 100 to 200 hours of work to complete, as the drawings must provide a clear, accurately dimensioned graphic description of the work to be done, and these drawings must be coordinated with the drawings of the other design professionals working on the same part of the project.

Experienced design professionals plan this step carefully and seek productivity savings. Computers, in particular, are beginning to bring some noticeable improvements in both speed and quality, but the human element is still key.

Selection of the Construction and Installation Teams and Purchasing

Once part or all of the construction documents are available, the next critical step is the selection of the builders, furniture and equipment manufacturers, and others who will provide the construction and other installed elements of the facility. Typically, the design team either manages the selection process or is an active participant with the client.

Experienced design professionals believe that if the right companies are selected, the remaining implementation phases are straightforward. Even one bad selection, however, can make completion of the project very difficult.

There are a number of choices available. In the selection of a builder, there are six major alternatives:

1. The most common procedure is for the construction documents to be completed and put out for a bid to companies attracted by public advertisement or selected from a list of prequalified general contractors.

2. For major educational facilities projects, a frequent choice is to have a construction manager (CM) work side by side with the design team.

During design, the CM gives advice on cost, schedule, and constructability issues. When the construction documentation nears completion, the CM bids all of the various subtrades and then provides a guaranteed maximum price (GMP) and becomes the general contractor.

3. For projects in which the scope is unclear or construction must start long before the completion of design, some clients retain a builder to work on a cost-plus basis. Most clients do not like the open-endedness of this method, but there are times when it is necessary. Because most public school work must be purchased by competitive bidding, this approach is limited to emergency work and projects in which the various parts of the work can be bid.

4 A variation in approach sometimes occurs where components such as sheetrock walls, outlets, light fixtures, playground equipment, and doors can be identified. The client may negotiate a unit price for each component and can then choose to buy as many units as he or she needs or can afford. This works for some projects such as window replacement programs, repaving of parking lots, and replacement of light fixtures.

5. An increasingly common option is *design/build*, whereby the client typically retains a team that includes both a builder and a design team, or a design team that includes a "builder" component. Some clients like the simplicity and the assumed higher degree of cost control. The success of the design/build approach, however, depends on the selection of a design/build team committed to the client's interests, inasmuch as the normal quality control provided by an independent design team is compromised. Because the design team works for or with the builder, it often cannot communicate concerns about quality and value directly to the client. For furnishings, the equivalent is the furniture manager, who bids furniture packages within the framework of a performance specification.

6. Since the 1970s an increasingly popular option has been construction management. During the design and construction documentation, the CM is a consultant to the client and the design team on cost, schedule, and constructability issues. This approach differs from the second option, however, in that the CM is a consultant to the client during construction as well. The CM may actually replace the general contractor, but does so on a fee basis. All of the construction subcontracts may be bid (as in the first option), but the CM—in his or her professional service form—does not guarantee the price. If the price is guaranteed, the CM can no longer work solely in the client's interest— the risks are too great.

The selection of an approach, as well as the selection of appropriate companies, is important and should be carried out in a systematic fashion. Advertising for bidders and hoping the right people show up to bid is rarely enough. Most experienced design teams and school districts research the options, identify the most qualified firms, solicit their interest, confirm their qualifications, and then—where public bid laws permit—limit the final proposals to the four to six best candidate firms. Again, AIA and other professional organizations have standard forms to facilitate the process: prequalification questionnaires, bid forms, contract forms, and other commonly required documents. Sometimes these forms are adapted by the client's attorney to fit specific project requirements, but they provide a helpful starting point.

In the case of many public school programs, the process, forms, and administrative procedures must be carefully planned to conform with the applicable bidding and purchasing procedures established by local or state law. These are often set out in documents available from the states' departments of education. For a summary of the laws and procedures that underlie most public bidding laws, the National Organization on Legal Problems of Education's *Planning and Financing School Improvement and Construction Projects* is good source (see bibliography).

A number of the same options are available in purchasing interior finishes, furnishings, and equipment. Dealers, who represent several manufacturers, or individual manufacturers will provide fixed-price bids for furniture and/or finishes. There are also many firms prepared to provide cost-plus services with or without a guaranteed maximum price, and there are a growing number of services offering the equivalent of a design/build approach.

Construction and Installation

With the start of construction and the production and delivery of furnishings and equipment, many additional companies and individuals take on major roles. In most educational facility projects, the design team is expected to provide both management and quality control throughout this process.

The management role typically includes administration of the various construction and supplier contracts; review of payment requests, change orders, claims, and related contract issues; and assistance in resolving problems in the field. On educational facility projects, both roles can require a major commitment of the design team's time. It is not uncommon for 20 to 25 percent of the design team's total project effort to be expended during this phase.

Occupancy

Schools require their buildings to be complete one to two months prior to occupancy by students. This time is necessary for teachers and staff to prepare. New schools are typically opened for the fall semester and sometimes in January, but are rarely opened midsemester.

The design team's work is not complete when the facility is ready for occupancy by the students. Virtually all clients moving into new facilities require assistance during the first few months.

The design team's tasks during the occupancy, or "commissioning," phase often fall into two categories: following up on incomplete construction, furnishing, and equipment issues, and organizing and transferring the information necessary to occupy and maintain the facility.

Most clients will not or cannot wait until everything is complete. They often choose to move in when the building achieves substantial completion—the point at which it can be safely occupied and used. Schools typically must be occupied before a term begins to permit teachers and staff to prepare for the start of classes. This circumstance often complicates the resolution of the open punch list (the list of still-to-be completed or corrected building items) elements.

Occupancy also often reveals construction, furnishing, and/or equipment that does not perform as intended. Sometimes these issues (such as an underperforming air-conditioning system) can be resolved with a limited amount of adjustment. Others require ongoing monitoring and additional work. Experienced design teams prepare their clients for the probability of some lingering issues and assure the clients that they will be there to help resolve them.

It is important, however, to wean clients from dependence on the design team for routine operation and maintenance. The first step in the weaning process is to collect and transfer to the client all operation and maintenance manuals, training information, and related information. This information should include a set of record drawings describing what was actually built. These drawings are usually prepared from marked-up working drawings provided by the contractors. In recent years it has become common for this information to be delivered in both electronic disk and hard-copy form. The electronic form can be a useful tool in future management of the facility by the client. Some design teams also prepare a reference manual containing samples, supplier data, and other information on all furnishings and finishes.

COMMON PROBLEMS AND CAUTIONS

The 11 steps outlined earlier constitute the process within which the design professionals must work. To properly serve most school facility clients, the design team must bring expertise to each step. The design team (in conjunction with the facility's owner/sponsor) is the thread that ties all 11 steps into a unified planning, design, and construction process. Thus, it is essential that design professionals be able to provide more than their particular technical service; they must also understand and be able to manage a very complex, multistep project delivery process. To be effective, design professionals should know not only how this process should proceed; they must also understand how it can go wrong. There are thousands of school construction programs each year. Some finish on time, within budget, and meet or exceed their objectives. Others encounter serious problems—some so serious that administrative staff lose their jobs, voters and boards lose confidence, and the school suffers long-term repercussions. Many of these problems are repeated in projects across the country. Ten of the most common and serious problems are discussed in the following paragraphs.

Failure to Plan

In some cases, careful planning may reduce the need for construction. For example, the need to build, a brick-and-mortar solution, may be avoided by revising class schedules or implementing other lower-cost solutions identified in the planning process. For example, one institution avoided most of a proposed building program by rescheduling the

---

TEN COMMON PROBLEMS IN SCHOOL DESIGN AND CONSTRUCTION
- Failure to plan
- Unclear and/or unrealistic goals
- Inadequate client leadership
- Selecting the wrong professional team for the wrong reasons
- Ineffective management
- Placing too low a priority on quality
- Poor cost management
- Failure to plan for maintenance
- A drawn-out or interrupted schedule
- Failure to match the project with the best available construction resources

---

school day and improving the departmental sharing of resources. Another avoided new construction by identifying and converting underutilized spaces within the district's schools. School building programs should be driven by curriculum, teaching, and learning needs. Not every demographic shift requires a construction response.

Often, however, brick-and-mortar solutions are necessary. Many districts under budgetary pressure have deferred maintenance projects for years. Others are responding to evolving education requirements. Even districts with significant declines in student population face space shortages. The incorporation of computer laboratories and other program changes require more rooms to serve the same number of children. Careful planning can minimize the need for building, but eventually all districts have construction needs. When the need for construction is identified by and justified through the planning process, planning ranks options in terms of effectiveness to meet demands and provides a clear, staged master plan for implementation.

Unclear and/or Unrealistic Goals

A building program is a complex but manageable task. The first step in effective management requires a clear statement of the program objectives. Many school systems ignore this step. Others fail to apply realism to their goal setting. Serious problems for a building program begin with goals that cannot be met because of a budget that is too low, a schedule that is too short, or an educational outcome that cannot be realized.

An unrealistic initial budget can haunt an entire building program. An initial budget estimate, publicly discussed, has a life of its own. It creates a target that everyone remembers and a standard for evaluating how well the program is managed. No school should ever publicly announce a budget target that is not based on a clear outline of all goals to be accomplished within the building program. A budget prepared at the beginning of a building program can be accurate for a project, but this happens only when it is preceded by careful planning and meticulous budget preparation processes.

The same care is needed in setting the other basic program goals. A frequent error is to expect too much from a renovation program. "Parity" between older and newer facilities is often not attainable even after amounts are spent that approach replacement cost. In some instances older facilities cannot be renovated to support modern teaching methodologies, new technology, or even current life safety requirements. The resultant compromises may point to replacement rather than renovation as the better, although harder to sell, course of action.

Goal setting, of course, should cover every other aspect of the program—from a program's ability to respond to future growth and change to a realistic target date for completion. These goals cannot be set arbitrarily but must evolve logically from a careful master-planning effort.

Inadequate Client Leadership

Selection of a strong, professional team does not relieve a school district of its role as the team leader. As any experienced design professional will quote, "You cannot create a good building without a good client."

Some tasks cannot be delegated. One of these, public presentation of the proposed building program, is typically an essential part of the client's leadership obligation as well as the design team's service. The core of an effective justification of need for a building program is an effective planning process. The school leadership must make sure that the results of this planning process are clear, defensible, and effectively presented.

All school spending plans face potential opposition. The easiest ways to attack a proposed building program include

pointing out lower-cost alternatives that were overlooked, highlighting shortcomings in the current management of the district's facilities, and asking questions about the accuracy of the budgeting and planning. If opponents can make a credible case concerning potential waste, lax management, or future cost overruns, a bond issue may be in trouble. If a bond issue fails initially, passage on a second round may be even more difficult. The result is often a reduced and compromised program in the future. The antidote is a thorough planning phase, with the plan properly reviewed and presented.

Selecting the Wrong Professional Team for the Wrong Reasons

Few school clients can analyze their needs and present a realistic plan without some technical assistance. They require professional advice from architects and engineers as well as legal and financial advisers. There are many architectural and engineering firms with the expertise to provide the planning, design, and project-management services required for a successful program. Legal and financial counsel provide guidance to ensure compliance with the expanding regulatory environment of public funding.

To identify qualified consultants able to work as a team with district personnel is a key step, which begins with a good selection process, such as that described earlier in this chapter. A professional team can be selected for the wrong reason, however.

The lowest fee proposal, or renderings, cost estimates of theoretical solutions, or other free services, are foolish bases for selection. Fees can be negotiated, in most cases, to acceptable levels. Free up-front work, completed on speculation, is rarely of any real value. A school design that is not produced in a close working relationship with the client is rarely appropriate. Most such studies rarely resemble the final, appropriate design solution. A successful school design comes from a careful process carried out by a design team that can bring design and management skills to bear over the several years it takes to implement a building program.

Ineffective Management

Although most school systems recognize their management responsibilities, a number of common errors in management compound the problems encountered in construction programs. In some cases, a district may fail to organize clear decision-making procedures. In others, micromanagement or poor interpersonal relationships between client and team members interfere with the coherent work process and team effort necessary for a successful building program.

There are several ways to organize management responsibilities for a building program:

- In some cases, the school or district administrative staff provides the day-to-day leadership and the board reviews, and approves the major policy issues (budget, team selection, major design choices, etc.).

- In other instances, the administration and board assume leadership and are supplemented by a building committee and/or additional staff with the skills to help manage the program.

- In the latter case, a building committee typically includes among its members a design professional, an attorney with construction experience, and a builder.

- Many schools also retain a professional project representative to provide day-to-day liaison with the design team and builder. This "clerk of the works" function can be ineffective if the person has limited experience or authority.

Whether the administrative staff or a committee has management responsibility, one individual should have authority for day-to-day decision making within the framework of the project plan. This individual should have the ability to build consensus among members of the committee and, when necessary, to make the decisions needed to advance the project even if a consensus does not exist. Clear allocation of responsibilities will go a long way toward enhancing program management.

Placing Too Low a Priority on Quality

The quality of a school building has a direct impact on the people who use it. A school building is a long-term—often 50 years or more—community asset. It provides the environment for learning. A well-planned and maintained school can facilitate its education program. A badly planned or maintained building can create barriers.

No school system wants to build a low-quality school, but poor quality may result. The most common culprits include an overemphasis on cost, an initial budget that is too low, planning only for the short term, failure to build in the capacity to grow or change in the future, and overreliance on outdated and unimaginative models.

One of the primary benefits a design team can provide the district is a clear understanding of the trade-off between cost and quality. The team must ensure that all participants in the planning process understand the differences between first cost versus life-cycle cost and short-term versus long-term needs. In addition, the design team should challenge traditional school building models and present the client with alternatives that reflect the client's specific needs and academic objectives.

Poor Cost Management

Most building programs are dominated by a focus on first cost, an overemphasis that stems from a fear of cost overruns. Construction costs—and even life-cycle costs—can be managed. There is no reason that a school program should not finish within budget, but this can be accomplished only with the help of an effective cost-management process.

An experienced design team can help a district set a realistic budget that properly reflects the district's goals, program, and master plan. Once the budget is set, the design team should present the options and their cost implications at each stage of the process. Thousands of planning and design choices are made during each phase of a building program, ranging from major program and floor plan choices in the early phases to the selection of specific building components (light fixtures, hardware, floor tile, etc.) in the later phases. For example, during schematic design a choice may be whether or not to air-condition, during

design development the location and type of equipment must be selected, and in creating working drawings there are many details to resolve. In a well-structured design process, the most important of the choices—as well as their costs and benefits—should be presented to the building program's decision makers.

It is particularly important, once decisions have been made, that the client and the project team stick to them. One of the most common sources of serious budget overruns in any building program is a team that changes decisions and adds scope during construction. Although some builders count on this eventuality to increase their job profit, most find it disruptive—and even the high markups they assign to the changes barely cover the costs and aggravation. Once the scope is set and the construction contract bid and awarded, the natural tendency to make changes—a common weakness of most design teams and their clients—should be strongly discouraged.

Failure to Plan for Maintenance

No matter how well built the facilities, they will not last unless they are maintained. An overemphasis on low initial construction cost (vs. life cycle cost) or poor choices in the initial planning can accelerate the need for a maintenance program. All building systems—from roofs to boilers—must be maintained. When properly maintained, their life span can often be extended. When school systems fail to plan for maintenance or balance their budgets by deferring essential repairs and preventive measures, they are increasing a long-term liability and cost. Schools across the country continue to pay a high price for this short-term thinking.

The design team can help a school system plan for and structure a maintenance program that will minimize life-cycle costs. No one, however, can eliminate the need for ongoing annual capital and maintenance expenditures. Owners should be careful in the selection of unduly complex controls and technologically advanced facility management systems that are costly and require sophisticated personnel to operate and maintain them. Sophisticated computer-based management of the mechanical systems, for example, may be too complex to be maintained and operated by a janitorial staff. Sometimes simpler is better.

A Drawn-Out or Interrupted Schedule

A school building program's leadership should not ignore the importance of momentum and continuity. A project that proceeds in a steady, orderly fashion from planning through implementation is far easier to manage. Not only is a longer process often more expensive, it can also lead to other problems. When a project stops and starts, or is stretched too far, decision making loses continuity. Key leadership or design team members will change, and the rationale for decisions will be obscured. Moreover, because even a well-run program can extend over four or five years, key team members can simply become exhausted by the process. Once a building program is initiated, there should be a commitment to seeing it through as quickly as possible, while the understanding of the need is clear and the team is fresh.

Failure to Match the Project with the Best Available Construction Resources

A strong client and an experienced design team are only two-thirds of the core leadership of a building program. The third part is the construction manager. Although selection of this team member is often constrained by public bidding laws, it is essential that a school seek out the best construction resources available, both at the management level and at the subcontractor level.

In some school systems the client itself brings in the management resources via a professional construction management service, additions to its own staff, or supplemental services from the design team. In other systems, there is an intense, proactive effort to attract bidder interest from construction companies with proven track records on comparable projects. What does not work is a passive reliance on advertising and word of mouth to attract the key construction resources.

The design team can help attract the right builders by investigating the local construction industry, contacting the preferred bidders, and designing the project to fit what local construction resources do best. A poorly planned building program can be packaged in a way that discourages local subcontractors because it is too big, has too short a schedule, requires too much sophistication, or has too onerous contract requirements. These errors can lead to higher prices or the wrong bidders.

With a good construction team, even a difficult project can run smoothly. Yet one bad major subcontractor can make the whole process difficult.

All ten of these problems can be avoided. In fact, many school systems initiate high-quality building programs that finish on time and within budget and enjoy broad public support. All building programs, however—even the most successful—face problems. A well-run program will surmount these challenges. The difference between a successful program and a program that encounters severe problems typically does not depend on the wealth of the school system. The difference is sound planning and effective management.

TRENDS IN SCHOOL PLANNING AND DESIGN

School building is influenced by many of the same general changes and trends that influence almost all building types, such as the general economy, construction costs, and development of new building systems and materials, but schools are also affected by issues that are specific to educational facilities. Among the most important issues and trends relevant to school design are the following:

- Enrollment trends
- Program requirements
- Condition of the existing facilities
- Schools as community centers
- Changes in school utilization

Enrollment Trends

One of the most important factors is the number and age of the students that must be accommodated by the school or school system. This has been the issue most vexing for many schools, because of the difficulty in predicting long-term trends. Many school districts saw steady declines until the mid-1980s. The graph below illustrates the trend in a typical small northeastern city. Schools were closed and converted to other uses just as the trend reversed. By the 1990s the same systems suffered overcrowding. As a result, many school systems now have professional staff or consultants addressing this issue. Private schools have had to focus on research and marketing to manage their enrollments.

▶ High school enrollment trends in a small city school district, illustrating the growth commonly experienced in many districts in the 1990s.

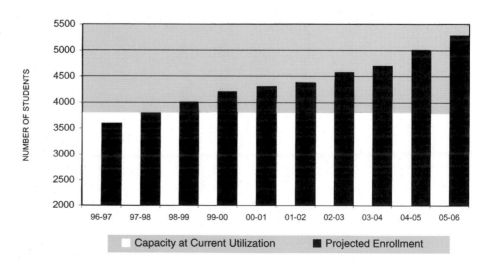

Program Requirements

Growth in the school-age population is only one of the reasons for the severe shortage of school space that began to appear in the 1990s in so many areas of the United States. A typical school today has to accommodate a very different program. In many school systems spaces must be created for special and remedial education, preschool programs, and classes for English as a second language (ESL). In most schools average class sizes have been reduced (from more than 50 in public schools approximately 28 to 30 years ago, to fewer than 22 today in many elementary schools), and new curricula have been added. Even more change can be expected to result from evolving teaching concepts.

Over the past decades the teaching of children has been based on a discipline-by-discipline model—in other words, a period for science, math, language, sociology, history, and so on. Typically, the sources of these subject matters were textbooks, supported by lectured instruction. More and more learning is now centered on projects, whereby teams of students attack a problem with a multidisciplinary approach, using any number of resources. This change in education methodology should influence the physical design of schools.

Classrooms can no longer be thought of in the traditional sense—having an instructor at the front of the room at the blackboard, with students at desks and chairs or tablet armchairs in regimented rows. Ideally the classroom needs total flexibility; however, total flexibility is difficult to achieve while there is still a need to bring utilities (power, data, or gas and water to lab benches, etc.) to student

locations. Infrared technology has not yet replaced the need for hardwiring. In addition, project-based instruction may require that a physical model or construct must stay in place during a period of study, which may last several weeks or months. Perhaps the future classroom has to be much larger, allowing for a traditional instructional area surrounded by clusters of project work areas. If multidisciplinary/multisource instruction is advantageous, then we may begin to see fewer single-purpose rooms, such as the biology lab or the computer lab, and instead a general classroom outfitted for student teams to have all of these resources at their immediate disposal. The computer laboratory is already beginning to disappear, as students need increasingly less pure computer and keyboarding instruction and teachers are more comfortable in having computers integrated directly into the classrooms.

Multidisciplinary/multisource instruction also supports the notion that teachers, more than students, will move from class to class. In other words, students studying a multifaceted project in a particular classroom (with all resources at their disposal) will have a specialist instructor visit the classroom. Middle schools are close to this approach. In kindergarten, this model has been used for years, with the creation of activity centers within the classroom and art and music teachers visiting the class. It is interesting to note that most state standards require larger classroom sizes for kindergarten than for upper grades. This is clearly inversely proportionate to the size of the student, but has been deemed necessary for the multidisciplinary/multiresource instruction

▲ *Some schools built early in the twentieth century, such as New Trier High School in Kenilworth, Illinois, have been maintained and modernized to remain examples of educational excellence in the twenty-first century. Designed by Perkins, Fellows and Hamilton.*

of the existing stock of school facilities. Nevertheless, there are more than 80,000 existing schools in the United States, and each such structure constitutes the core resource to be considered in the planning of any school building program.

Schools as Community Centers

School facilities need not be just for children. Lifelong learning (adult education) programs, the increasing incorporation of early childhood programs in school campuses, the desire by other age groups to use school athletic and cultural (theater, art, etc.) facilities, and the limitations on land and funds for duplicate community facilities are all encouraging a trend to treat schools as community centers rather than isolated precincts for teaching children and adolescents. The implications of this broader community use tend to promote a closer integration with other community facilities such as the park system and library. Community use also can lead to greater space requirements to provide for both students and adults. Art studios may need storage, athletic facilities may need separate locker rooms, and some facilities— such as a theater or auditorium—may have to be larger or better equipped to accommodate broader community use. Balancing the increased costs, however, is the increased community support that this wider usage should generate.

Changes in School Utilization

In recent years more school systems have been experimenting with changes in the traditional school hours and year. Such utilization has gone far beyond traditional summer school and after-school programming. Some schools are experimenting with longer school days

traditionally used at lower grade levels. A few decades ago, open-plan schools, or classrooms without walls, were the rage. This trend, for the most part, failed, and many open-plan schools were renovated, with hard walls built to divide class areas. Perhaps this physical model was flawed, but it may also have failed because teaching methodologies had not yet advanced to the same state as the physical model.

Condition of Existing Facilities

If properly maintained, the shells of most school buildings can last more than 100 years. Many of their other systems, however, become obsolete much sooner. Because of budget pressures or poor planning, or for other reasons, obsolescence and severely deferred maintenance are common across much

▲ At the Community Education Village in Perry, Ohio, the community shares fitness, swimming, auditorium, and music spaces with a K-12 school. Perkins & Will Architects. (Photograph by Hedrick/Blessing.) ▶

and year-round programming. This innovation is, in part, a response to the need to accommodate more class hours without building new facilities, but it is also a response to the need for greater flexibility and access. Adults and others need programs that are available in the evening and on weekends. Even some children can benefit from a school year that is not confined to the traditional September-to-June span. And, as noted earlier, many schools are being opened to broad community use.

Even during the school year, schools are experimenting with nontraditional scheduling. Instead of the usual 50-minute periods, some are using block scheduling, whereby classes are taught in longer periods, but not every day.

Such change puts more pressure on facilities by reducing or eliminating the periods when modernization, maintenance, and repairs are traditionally performed. Thus, schools are having to give greater attention to robust materials and systems that require less maintenance and have longer useful lives. Many schools are also experiencing pressure to be air-conditioned so that they can be used during the summer.

UNIQUE DESIGN CONCERNS

Beyond the general trends are a number of design imperatives that influence most schools. Among the most important are the following:

- Making the school an inviting place for children and adolescents
- Size
- Technology
- Flexibility
- Regional influences
- Energy conservation
- Sustainability
- Security
- Storage

Making the School an Inviting Place for Children and Adolescents

One of the major problems the school designer must consider is

the "first impression" [the] building gives. Those of us who began our education in one of those big, ugly, fortresslike school buildings remember that First Day as a frightening experience. The grim face of the building was awesome; it was bullying. Here was a witches' castle, a place of fierce teachers and cruel older

children.... But just how can a school building be made to say "welcome"? First, both the school building and approach should be designed with just that in mind. Open-armed and friendly, they greet the student without overwhelming. (Perkins 1957)

Size

The ideal size for schools has been widely debated for decades. In former Harvard president James B. Conant's influential 1959 study, *The American High School Today*, he noted, "The enrollment of many American public high schools is too small to allow for a diversified curriculum except at exorbitant expense" (p. 77). Because of the inherent problems and inefficiency of small schools, this milestone study recommended consolidation of many smaller districts.

Today, however, the debate is often more about schools being too large to be manageable and sensitive to the needs of the individual child. A 1995 study by Valerie Lee at the University of Michigan and Julia Smith at the University of Rochester published research arguing that 600 to 900 students is the ideal size.

There is, of course, no magic number for any school or even any class, but there are guidelines, as discussed in chapter 1.

Technology

As discussed in chapter 10, technology is finally having a profound impact on school design. The growing use of computers, Internet access, and other technologies have all become major design issues.

Flexibility

Change is inevitable and accelerating. School design today must assume both

▶ *Computers are now found in most libraries and classrooms as in this new school, the South Lawrence East School, in Lawrence, Massachusetts. Earl Flansburgh + Associates, Inc. (Photograph by Wheeler Photographics.)*

▼ *Typical layout for a computer classroom.*

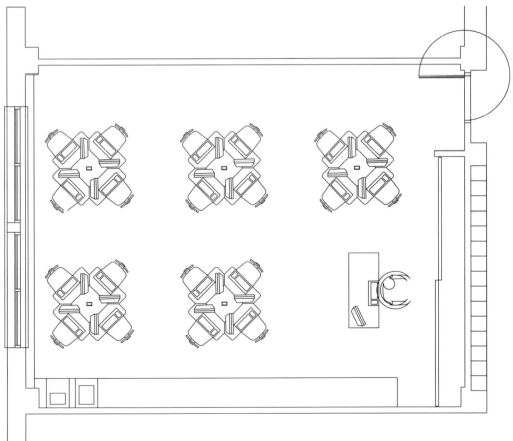

growth and contraction in future enrollment; changes in average class size; new technology, teaching concepts, and curricula; and other issues that will require significant adaptation. In the 1960s one response was the open-plan school—a concept that involves the inclusion of large open spaces within the school. These large spaces were supposed to encourage flexible teaching, larger group teaching situations, and other less traditional teaching approaches. Many teachers never committed to the concept, and the spaces themselves were often anonymous, unattractive, and hard to use. Now many of these earlier experiments with flexible design have been subdivided into traditional classrooms.

Even though these earlier efforts may have been misdirected, the issue remained. Today more typical responses include the following:

- Plans that facilitate the combination of spaces

- Circulation patterns and site planning that allow for future additions

- Technology distribution that facilitates replacement and expansion

- Increased use of demountable partitions to permit reconfiguration of space

- Mechanical/electrical distribution designs that can easily accommodate changes in partition layout

These are just some of the techniques that are used to build in flexibility. Unfortunately, such built-in flexibility is still the exception in school design. Most existing schools and too many new buildings have been designed to a more rigid model. George H. Wood wrote in *Schools That Work* (1992):

It should come as little surprise that in rooms with all desks facing the front (some bolted to the floor) the predominant mode of instruction will be lecture, drill, and recitation. Hands-on experiences require classroom arrangements that facilitate movement, group work, and varied activities. Why then are classrooms so oppressively alike in arrangement and decor?... Part of the answer is in the way schools equip classrooms. Individual desks are the norm, as opposed to tables, lounge chairs, or workstations. The rooms themselves, especially in schools built during the 1950s, are a testament to the lack of imagination of most school architects. Carbon copies of one another, designed to meet square footage requirements, each room is adaptable to any program—as long as the program works well in an open square or rectangle with windows on one side, chalkboard on another, and little or no storage or private space for teachers or students (pp. 122–123).

Regional Influences

Schools in different parts of the country should reflect their particular regions. At times school design relied too heavily on national models, but more recently styles reflecting regional building traditions, different climates, and other variables have reemerged. Buildings that use a lot of wood are common in the Northwest, and stucco and concrete are the common materials in Florida and the Southwest. Campus-plan schools, where the components are in separate buildings, are more appropriate in milder climates. Schools in regions where the circulation can be in open corridors—as in Southern California and Florida—often have a

In 1957 Lawrence Perkins made the following observation: "Traditional classroom design, with its rigidly arranged seating, high-silled windows on the left, and authoritarian location of the teacher, was based on several assumptions: That all students were right-handed. That daylight beamed on just a few rows was enough for the whole room. That neither teacher nor students should ever move into groups, or change location. That teacher-to-student lectures, recitations, and at-desk study were the sole activities in the classroom. That the world around the classroom had nothing to teach the student... Today's classroom design [should be] based on other principles, most basic of which is flexibility—flexibility to keep pace with changing concepts of education's role in society, and of the teacher's role in the learning process. Also, the classroom must reflect the teaching methods of the school; it must be an efficient tool and a suitable atmosphere for education, regardless of the educational approaches used" (Perkins 1957, p. 23). This basic principle is still valid today.

much lower overall size (or net to gross square foot ratio) because of the reduced requirement for enclosed circulation.

Energy Conservation

The oil embargo of 1973 made energy conservation an important consideration in building design. Even though energy prices have declined since then, it remains a significant design issue. In the first years of the energy conservation movement, this issue led to some very unfortunate concepts: very compact floor plans to reduce the amount of perimeter exposed to heat loss or gain; overinsulated, tight buildings that often created indoor air-quality problems; and even the concept (briefly implemented in Florida and a few other locations) of windowless schools. Although the desire to minimize operating costs and greater public awareness have kept energy conservation an important issue, there has been a trend toward more natural design responses. There has even been a

return to earlier design traditions that facilitated cross-ventilation, the use of overhangs and other shading devices to reduce solar gain, and building orientation to maximize the use of natural light to illuminate spaces. This subject is discussed further in chapter 6.

Sustainability

Closely related to energy conservation is the issue of sustainability, covered in more detail in chapter 6. The basic principles of "green" architecture (use of renewable resources, energy conservation, daylighting, avoidance of materials that cause indoor air pollution, etc.) are being incorporated in school design.

Security

Security has, unfortunately, become a major issue in many school districts. In some cases it even includes designs that limit access, provide for video surveillance, or permit screening for weapons. In many others it involves the incorporation of the basic principles of "defensible space" design, such as the elimination of spaces that are not subject to random or constant visual supervision, and functional locks and other devices to discourage opportunistic crime and vandalism. In some particularly difficult areas, schools have had to be designed to provide a safe island in an otherwise dangerous neighborhood.

Storage

Storage may seem at first to be a programmatic detail, but it is typically an important issue in supporting a teaching program. As Lawrence Perkins noted, "Ask any teacher about basic requirements for classroom and school design. Storage space ranks high on the list" (Perkins 1957, p. 34). Teaching requires a wide variety of materials, and both the classroom and school must meet this need.

CHAPTER 4

SITE PLANNING

SITE SIZE

In addition to building size, there are several other exterior elements to be considered in determining site size:

- Administration/faculty parking
- Visitor parking
- Student parking
- Bus drop-off areas
- Service/loading areas
- Playing fields
- Playgrounds for younger-age children

Requirements for overall school size sizes are relatively consistent between many states. See, for example, the table below.

In determining site size, the design team must also take into consideration the buildable areas of the site. This includes reviewing regulations for wetlands, easements, and setbacks as well as reviewing topography and other natural features that may not easily accommodate buildings or playing fields.

SITE CIRCULATION

Designing to mitigate conflicts between the several types of vehicular circulation (buses, parents', staff members, and service vehicles) and pedestrian circulation is one of the most difficult site development tasks. In addition to determining the amount of parking required, it is also important to determine the amount of busing and anticipated parent/caregiver drop-off, which varies

TYPICAL STATE SITE REQUIREMENTS		
	Basic Acreage	Additional Acreage per 100 Pupils in Ultimate Enrollment
New York		
Grades K–6	3	1
Grades 7–12	10	1
Florida		
Primary	3	1
Elementary	4	1
Junior High, Junior-Senior, or Senior High	10	1
High or Combined Elementary and High	10	1
Virginia		
Primary or Elementary	4	1
Middle School, Intermediate, or Junior High	10	1
Senior High or Combined School	10	1

with grade level, location, and demographics. The vehicular circulation types (bus drop-off, parent/caregiver drop-off, and parking) should be kept as separate as possible, and the walking routes of children must be kept clear of these areas. Bus drop-off areas must be designed so buses do not have to back up and children do not have to leave the safety of sidewalk areas to board. Bus stack areas must also be considered. In designing entrance drives, it should be noted that most traffic enters and leaves the site at the same peak times. These roadway systems must be designed to be long enough and wide enough to allow for this traffic. In addition, emergency vehicles must have access even during peak traffic events.

FIELD SIZES

The table opposite shows approximate sizes for playing fields. Check the local league or school division regulation

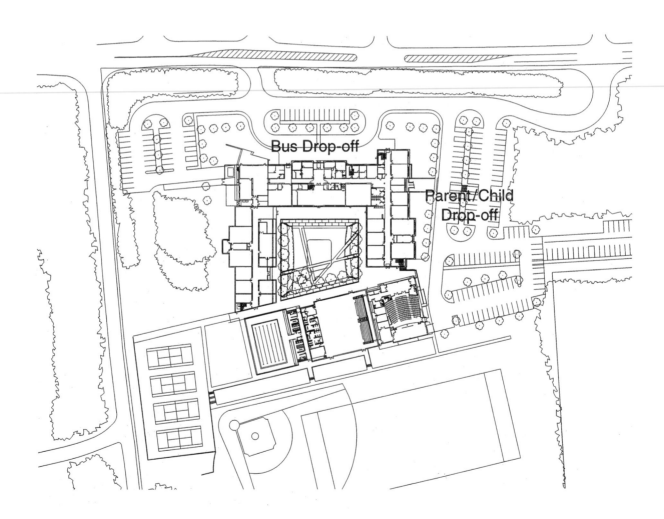

Bus Drop-off

Parent/Child Drop-off

PLAYING-FIELD SIZES	
Activity	**Space Requirements**
High school basketball court	50 ft x 84 ft—playing area only, without bleachers or out-of-bounds area
Football	360 ft x 160 ft—playing area only, without bleachers
Little League baseball	175 ft long along foul lines to end of outfield, approximately 60 ft between bases, and approximately 257 ft from home plate to the end of center field
Lacrosse	159 ft x 330 ft
Soccer	195 ft x 330 ft
Tennis courts	60 ft x 120 ft (fence line to fence line)

standards for each when determining final layout. It is also important to locate these fields with appropriate solar orientations. It is typical for courts and fields to be oriented north-south when feasible.

In many instances, where field space or costs are limited, playing fields are used for multiple sports. For example, lacrosse and soccer fields become interchangeable and restriped from one semester to the next. In most cases a football field is placed within a quarter-mile track.

SITE-DESIGN CONCEPTS

Some school buildings are single structures; students do not leave their building during the day except for physical education. Other schools are designed as separate buildings, whereby a campus is created, allowing children to move from building to building throughout the day. In some public schools and in many private schools, grade levels from prekindergarten

through senior year share the same site; thus, an educational campus is created.

In some instances, all grade levels share central facilities (such as the gymnasium, food area, and auditorium). For example, a single site may contain an elementary classroom building, a middle school classroom building, a high school, and a student center building housing the gym, cafeteria, auditorium, and other areas.

At other campuses, separate buildings house art or science facilities, similar to a college campus. In deciding to create a campus school, the designer should consider whether it enhances the school's educational objectives and whether the climate is appropriate for walking from building to building. Security must also be addressed. A single structure with a single or limited number of access points is clearly easier to secure and monitor than an open campus setting. Campus settings, or separate buildings, are typically found

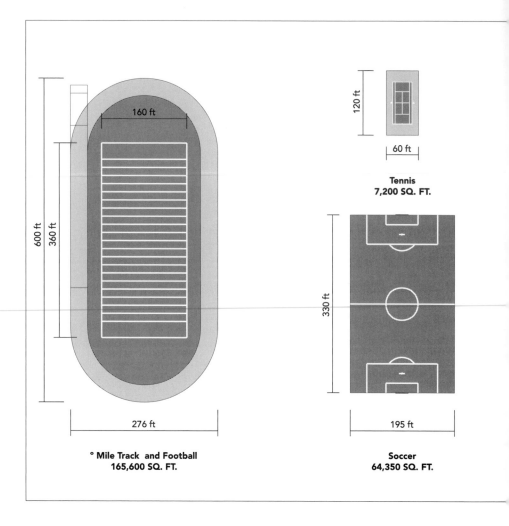

120 ft

60 ft

**Tennis
7,200 SQ. FT.**

160 ft

600 ft

360 ft

330 ft

276 ft

195 ft

**° Mile Track and Football
165,600 SQ. FT.**

**Soccer
64,350 SQ. FT.**

▶ *Regulation sizes for
high school football,
tennis, soccer, baseball,
and softball.*

where one or more of the following conditions are present:

- Private residential school

- Preparatory school desirous of a college image

- Community schools where kindergarten through 12th grade are housed on a single site

- Moderate climatic conditions

- Schools with large enrollments

In developing an organizational strategy for a school, the designer must consider many factors. Adjacencies between school program elements are contingent on the following major issues:

Entry sequence. How do students enter school each day, and where do they go? Do they immediately report to a homeroom or do they first gather in a larger area such as the gym or cafeteria? How do staff and faculty enter the building? How does the public enter the

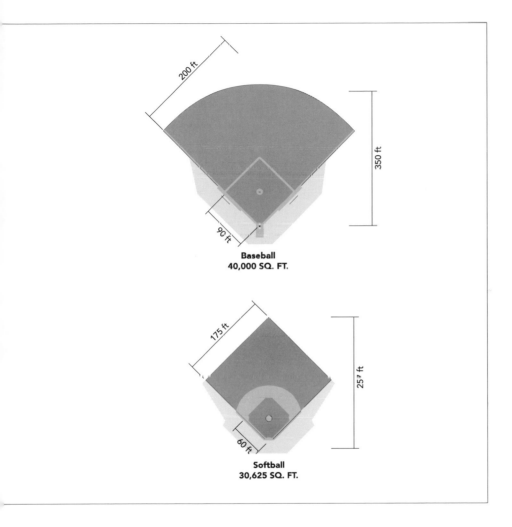

Baseball
40,000 SQ. FT.

Softball
30,625 SQ. FT.

building during the school day? Is central administration the security checkpoint? How does the public enter the building for larger community events? Is the entry sequence different in inclement weather?

Most schools have more than one entrance; many have ceremonial/formal entrances and additional entrances that are more frequently used for entry by students. In warm climates, many schools have direct exterior access to classrooms, with outdoor breezeways and corridors.

This organizational strategy reduces square footage and, ultimately, construction costs. It also reduces the ability to monitor or control entrance to the building.

Internal circulation. During the school day, where do students have to go and how often? Do some travel the corridors as a class, such as in elementary school, while other classes are in session? Do they travel individually at each class period, such as in upper grade levels? How much time is allotted between periods, and how far are distances? How are student lockers used and distributed in the school?

School size. How large is the school's enrollment? Is there a need to create subgroupings within the building to mitigate the anonymity found in facilities with large enrollments? If subgrouping is a goal, what are the differentiating factors for grouping: by grade level, by full-grade microcosm spectrums such as "houses," by different magnet programs, or otherwise?

Teaching methodologies. What are the teaching methodologies employed? Is there a magnet or multiple magnet program? Is there a team teaching approach?

Efficiency/cost. The amount of corridor space needed to serve each room in the building is a major component in the determination of building efficiency and resultant costs. Different organizational strategies yield varying efficiencies. Compact plans tend to be lower in first cost but are often not the best

educational environment. Typical configuration options are discussed in chapter 2.

Natural light and views. Almost all spaces in a school building can benefit from some amount of natural light. Many rooms require certain amounts of light by local codes and regulations.

Site access. Many spaces, including lower-age-group classrooms, benefit from direct access.

Service access. Which program elements require direct service, such as auditorium stage areas, kitchens, gymnasiums, mechanical areas?

Solar orientation and related issues. The siting of the building can influence the amount of artificial lighting required, the potential solar heat gain, the ability to use natural ventilation, and other factors.

Accessibility. All school sites are now expected to provide barrier-free access. This subject is well illustrated in the U.S. Department of Justice's technical-assistance updates.

CHAPTER 5
CODES

Almost all construction is governed by a variety of codes and related regulations. Because of the importance of the health and safety of children, school buildings are among the most carefully regulated. Many states, for example, have at least eight to ten codes that govern the construction of all a school's major building systems.

The National Conference of States on Building Codes and Standards (NCSBCS) has published an extremely useful directory of the relevant codes that apply in each state as well as in the cities that have their own supplemental codes. The *Directory of Building Codes and Regulations* can be obtained from the National Conference of States on Building Codes and Standards, 505 Huntmar Park Drive, Suite 210, Herndon, VA 22070 (703–437–0100).

In addition, most states also have detailed regulations written specifically to govern school building design and construction. Some of these are more than 100 pages long and cover everything from space standards (also discussed in the chapter 1) to bidding procedures to specific provisions for emergency evacuation. Many of these regulations are also available on the Internet.

In general, all of this regulation is directed at seven primary issues: life safety; adequate space and facilities for teaching, appropriate building systems and construction practices, public policy

NCSBCS CODE SUMMARY, MINNESOTA						
Type of Code	**State Code**	**Technical Basis**	**Applicability**	**Preemptive Application**	**Administration**	**Enforce.**
Building	State Building Code	1994 UBC with state amendments	All buildings	Mandatory. Local jurisdictions may not amend.	1	1 or Local
Mechanical	Minnesota Mechanical Code	1991 UMC with state amendments	All buildings	Mandatory. Local jurisdictions may not amend.	1	1 or Local
Plumbing	Minnesota Plumbing Code	State-written	All public buildings or buildings connected to public use water or sewer system.	Mandatory. Local jurisdictions may not amend.	1,2	2 for public bldgs. or Local
Electrical	State Building Code	1996 NEC	All buildings	Mandatory. Local jurisdictions may not amend.	3	3 or Local
Energy	Minnesota Energy Code	State-written	All buildings	Mandatory. Local jurisdictions may not amend.	4	1 or Local
Gas	Minnesota Mechanical Code	1991 UMC with state amendments	All buildings	Mandatory. Local jurisdictions may not amend.	1	1 or Local
Fire Prevention	Fire Safety, Chapter 7510	1991 UFC with state amendments	All buildings	Mandatory. Local jurisdictions may amend to make more stringent.	5	5 or Local
Life Safety	Fire Safety, Chapter 7510	NFPA 101, 1991 edition, as supplement to fire code	All buildings	Mandatory. Local jurisdictions may amend to make more stringent.	5	5 or Local
Accessibility	State Building Code	1994 UBC, Chapter 11 and Appendix Chapter 11, with state amendments	All buildings	Mandatory. Local jurisdictions may not amend.	1	1 or Local

Source: *Directory of Building Codes and Regulations*, April 1998. National Conference of States on Building Codes and Standards Inc., p. 96.

(historical preservation, energy conservation, accessibility for disabled persons), enforcement, fiscal and anticorruption controls, and land-use policy.

The codes are applied unevenly to public and private schools. Public schools are often subject to state rather than local regulation. Therefore, they are often exempt from local land-use controls. Private schools, on the other hand, may be subject to local land-use controls but are often exempt from meeting state department of education standards for classroom size and other factors.

LIFE SAFETY

The most important issue in the development of any code is life safety. For obvious reasons, all state and local codes—as well as enforcement—start with this issue. The key life safety considerations built into the codes include fire safety, environmental safety, and elimination of hazards.

1. *Fire safety*. The following are key issues in fire safety:

- Reduction of the likelihood of fire through use of noncombustible materials in construction. For example, wood-frame construction is discouraged or prohibited in many states, and there are often restrictions on the use of flammable interior finishes.

- Reduction of the potential of fire-related structural collapse. Many codes require structural assemblies that will withstand some period of exposure to fire.

- Early detection through the use of smoke and/or heat detectors—particularly in highly hazardous areas

such as kitchens and mechanical spaces—is now commonly required.

- Fire and smoke containment through use of compartmentalization and rated assemblies between floors is also commonly required. Highly hazardous areas, including mechanical rooms, storage areas, and the like, are typically to be enclosed with fire-rated walls, floors, and ceilings.

- Fire suppression through mandatory installation of extinguishers, fire-suppression systems in highly hazardous spaces such as kitchens, and, increasingly, the use of sprinklers. The National Fire Protection Association points out that there has never been a multiple-death fire in a building with a functioning sprinkler system.

- Evacuation in case of fire or other emergency is the most universal concept built into the codes. Almost all codes require that there be two means of egress from most spaces. For classrooms, this is typically accomplished by having one exit go into a fire-rated corridor leading to a fire stair or directly outside, combined with an "escape window" or door to the outside. Providing a choice of evacuation routes—in case one is blocked—is fundamental. Most codes also define exit widths and the spacing of fixed seating in larger spaces such as gyms and auditoriums.

Typical of the standards applied are those in the New York State education department's *Manual of Planning Standards*:

Main corridor width without lockers 8 ft
Main corridor width with lockers
one side   9 ft

Main corridor width with lockers
    two sides   10 ft
Secondary corridor without lockers 6 ft
Secondary corridor with lockers
    one side   7 ft
Secondary corridor with lockers
    two sides   8 ft
Auditorium and cafeteria required
    exit units   Net sq ft ÷ 600
Back to back spacing of
    seating   Not less than 33 in.
Minimum clear distance between
    seating in the up position   12 in.
    continental seating   16 in
Maximum number of seats if aisles at
    each end   15

- *Fire fighting.* Some codes require emergency and fire access to all sides of a school building. They usually establish requirements for the standpipe, hydrant, or other devices required for fire fighting. Typical requirements call for hydrants to be located so that any fire can be reached with 500 ft of hose and that they be able to provide 500 gallons per minute.

2. *Environmental safety.* The codes dealing with environmental safety issues vary from state to state; the following are among the most common:

- Required ventilation (see "Ventilation" in chapter 8) and indoor air-quality standards (see "Environmental Quality" in chapter 6)

- Required removal or containment of asbestos

- Required removal or containment of lead-based paint

- Requirements for food-service equipment (stainless steel, easily cleaned, etc.) and food-preparation and servery spaces

- Requirements for safe drinking water and water fountains

- Minimum lighting standards (see chapter 13)

3. *Elimination of hazards.* Most state codes and departments of education also try to minimize potential hazards. Typical requirements and prohibitions in the codes include the following:

- Use of flooring materials that minimize slipping

- Marking of glazed doors and sidelights

- Use of safety glass or glazing within 18 in. of the floor, corridor glazing within 48 in. of the floor in corridors, and glazing in areas such as a gymnasium

- Site designs that minimize pedestrian-vehicular conflicts, with particular emphasis on drop-off and pickup areas (see chapter 4)

- Physical restrictions on access to highly hazardous spaces such as boiler rooms, electrical closets, etc.

- Elimination of overhead power lines that cross school property

- Restrictions on the location and use of high-pressure boilers

- Availability of emergency showers in chemistry classrooms

- A variety of guidelines for natural gas use and distribution

- Prevention of child access to electrical heating devices

SPACE STANDARDS

Most states establish standards for classroom size as well as the sizes of many other school facilities. This subject is discussed in Chapter 1. It should be noted, however, that meeting these standards may not be required in private and parochial schools.

APPROPRIATE BUILDING SYSTEMS AND CONSTRUCTION PRACTICES

The largest quantity of code material regulates the selection of appropriate building systems and methods of construction. The Building Officials and Code Administrators (BOCA) International Code is one of the most widely used compendium of building codes. Many of its codes also refer to other codes or standards, such as those of the National Electrical Code (NEC); the American Society of Heating, Refrigerating, and Air-Conditioning Engineers (ASHRAE); and the American National Standards Institute (ANSI). State codes typically include separate codes or sections of the code for mechanical, electrical, and plumbing systems.

PUBLIC POLICY

Schools are often subject to laws and codes passed to further a certain public policy, such as historic preservation, energy conservation, and/or accessibility for disabled persons.

1. *Historic preservation.* Preservation regulations vary widely across the United States. In some states, schools are exempt. In others, a school designated as a landmark or historically significant may involve additional public reviews, restrictions on renovations and additions, and/or a prohibition against demolition.

2. *Energy conservation.* Most states have an energy code, which usually focuses on the energy performance of the building envelope. (See chapter 6.)

ACCESSIBILITY

One of the most discussed—and often misunderstood—code issues is the Americans with Disabilities Act (ADA). Many people think it is a building code when it is, in fact, a civil rights law whose intent has now been built into many existing codes. The general intent of this important legislation is stated in Title II of the law: "Subject to the provisions of this subchapter, no qualified individual with a disability shall, by reason of such disability, be excluded from participation in or be denied the benefits of services, programs, or activities of a public entity, or be subjected to discrimination by any such entity."

Although the law applies only to a "public entity," ADA's supplemental technical guidelines and most building codes have been developed or revised so that they apply to virtually all schools—even private schools. They apply to faculty and staff, students, and—in the case of some school facilities that have community functions—the general public.

This section of this chapter summarizes some of the guidelines that generally guide the application of this law and the related codes, but these have been subject to myriad local and state variations and interpretations. This discussion should not be considered either legal advice or an interpretation of every accessibility code, but is intended as a framework to help in understanding and interpreting this evolving area of building regulation. For a more complete discussion of the legal issues, the National Organization on Legal Problems of Education's (NOLPE) *Planning and Financing School Improvement and Construction Projects* has an informative chapter, and technical guidelines are typically provided in state or local accessibility codes as well as in the ADA and ANSI guidelines. Probably the best source on this topic is *Compliance with the Americans with Disabilities Act: A Self-Evaluation Guide for Public Elementary and Secondary Schools*, published by the U.S. Department of Education, Office of Civil Rights.

Although most people are aware of the need to create an accessible route for the mobility-impaired individuals to all functions, ADA also covers other disabilities, including sight, hearing, and other impairments. Thus curb ramps, elevators, properly sloped ramps, accessible toilet stalls, accessible telephones and drinking fountains, and other such accommodations are not necessarily enough. Alarms suitable for hearing-impaired persons, hardware appropriate for people with hand impairments such as arthritis, and other changes may be needed as well. The codes in most states establish the minimum standards, but the definitions of disability are still evolving.

An area that is the subject of particular debate is the degree to which design guidelines should be adjusted for children. Some code officials believe that children should learn to use the same aids as the general public, whereas others argue for aids that reflect children's size, strength, and experience.

The main issue facing school systems, of course, is what to do with the barriers in existing facilities. There are choices. For example, a school can use ramps, lifts, or elevators to permit a disabled student to get to the library, or it can have an aide take a book cart to each classroom. The spirit of law, however, requires the barrier-free route because it offers library services to disabled students in the same setting as others.

The regulations suggest several possible methods of compliance:

- Redesign of equipment
- Reassignment of services to accessible buildings
- Assignment of aides to beneficiaries
- Home visits
- Delivery of services at alternative accessible sites
- Alteration of existing facilities
- Construction of new facilities
- Use of accessible rolling stock or other conveyances

New buildings built or significantly altered after January 26, 1992, however, are to be designed and built so that they are "readily accessible to and usable by individuals with disabilities." The state codes are now reasonably clear, but the federal government references the *Americans with Disabilities Act Accessibility Guidelines for Buildings and Facilities* (ADAAG), published as 59 Fed. Reg. 31,676 (1994). Some state codes reference the Council of American Building Officials (CABO) American National Standards Institute (ANSI) standards, CABO/ANSI A117.1–1992 and A17.1–1987.

Most codes also outline the enforcement procedures that will be used.

FISCAL AND ANTICORRUPTION CONTROLS

State laws and other regulations typically govern the purchasing of design services, construction, equipment, and furnishings.

Although most states permit qualification-based selection of professional services, construction, equipment, and furnishings are typically purchased via a competitive bidding process. The NOLPE monograph *Planning and Financing School Improvements and Construction Projects* mentioned earlier also has a good chapter on this subject, "Fundamentals of Competitive Bidding."

Many districts also impose a number of disclosure and procedural requirements to avoid conflicts of interest and other problems. After this screening, most jurisdictions require the school to award the contract to the "lowest responsible and responsive bidder." A responsible bidder is one "who has the capability to perform the contract requirements and the integrity and reliability which will assure good faith performance." A responsive bidder is one "who has submitted a bid which conforms in all material respects to the Invitation for Bids."

LAND-USE POLICY

Many states exempt public schools from most local land-use controls. Private and parochial schools, as well as a minority of public schools, may be subject to some or all of the following:

- Planning and/or Zoning Board review, which typically focuses on issues such as vehicular access, storm water management, landscaping and other site planning considerations, as well as compliance with the height, setback, lot coverage, parking, and other requirements of local zoning.

- Coastal Zone, State Historic Preservation Office, and other reviews, which typically deal with one of the public policy issues noted earlier in this chapter.

- Board of Architectural Review scrutiny, which typically focuses on the materials and aesthetics of the proposed design.

- State or local department of transportation regulations, which often govern the road improvements, curb cuts, and other actions necessary for vehicular access.

- Environmental-impact review, which is often mandated in the expenditure of significant public monies.

CONCLUSION

Navigating the increasingly complex code and public-approval environment has become a major task for most schools and their planning and design teams. It is not unusual for the various reviews to add 6 to 18 months to the time normally required to plan, design, and start construction of a school.

CHAPTER 6

ENERGY AND ENVIRONMENTAL ISSUES

The 1973 oil embargo is generally regarded as the beginning of broad-based concern about energy conservation in the United States. The growing interest in "green" or "sustainable" design has been a natural extension of the greater public awareness of the economic and environmental costs of wasting nonrenewable resources. The first part of this chapter discusses the major issues of energy conservation in school design, and the second discusses energy conservation in the context of the broader concern for environmentally sensitive design.

Typical of the growing interest in energy and environmental issues is Southern California Edison's (SCE) "Rethinking the Portable Classroom" initiative, a yearlong study to improve the design and performance of this ubiquitous addition to many schools. The initiative places particular attention on:

- Daylighting
- Energy reduction
- Low-emission materials
- Siting
- Long-term durability

ENERGY CONSERVATION
Energy conservation in schools has focused on the six major consumers of energy in this building type:
- Lighting
- Heating
- Air-conditioning
- Domestic hot water
- Ventilation
- Miscellaneous other pieces of mechanical and electrical equipment (pumps, elevators, computers, kitchen equipment, audiovisual equipment, etc.) found in many school buildings

New technologies and systems are continuing to be developed in each area, but some of the most effective conservation techniques remain the commonsense design solutions developed long before energy was cheap and plentiful.

Lighting
Some of the most dramatic conservation gains have been made in lighting. In the 1960s the typical design standard for lighting called for 2 to 3 watts per square foot for classroom lighting. Today the same or better lighting levels can be achieved with 0.7 to 0.9 watts per square foot. The source of these dramatic reductions can be traced to the development of high-efficiency ballasts, high-efficiency lamps, and fixtures that are more efficient in directing low-glare, adequate light levels to the work surface. (These more efficient fixtures and their incorporation in school design are also discussed in chapter 13.) In terms of energy conservation, many school systems have found complete replacement of their older lighting to be cost-effective.

Some further reductions in lighting usage have also been achieved by a combination of simple technology and commonsense operating procedures. Among the more common are the following:

- The obvious step of turning out lights when a room is not in use.

- Similarly obvious is the reduction of lighting to the levels actually needed for a task. In the past, lighting standards were often unduly influenced by manufacturers and energy suppliers. As a result, many schools have excessive lighting levels.

- The use of double circuiting so that only the number of light fixtures required are turned on. In many classrooms, half the fixtures will provide the desired lighting levels during a normal sunny day. Photocells also are used in some areas—such as the major public areas and circulation spaces—where more automatic adjustment of light levels using this technology may be justified. Photocell-actuated lighting can also be appropriate in some exterior applications.

- The use of time clocks and motion detectors to automatically turn off lights in spaces that are not in use. Motion detectors (if not a code requirement) have not been cost-effective in many classrooms but can work well in smaller spaces that get sporadic use.

- There are many central-lighting, programmable control systems available to manage clocks and lights automatically with digital controls.

- Designing the school to maximize the use of daylight. As discussed in chapter 13, however, it is important that natural light be used properly.

High-intensity direct sunlight on a school desk is not a good alternative to the proper balance between artificial and natural light.

- Use of low-energy fixtures, such as light-emitting diode (LED) exit lights and high-pressure sodium lamps for parking lots, is important where permitted by code. LED fixtures have a long expected life, and sodium vapor lighting produces twice as much light per watt as mercury vapor lighting and five times per watt as incandescent fixtures. Sodium vapor, however, may cause disturbance to neighboring homes and may not provide a pleasing color rendition.

Heating

Until the increased use of air-conditioning in schools changed the equation in many school systems, the next major consumer of energy was heating. This was a major focus of the initial efforts toward energy conservation. Tighter building envelopes, more compact floor plans, greater insulation, more efficient heating systems, lower heating levels, more sensitive controls, and more exotic measures were all tried by hundreds of schools and school systems. As energy prices declined and the negative consequences of some measures (poor indoor air quality, oppressive designs with little natural light in many spaces, discomfort, disappointing savings, etc.) became apparent, a more balanced view of energy conservation in the heating system has evolved.

By the late 1990s the most common areas of emphasis in heating conservation were the following:

- Tightening the performance of the building envelope by adding wall and roof insulation, building vestibules for the main entrances, and weather-stripping doors and windows.

- Improving the balance and increasing the number of room-by-room controls of the heating system to eliminate the need to open windows in some areas of the school on cold days to compensate for excessive heat. This is a common problem in older schools, where poor operating and maintenance procedures allow solar gain on one facade to be counteracted by opening windows.

- Improved controls, including direct digital controls, which more quickly and efficiently adjust heat levels in a space to reflect changes in occupancy and solar gain. Night setback thermostats and other controls are now common as well. These setback controls are often combined with morning warm-up and evening cool-down controls, as well as heating water reset according to outside temperature.

- Window replacement is a common concern. Unless a school's windows have to be replaced because of rot or other functional deficiencies, replacing the large windows common in most schools is rarely justified by the energy savings alone. If other factors help to justify the change, and new windows are installed, there can be a significant increase in the thermal performance of the building envelope, as well as a reduction in the need for painting, repair of balances, and other routine maintenance. Unfortunately, many schools have replaced their large, attractive wood windows with cheap residential windows with inappropriate anodized finishes, on the grounds of low first cost. These windows are often too thinly structured to fill the entire opening, and a fixed metal panel is added to fill in the top of the opening. These windows not only disfigure the schools, but often fail early because they were meant primarily for the smaller openings typically found in apartment buildings. There is no reason for this mistake inasmuch as there are many competitively priced high-performance window systems available.

- The addition of "Low E" coatings to windows is now common. This technological innovation significantly improves the performance of the windows and often approximates the benefits of insulated (double-glazed) window units.

- More efficient boilers and related systems save energy costs through flue gas heat recovery, flue dampers, dual-fuel combustion, high-efficiency combustion, and other features. In addition, it is often recommended that boilers be selected to more efficiently match the heating demand (e.g., modules of 50 to 60 percent of demand to operate at low loads).

- More efficient distribution systems, such as variable speed pumping, and independent zoning for temperature control help to reduce the heating and cooling energy lost in distribution.

Air-Conditioning

In recent decades more schools have air-conditioned more of their facilities to improve teaching conditions and to make the schools suitable for year-round use. In many school districts air-conditioning has become the standard, rather than a luxury feature for a few priority spaces (such as the principal's office). This shift has added a significant new source of energy consumption.

Among the major steps that schools are taking to control the increase in energy consumption caused by this new demand are the following:

- Use of separate systems to serve areas with unique usage profiles (e.g., auditoriums, computer-intensive areas, offices, community centers, etc.).

- Steps to reduce the power required by a system's fans, often the major energy uses in an air-conditioning system. This has been accomplished in part with variable-speed fans, use of radiant cooling (common in Europe but still rare in the United States), and lower-temperature air supply.

- Utilization of high-efficiency heating, ventilation and air-conditioning (HVAC) equipment, variable-speed drives on the fans, high-efficiency motors, and refrigeration equipment with good (EER) ratings.

- Use of roof insulation, Low E window coatings, and lighter-colored roofing materials to reduce the cooling load.

- Strategies employed to minimize solar gain through glazing while maximizing the penetration of daylight, include massing, orientation, use of deciduous trees, light shelves, glazing analysis, reflectivity, etc.

Ventilation

Ventilation is a mandatory part of most codes, and it contributes to energy consumption in two primary ways: via the energy used when ventilation air is heated, cooled, and/or dehumidified and the energy required to operate the fans in the system. The primary energy-saving opportunities in ventilation include the following:

- Heat-recovery systems that transfer the exhaust heat to the incoming cold air or, reciprocally, the exhaust "cooling" to the incoming hot, humid air.

- Installing a warm-up cycle during fan start-up on cold mornings. Energy savings will result form heating indoor air, instead of colder outdoor air, to bring the building up to temperature.

- The installation of relief vents and exhaust systems if necessary to relieve pressurization for rooftop units with inadequate relief vents.

Reduction in Other Energy Demands

There are further energy demands that can be reduced. Microprocessor-based energy management and control systems (EMCS) can be very cost-effective in controlling HVAC systems (e.g., start/stop, temperature reset, system optimization, maintenance logs, etc.).

Schools are incorporating an increasing number of mechanical and electrical devices, such as television, VCRs, computers, audiovisual equipment, kitchen equipment, specialized vocational teaching equipment, and elevators, all of which demand energy. Some of these systems can be controlled by EMCS to minimize waste. Energy input ratings, available for much of this equipment, should be evaluated as part of the performance specifications.

Domestic Hot Water and Other Plumbing-Related Energy Demands

Although it is not a major source of energy consumption, water usage is an important energy and environmental consideration. Among the conservation measures most frequently employed are the following:

- The most obvious is the repair of leaking faucets. Although this problem appears to be minor, it is often a significant source of waste.

- Installing low-flow devices for showers and sinks and low-water-usage toilet fixtures.

- In some warm-weather states, solar power has been employed to provide domestic hot water and for other uses. During a period of low energy cost, however, few such applications can be justified by cost savings alone.

- Use of energy-efficient separate domestic hot-water heaters to allow the large heating boilers to be shut off during mild weather.

- Operating with lower hot-water temperatures (120° F vs. 140° F).

Calculating the Costs and Benefits of Energy-Conservation Measures

There are many methods of calculating the costs and benefits of energy-conservation measures, but probably the most common (and most widely accepted) is the simple payback calculation. With this method, the projected cost of the measure (for example, the cost of a program of light-fixture replacement or more efficient boilers) is estimated. Then the projected annual savings in gallons of fuel oil or kilowatt hours are converted to dollar savings. The cost of the measure is then divided by the savings to yield an estimated payback period—in other words, an approximation of the time it will take to recover the capital cost of the measure with the money saved from lower operating costs. When the payback period is less than seven or eight years, many school systems consider it a worthwhile investment. Some will even consider payback periods of ten to twelve years adequate to justify the change.

The payback method is a useful, if somewhat crude, tool. Its reliability depends on the accuracy of the estimates of both costs and savings. Estimates of savings and costs for replacement of light fixtures are relatively easy to calculate, but many other measures are far less exact. Most require the input of an engineering or energy-conservation professional, who often uses more sophisticated methods of calculation, such as the life-cycle cost analysis. This technique is summarized in chapter 19.

Solar Energy and Geothermic Systems, Passive Heating and Cooling, and Photovoltaics

Schools are logical uses of solar energy, because the building use is typically concentrated during the day, when energy from the sun can be used to maximum benefit. The low cost of fossil-fuel energy in the 1990s has slowed the introduction of solar and other renewable energy systems. Steady technological advances, increased public awareness and concern, greater design team sophistication, and government support have continued to stimulate experimentation with application of these techniques.

The following are among the systems being used in schools:

- *Active solar thermal.* Solar panels are used for hot-water production and part of the heating load. These systems are often tied into a school's conventional hot-water production system. Many school districts throughout the United States have experimented with this technology and participated in demonstration projects. The Ferry Pass Middle School, in Pensacola, Florida, offers just one of a number of high-profile demonstrations designed to stimulate active solar use.

- *Passive solar.* Building envelopes can be designed to reduce solar gain for cooling and increase solar gain for heating.

- *Photocell-controlled lighting.* Photocells can control the amount of lighting needed both within classrooms and in outside installations such as parking lots. This technique, combined with proven daylighting design, can significantly reduce lighting energy demand.

- *Photovoltaics (PV).* PV technology is steadily advancing, and a growing number of school districts have installed such systems. In most cases these systems are designed in combination with normal grid-supplied electricity. For example, it is possible for a school to use such a system to run the electric pumps and blowers of a solar thermal desicant air-conditioning system at high speed on a sunny afternoon, and then switch over to grid-supplied power for the low-speed, nighttime demand.

Demonstration projects in Maryland, Michigan, Wisconsin, and many other states have been targeted for schools, and the results have been encouraging. For example, SolarWise for Schools installed this system in three Wisconsin schools. The annual output and environmental impacts of the three systems are shown in the opposite table, along with projections for the additional 60 schools in WPSC territory if they receive solar-electric systems.

Other energy technologies are also being tested in schools:

- *Geothermal.* Low-level geothermal systems use geothermal heat pumps and water in wells, where the water stays at a constant temperature. Proponents of this system point to its use of a nonpolluting renewable resource, lower operating costs, reduction in rooftop equipment, and other advantages. There are also geothermal systems that use naturally heated water, but there are no prominent examples of their use by schools.

- *Wind generation.* A school in Spirit Lake, Iowa, has housed a demonstration project for wind-generated electrical power. Its wind turbine generates more power than is consumed by the school. The payback calculation was enhanced by a Department of Energy grant, but according to the school's figures, even without the grant the annual savings are almost enough to justify a normal capital investment by the school.

Building Envelope
The energy performance of many new buildings is now governed by code.

IMPACT OF SOLAR-GENERATED SYSTEMS						
	Annual Energy Output (kWh/year)	Annual Cost Conserved (lbs/year)	Annual Avoided Emissions (lbs./year)			
			CO_2	SO_2	NO_2	Particulate
Current impacts (3 schools; 12 kW each)	50,000	68,100	120,000	560	640	20
Projected impacts (60 schools, 4 kW each)	332,000	454,000	800,000	3,700	4,270	140

Source: *Solar Wise for Schools*, http://www.wpsr.com/foundat/Monsumm.html#anchor707504

Typical of the energy code requirements are those based on the American Society of Heating, Refrigerating, and Air-Conditioning Engineers' (ASHRAE) Standard 90.1–1999. In existing buildings, retrofits are frequently used to upgrade the energy conservation performance of the building envelope. Among the more common envelope upgrades are the following:

• New thermal pane or Low E glazed windows

• Additional roof insulation added during roof replacement

• Additional wall insulation

• The addition of vestibules

• Weather-stripping and other actions to reduce air infiltration and heat loss

As noted in a following section, however, care must be taken to balance the energy savings of a tighter building envelope with the steps necessary to preserve indoor air quality.

Building Siting and Orientation

Energy, as considered in building siting, is discussed in chapter 4.

SUSTAINABLE DESIGN

Along with energy conservation, sustainable, or "green," design has emerged in the last two decades as a major consideration in the planning and designing of all building types. In 1996, for example, the City of Seattle public utilities partnered with the Seattle public schools to promote sustainability. Other schools have built sustainability into their curricula as well as their building programs.

Among the major issues that are considered in any "green" building are the following:

• Energy efficiency

• Water conservation

• Solid waste management

• Resource-efficient building materials

• Environmental quality

Each of these issues has been translated into specific design and operational decisions for a growing number of school buildings.

Water Conservation

To date, most water-conservation efforts have focused on the selection of low-consumption toilet, shower, and other plumbing fixtures. However, in some areas landscape design and low-consumption irrigation techniques are also major water-conservation issues.

However, gray-water systems are also being considered, which include the use of waste water from lavatories and showers for irrigation or cooling towers.

Solid Waste Management

Many schools are trying to reduce the quantity of solid waste and have increased the amount of recycling and use of materials with recycled content. These measures, which add to the amount of storage a school needs, are affecting the choice of materials specified by a design team.

Resource-Efficient Building Materials

The materials used in renovation or new construction constitute another significant issue. Are the materials:

- Produced locally?

- Developed from sustainable or renewable resources?

- Salvageable if the structure is demolished later?

- Manufactured in a process that creates toxic by-products?

- Used in a way that results in post-installation off-gassing?

- Easily maintainable and durable?

All of these concerns must be balanced with such issues as performance, aesthetics, cost, codes, and the many other criteria that should be used to select any material or system. Buildings made of rammed earth or hay bales; triple-paneled, organic-filled windows; and

natural wool carpeting appear in articles on green architecture, but they are not likely to be relevant to school projects.

Environmental Quality

The oil embargo and energy crisis of the 1970s caused the owners of most buildings—including schools—to tighten the building envelope and reduce the infiltration of outside air. These measures are often cited as the primary cause of the well-documented health problems that have resulted from poor indoor air quality.

In fact, the causes of many specific indoor air problems are complex, and it is clear that inadequate flow of outside air into a building is only one cause. As more schools are air-conditioned, aging systems, dirty ducts, and deferred maintenance are also issues of concern.

ASHRAE has addressed this issue with the recommendations in its published Standard 62–1989. In many outdoor weather conditions, increased ventilation not only improves indoor air quality but reduces cooling energy consumption. Well designed and controlled air-economizer systems can readily achieve this objective. The Occupational Safety and Health Administration's (OSHA) indoor air-quality (IAQ) rules and the Environmental Protection Agency's (EPA) "Tools for Schools" kit both refer to this standard. (American School and University 1998).

Other issues are addressed by common sense, better maintenance, and growing knowledge about the emission of volatile organic compounds (VOC). More attention is now paid to the location of air intakes away from the sources of building or vehicular exhaust, to regular cleaning of HVAC ductwork, to better ventilation in special-use classrooms (chemistry, biology, fine arts, etc.), to the selection of better air-filtration systems, and to regular vacuuming of carpets and other dust- or mold-trapping materials.

At the same time, more design teams are being careful to specify materials such as paints and adhesives that are certified as "low emitting" in regard to VOCs.

There are, of course, related concerns about the exterior environment as well. Probably the most commonly discussed topic has been the need for reduction of ozone-depleting compounds in refrigeration, fire suppression, and other systems.

Environmentally Sensitive Site Development

Those concerned with renovation and new construction of school buildings are noting the impact of site design on the natural environment. Mandatory environmental impact reviews and stricter environmental regulations have greatly reduced this impact. Some design teams are placing greater emphasis on reducing the building footprint, decreasing disturbance of site areas, and protecting a site's important natural features.

Caveats

Much of the initial work on sustainable design has been oversold. Most of the concepts summarized in this chapter should be considered in building design, but in many of the highly publicized projects by the pioneers in this field, the achievements have been overstated and the costs understated. Nevertheless, environmentally sensitive design will continue to be an increasingly important issue in school building design.

CHAPTER 7
STRUCTURAL SYSTEMS

Because of differences in age, geographical diversity, design team preferences, various federal, state, and local codes, construction costs, and many other factors, virtually every common structural system—and some unusual alternatives—have been used in school construction. Masonry bearing wall, wood frame, poured-in-place concrete, precast concrete, steel frame, and Teflon-coated fiberglass fabrics are just a few of the systems employed. Therefore, it is not possible to provide general guidelines for the selection of the appropriate structural system.

It is possible, however, to summarize ten of the typical factors that school systems and their design teams consider in evaluating structural systems as discussed in the following sections.

BUILDING LIFE

Most schools are built to last a long time. Although virtually all structural systems can last indefinitely if properly maintained, most new schools prefer structural systems with indefinite life spans and minimal maintenance requirements, such as concrete, steel, bearing wall, and the like. Cost, however, can distort this preference. To reduce first cost, many school buildings use exterior wall systems such as structural stud back up to masonry veneer and exterior insulated facade system (EIFS). The reduction in first cost is usually accompanied by higher maintenance cost and a shorter system life span.

FIRE SAFETY

Although most fire experts will note that the structural system has little to do with fire safety in a typical low-rise school structure, a growing number of codes now direct or encourage the selection of fire-resistant structural systems, such as fireproofed steel, concrete, glue-laminated beams, and the like.

SEISMIC CONSIDERATIONS

A building's ability to withstand seismic events is probably of greater concern than the combustibility of the structural system. An increasing number of states are recognizing the potential dangers and are addressing seismic design in their codes. Seismic design, however, can significantly affect the choice of systems as well as their cost and flexibility.

FLEXIBILITY

Bearing-wall construction was common in older schools—and is frequently used even today. A bearing-wall structure, particularly when the partitions between classrooms or the corridor walls are load bearing, is one of the least flexible systems. Poured-in-place concrete walls and a number of other systems create similar constraints. In an era of accelerating change in educational environments, flexibility is important. Thus, the selection of a structural system should not preclude or inhibit future reconfiguration of space or additions to a school. At one time, during the 1950s and 1960s, flexibility was such a major consideration that it led to prototypes— such as in the School Construction Systems Development (SCSD)—that were developed around the concepts of speed and flexibility.

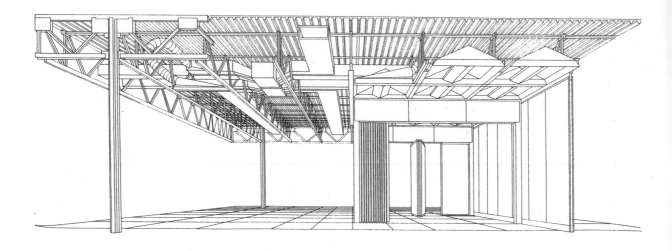

▲ Illustration of the systems integration built into the SCSD prototype.

COST

The structural system typically makes up 10 to 15 percent of the construction costs of a new school. Most school systems and their design teams try to minimize this part of the budget (subject to code, flexibility, life expectancy, and other considerations). The cost-effectiveness of any system will vary according to changes in market conditions, regional preferences, code requirements, relative labor and material costs, and other factors. Nevertheless, the choice of lowest cost is typically the system that combines the local construction industry preference with simple fabrication and readily available materials.

Although the structural systems of schools are rarely complex, as compared with other building types, one of the challenges to cost control is the lack of repetition. The specific needs of the different areas in a school call for a variety of heights, bay sizes, cladding requirements, and even utility systems. Repetition—a typical goal in simplifying a structure and managing cost—is very

hard to achieve in the design of a school's structural system.

Among the issues that any school structure must address are code requirements. Typical of the basic code requirements are the loads that the structure must support. The specifications of New York's code, for example, are shown in the opposite table.

AESTHETICS

The structural system can be a major aesthetic consideration in the design of schools. Some architects have chosen to express structure with dramatic effect, as shown in the illustrations on pages 126 and 127.

LONG SPAN SPACES

Typically, the most structurally complex spaces are the large ones—cafeterias, gymnasiums, auditoriums, swimming pools, and the like. Where availability of land is not a constraint, these spaces are typically designed as one-story structures and rarely have other structures above them. These spaces use most of the

MINIMUM LIVE LOADS, NEW YORK STATE		
Occupancy	Uniform Live Load (psf)[a]	Concentrated Load(pounds)
Assembly areas:		
Fixed seats	60	
Lobbies	100	
Movable seats	100	
Platforms (assembly)	125	
Projection and control rooms	50	
Stage catwalks	40	
Stage floors	125	
Gymnasiums, main floors, and balconies	100[b]	
Libraries		
Reading rooms	60	1,000
Stack rooms	150[c]	1,000
Corridors above first floor	80	1,000
Schools		
Classrooms	40	1,000
Corridors above first floor	80	1,000
First-floor corridors	100	1,000

[b] In addition to the vertical live loads, loads of 120 pounds per lineal foot on footboards and seatboards shall be utilized. Lateral sway-bracing loads of 24 pounds per lineal foot parallel to and 10 pounds per lineal foot perpendicular to seatboards and footboards shall be utilized. [c] The weight of books and shelving shall be computed utilizing an assumed density of 65 lb/ft^3 and converted to a uniformly distributed load, which shall be utilized if this load exceeds 150 lb/ft^2 [e] 1 psf = 47.9 Pa; 1 pound = 4.4 N.

Source: BOCA National Building Code, 1996 (pp.16–8, 16–9).

typical long-span material options, such as steel, trusses, precast concrete, and glue-laminated beams.

PREFABRICATED AND PREENGINEERED STRUCTURES

Many school systems investigate the cost-effectiveness of prefabricated and preengineered structures. Prefabricated structures are widely used to provide temporary classroom space, but their attraction typically is speed of acquisition rather than cost or quality. Thus, the primary reason prefabricated structures are used is to solve short-term shortages of space. They are most commonly used for long-span spaces such as gyms and field houses. Such structures can often be planned, acquired, and made operational in less than a few months. More permanent factory-built structures are also used in some school programs.

Preengineered structures—used particularly for long-span spaces—are quite common. The major advantage of such structures is the reduction in design, fabrication, and delivery time. The costs are not necessarily significantly different from those of other structural alternatives.

Preengineered structures also have disadvantages. Many require pitched roofs with greater volume to heat and cool and more complex interior partitioning. Another disadvantage of many of these structures is the metal siding and roofing used as an exterior cladding material. Many of these metal cladding systems have limited lives and are viewed as unattractive.

FOUNDATIONS

In more developed areas, available sites often pose problems, one of which is poor soil conditions. As a result, early geotechnical analysis is important. In most cases an analysis should be performed prior to site acquisition. More detailed analysis is also often necessary at the start of construction inasmuch as the initial tests are only spot checks.

▶ *The Wilbert Snow Elementary School in Middletown, Connecticut, designed by Jeter Cook & Jepson Architects, illustrates the aesthetic potential of an expressed wood structure. (Photograph by Woodruff Brown Photography.)*

▶ *Example of exposed wood and steel structure used for aesthetic effect. Lincoln Elementary School, Lincoln, Massachusetts. HMFH Architects. (Photograph by Wayne Soverns Jr.)*

▼ *Example of exposed wood and steel structure used for aesthetic effect. Andover High School, Andover, Massachusetts. Earl R. Flansburgh & Associates, Inc. (Photograph by Wheeler Photographics.)*

SPECIAL ISSUES

There are a number of other structural issues that arise in some school planning programs:

- Special consideration must be given to the selection of the structural system for swimming pools. The high humidity and chemicals used corrode many structural systems and are a frequent source of problems.

- The desire for flexibility has led many schools to use operable partitions between spaces. In most spaces—and especially in large ones such as gymnasiums—these partitions create a significant structural load (and associated cost) that many school systems, and some design teams, fail to recognize in the initial budgeting.

- There are continuing experiments with structural systems—such as Teflon-coated fiberglass—for roofing large spaces such as tennis and pool areas.

Overall, structure is a less challenging issue in school design than in the design of other building types. Nevertheless, the proper planning and design of the structural system are important to a school's long-term life.

CHAPTER 8
MECHANICAL SYSTEMS

The American Society of Heating, Refrigerating, and Air-Conditioning Engineers (ASHRAE) is probably the best general source of mechanical systems information. The *1999 ASHRAE Handbook* (ASHRAE 1999) provides an introduction to the major issues. The lists of issues, supplemented with the advice of several experienced school design professionals, are summarized in the following sections.

GENERAL

Interior Environment
The interior environment has a direct impact on a school's occupants. Inadequate heating, cooling, humidity control, air cleaning, and ventilation can all impede learning.

Simplicity
Most schools cannot support sophisticated engineering and maintenance staff. Therefore, systems should be easily understandable and maintainable. Ideally, boilers, chillers, pumps, and air-handling equipment should be in easily accessed enclosed rooms, with space around the equipment adequate for service and replacement of major components when needed.

Life-Cycle Analysis
As long-term owners know, schools are ideal candidates for life-cycle cost analysis. In selecting systems, schools should be aware that energy savings and lower maintenance costs often justify the higher first costs of more efficient systems. (See also "Energy Conservation" in chapter 6.)

Ability to Accommodate Growth and Change
Because schools often have to grow and change, mechanical systems should be designed to accommodate change easily. Piping should not be buried in concrete, mechanical rooms should be expandable, and so forth. Boiler equipment should be designed in modules so as to be easily expandable and to provide redundancy, with no unit providing more than two-thirds of peak heating demand.

Ventilation
Mechanical ventilation is required by code for virtually every school space. The *ASHRAE Handbook* recommends ventilation rates. ASHRAE Standard 62.1 (latest version) is more current, with addenda, and is often the basis for the ratios in codes. Typical of such rates used in schools are those in the state of New York's *Manual of Planning Standards:*

Occupied areas	15 cfm* per occupant of perimeter area
Locker and shower rooms	1 cfm per sq ft of floor area
Toilets	2 cfm per sq ft of floor area
Kitchen-dishwashing	100–150 cfm per sq ft of floor area

Air-Conditioning
An increasing number of schools have incorporated air-conditioning to improve the teaching environment and allow year-round use. In hot, humid climates air-conditioning and/or dehumidification is also used to prevent mold and mildew.

*cfm = cubic feet per minute

Impact of Program

Year-round school, adult education, night classes, community use of auditorium or athletic facilities, and other program variables can have a significant impact on selection of appropriate mechanical systems.

Regional Variability

There is still great variability between school districts, and even within school systems. Age, budget, and program, as well as climate, make it hard to generalize. Nevertheless, the table below, a modified version of an ASHRAE table, summarizes "recommended winter and summer design dry-bulb temperatures for various spaces common in schools."

Indoor Air Quality

A school's indoor air quality (IAQ)

should be a major consideration. See "Environmental Quality" in chapter 6.

Noise and Vibration

Mechanical systems produce noise and vibration that must be controlled. The location of mechanical rooms and the selection of partition materials are critical in school design. Major equipment should have vibration isolation mountings, particularly with a suspended floor. Piping in mechanical rooms should have vibration-isolation joints and hangers. See also chapter 12.

Program Area

The space required for mechanical systems varies widely inasmuch as some schools provide limited mechanical services with rooftop equipment and others have central mechanical areas for sophisticated heating

RECOMMENDED DESIGN TEMPERATURES			
Space[a]	Winter Design, °F	Summer Design, °F DB	Summer Design, RH = (%)
Laboratories	72	76–78[d]	50–55
Auditoriums, libraries, administrative areas, etc.	72	76–78	50–55
Classrooms			
Prekindergarten through grade 3	75	76–78	50–55
Grades 4 through 12	72	76–78	50–55
Shops	72	76–78[b]	50–55
Locker, shower rooms	75[d]	c,d	
Toilets	72	c,d	
Storage	65	c,d	
Mechanical rooms	60	c	
Corridors	68	78–80[b]	60[c]

[a]For spaces of high population density and where sensible heat factors are 0.75 or less, lower dry-bulb temperatures will result in generation of less latent heat, which may reduce the need for reheating and thus save energy. Therefore, optimum dry-bulb temperatures should be the subject of detailed design analysis. [b]Frequently not air-conditioned. [c]Usually not air-conditioned.
[d]Provide ventilation for odor control. DB = dry-bulb temperature. RH = relative humidity.

and air-conditioning equipment. Most school programmers allocate 4 to 6 percent of total area for mechanical and electrical spaces in a new building prior to design. Engineers argue, however, that if air handlers are within the building, they can take up 6 percent by themselves. This percentage is lower if the heating, ventilation, and air-conditioning (HVAC) equipment is housed in rooftop package units.

Construction Budget

Mechanical systems costs (not including electrical or plumbing) also vary widely, ranging from less than 10 to 15 percent of the construction budget for schools that require only heating and ventilation, to more than 15 to 25 percent of the budget in air-conditioned high schools that include a pool, auditorium, and sophisticated science rooms.

PRESCHOOL AND KINDERGARTENS

Some of the specific issues regarding mechanical systems in preschool and kindergarten are discussed in the following paragraphs.

Use of Existing Facilities

Many early childhood programs must adapt spaces originally designed for other uses. Thus, their mechanical systems are often retrofits or replacements. Many old heating systems can be retrofitted, with temperature-control valves added at each space-heating element to provide improved temperature control.

Warm Floors and No Drafts

Because young children often play or sit on the floor, a warm floor with minimal drafts is important. To this end radiant heating, including in-slab systems, can be effective. Air supply intakes should be located to minimize drafts. Floor-mounted heating equipment with exposed hot surfaces or sharp edges should be avoided. In addition, care should be exercised in zoning to avoid overheating and slow "pickup."

Hours of Operation

Many school programs operate from early in the morning to early in the evening to match parents' working hours. The design of systems should assume 12 to 14 hours of operation for these programs and minimal night and weekend use.

Ventilation

Well-designed provisions for ventilation and humidity control, to minimize formation of microbial growth and the spread of communicable diseases and odors, are particularly important. The location of air intakes and the selection of filter media are critical; use of duct lining that when damp can be a source of mold, is discouraged.

Teacher Work Spaces

Teacher work spaces may call for a separate temperature control zone.

ELEMENTARY SCHOOLS

The HVAC requirements of elementary schools incorporate some of the preschool requirements but also have their own special issues.

Program Areas

Elementary schools typically are more complex programmatically than preschool facilities. Gymnasiums, auditoriums, and cafeterias are often part of the program, as are specialized teaching spaces (media center, music, art, etc.).

Hours of Operation

An elementary school's primary hours of operation are from 7:00 a.m. to 3:00 p.m. Usually, the peak cooling load occurs in the afternoon, and peak heating demand is in the morning at start-up.

Basic Classroom HVAC Needs

The basic ASHRAE recommendations for classroom HVAC systems include the following:

- Heating and ventilation in all classrooms
- Air-conditioning for classes used year-round in warm, humid climates
- Summer dehumidification in humid climates
- Economizer cycles for use during winter months
- Separate temperature-control zone for each classroom

Gymnasiums

Gymnasiums often have independent systems to accommodate a variety of uses, both during and after normal school hours. Locker rooms, if provided, are typically positioned so they can be vented directly to the outside; toilets and/or showers are also provided. These spaces require a great deal of ventilation. Air may be transferred from adjacent spaces to make up for that displaced by exhaust requirements.

Administrative Areas

Administrative areas typically are occupied beyond normal class hours and when school is not in session. They are often served by separate systems and are air-conditioned. At the very least, they should be designed to permit future air-conditioning.

Science, Art, and Computer Rooms

An increasing number of elementary schools have dedicated teaching spaces for science, art, computers, and other classes. Odors, such as caused by animals in science rooms and some art media, require adequate ventilation. These spaces should have sufficient exhaust (that is, exceeding air supplied) to yield a negative pressure relative to adjacent space. Computers almost always require air-conditioning, and a separate system is usually desirable for computer labs and server rooms.

Libraries and Media Centers

In most climates libraries and media centers should be air-conditioned to better preserve their books and other materials. Humidification may also be considered to alleviate excessive winter dryness. Large temperature and humidity variations throughout the year should be minimized.

MIDDLE AND SECONDARY SCHOOLS

Middle and secondary schools share the mechanical systems requirements of elementary schools, but they have more varied facilities as well as different hours of use. Some of the issues involved in providing systems for the additional spaces in such facilities are discussed in the following paragraphs.

Auditoriums

Auditoriums require an especially quiet and draft-free system. Air-conditioning is increasingly common because of year-round and community use. Independent systems should certainly be considered. In addition, auditorium design should take into consideration a number of other factors:

- The ability to precool the building mass can reduce the volume of air-conditioning required during peak occupancy for programs lasting just a few hours.

- Proper placement of air-supply intakes and exhaust outlets (low in the space) can facilitate stratification of much of the generated heat above the occupied zone. This can also reduce the load on the equipment.

- Careful air distribution is important to minimize drafts. Some air should be exhausted near or in the ceiling to remove pockets of hot air.

- Returns near seating where face velocities exceed 275 ft per minute (fpm) may cause objectionable noise and drafts.

- Mechanical equipment rooms should be buffered from seating and stage areas to avoid acoustical problems.

- Lobbies and ancillary spaces such as toilet rooms have different heating and cooling requirements and should probably be served by separate systems or temperature-control zones.

- Stages require special consideration because of the unusual loads created by lighting and the activities on stage. Exhaust mechanisms are often included high in the space near the lights. However, care must be taken to minimize stack effect by creating low air velocities, wide distribution, and properly designed exhaust equipment.

Computer Classrooms

Some cooling is typically required in computer classrooms, as well as humidity control.

Science Classrooms

Science classrooms may require fume hoods with special exhaust systems, as well as a makeup air system. At minimum the ventilation system should be carefully designed to maintain negative pressure relative to adjacent spaces, even when some fume hoods are not in operation. Independent temperature control should be provided for each science classroom.

Natatoriums and Ice Rinks

Natatoriums and ice rinks require special heating, air-conditioning, and dehumidification systems. There are also a number of further requirements:

- A natatorium design must address humidity control, ventilation requirements for air quality (outdoor and exhaust air), air distribution, duct design, pool-water chemistry, and evaporation rates. A humidity-control system will not work if any of these items are overlooked.

- A natatorium requires year-round relative humidity levels between 40 and 60 percent for comfort, energy conservation, and protection of the building.

- Strategic use of glazing should be studied carefully to avoid condensation and "fogging."

- Ice rinks present equally complex design challenges. The mechanical system must be designed to reduce refrigeration loads, avoid fogging (owing to introduction of moisture-laden outside air), deal with the heat load of lighting, skaters, and spectators, and address a number of other special technical issues.

TRADITIONAL HEATING AND COOLING SYSTEMS FOR OLDER SCHOOLS

HEATING AND VENTILATION

SCHEMATIC DRAWING	DOES THIS SYSTEM:	VENTI-LATE AND FILTER AIR?	CONTROL TEMPER-ATURE?	CONVERT TO SUMMER COOLING?	REMARKS	COST COMPARISON
Unit Ventilator (with finned tube extensions) under windows; pulls outdoor air through louvers, heats, and disperses it about room with fans; exhaust air is carried out by ducts above corridor ceiling; a two pipe hot water or steam system		Yes	Very good in all seasons; quick and sensitive	No, except for forced air circulation	Occupies considerable space in classroom, but little in central heating room; if not carefully maintained, fans may get somewhat noisy	installation cost
	Unit ventilator, similar to one above with addition of chilled water lines to central compressor room for summer cooling	Yes	Very good in all seasons; quick and sensitive	Yes	Occupies considerable space in classroom, but little in central heating room; if not carefully maintained, fans may get somewhat noisy	operating, power and fuel cost for 20 years
Finned baseboard convector, extending across exterior wall near floor level; Air is warmed by convecting surfaces, rises, crosses room; central duct for ventilation and air supply is in corridor; a two pipe hot water or steam system		Yes	Fair in all seasons	Yes, but only if ducts and piping are insulated and special drainage system is provided in original installation	A quiet system; requires little classroom area but considerable central fan room area	
	Finned tube convector, hung on wall under windows; air enters through window, is heated, rises in convection pattern, and is exhausted through ducts in corridor ceiling; a two pipe hot water or steam system	No	Fair in spring and fall, poor in winter (except in mild climatic areas)	No	A quiet system; requires little classroom area and moderate central heating room area	
Metal pan radiant ceiling; prefabricated metal units make up ceiling and contain pipeways for two pipe hot water system; heat radiates downward; air is supplied and exhausted by ducts		Yes	Good in all seasons	Yes, but only if ducts and piping are insulated and special drainage system is provided in original installation	A quiet system; requires no usable space in classroom and moderate area in central heating room; pan ceiling may also include acoustical treatment	
	Forced warm air, delivered into room through grills under windows; air is mixed in fan room, sent through floor ducts and exhausted through corridor ceiling ducts	Yes	Very good in all seasons	Yes, but only if ducts and piping are insulated and special drainage system is provided in original installation	A quiet system at normal velocities; requires moderate space in classroom, but considerable area in the central heating room	

Source: Walter McQuade, ed., *Schoolhouse* (New York: Simon & Schuster, 1958), pp. 181–182.

SCHEMATIC DRAWING	DOES THIS SYSTEM:	VENTI-LATE AND FILTER AIR?	CONTROL TEMPER-ATURE?	CONVERT TO SUMMER COOLING?	REMARKS	COST COMPARISON
Hot and cold air, delivered by ducts to mixing box beneath floor of room; mixed air is introduced into class-room through grills under windows and exhausted through corridor ceiling ducts		Yes	Very good in all seasons	Yes, but only if ducts and piping are insulated and special drainage system is provided in original installation	A quiet system; requires moderate space in the class-room, but consider-able space in the fan room	installation cost
Radiant floor slab; contains pipe coils through which hot water (a two pipe system) is circulated; air is supplied and exhausted through corridor ducts		Yes	Good in all seasons	Yes, but only if ducts and piping are insulated and special drainage system is provided in original installation	A quiet system, requires no useful space in the class-room and moderate space in the central heating room; needs careful temperature control; heat lag is sometimes a problem	operating, power and fuel cost for 20 years
Direct fired unit; ceiling-hung, it heats the room air which, after circulating, is exhausted through ceiling ducts; natural gas fired		No	Good in fall, fair in spring and winter	No, except for fan effect	Noisy; occupies considerable space in the classroom, but no space in the central heating room; seldom used in classrooms	
Electric panels, set in ceiling, radiating heat downward; air is supplied and exhausted through corridor ducts		Yes	Good in all seasons	No, unless complete system is added to utilize ductwork in the corridors	A quiet system; requires no space in the classroom and little space in the central fan room	
Cast iron radiator; roof fan exhaust; two pipe hot water system		No	Fair in spring and fall, poor in winter	No	Roof fan might become noisy; radi-ators take up considerable space in the classroom, are difficult to keep clean, and are hazards unless enclosed	

- Ventilation must be adequate to avoid high content ratios of exhaust fumes from an engine-powered ice resurfacing machine (Zamboni).

Vocational Education Spaces

There are a wide variety of vocational education spaces. Many require special mechanical systems:

- Automechanic instruction typically requires outdoor air supply, an exhaust system that can deal with odors and fumes (such as carbon monoxide), and controls that maintain the negative pressure of the space.

- Other industrial arts shops often have special requirements to accommodate the exhaust, dust, and heat associated with painting, welding, soldering, and similar activities.

- Home economics spaces often produce high heat loads resulting from cooking, washing, drying, and sewing equipment, and the plumbing and HVAC systems should be designed to handle such demands.

CONCLUSION

Although the systems selected will vary from school to school, many of the common issues discussed in this chapter are likely to be relevant.

CHAPTER 9

ELECTRICAL/COMMUNICATIONS SYSTEMS

REFERENCE STANDARDS

The most important reference standards for a school's electrical systems are the following:

NFPA 70–National Electrical Code

NFPA 101–Life Safety Code

EIA/TIA 568-A—Commercial Building Telecommunications Standard

EIA/TIA 569—Commercial Building Standard for Telecommunication Pathways and Spaces

EIA/TIA 607—Grounding and Bonding

ADA—Americans with Disabilities Act

IMPACT OF TECHNOLOGY

As in business, personal computers are proliferating throughout the country's educational system. The United States Department of Defense Education Association's Technology Program Standards call for one personal computer per two students throughout its worldwide program. This concentration of technology affects the design of electrical systems in many ways.

Although the design unit power density for lighting systems is decreasing to approximately 1.0 to 1.5 watts per square foot in classroom occupancies, the density for receptacle power is now up to 3.0 to 4.0 watts per square foot.

In providing branch circuits for devices that utilize power supplies to convert AC power to DC for use within solid-state equipment such as computers, printers, and even fluorescent lighting fixtures with electronic ballasts, the effects of harmonics on the power system must be considered. In the common practice of using three-phase homeruns for receptacle circuits, with a common neutral conductor, the neutral will likely be carrying more current than any of the three-phase conductors because of third harmonic currents. Thus, from a practical perspective, neutral conductors must be enlarged or, alternatively, each circuit must carry its own neutral.

The increase in power density also implies larger electrical distribution equipment and transformers. These devices are likely sources of electromagnetic interference (EMI). Because the effects of long-term exposure to high levels of EMI on people are not known, it is appropriate to practice "prudent avoidance." That is, because EMI levels are inversely proportional to the distance from their sources, it is prudent to avoid locating electrical panel boards, transformers, and so forth within 8 ft of classrooms, offices, and other areas occupied by people for more than a few minutes at a time.

Many jurisdictions allow the use of flexible, metal-clad cable for the concealed installation of branch circuits, rather than the traditional method of wiring in conduit. Although there are potentially considerable first cost savings in using the metal-clad cable method for both lighting and branch circuits, there is a downside that must be considered. As discussed earlier, technology in the classroom is rapidly changing, and thus the electrical infrastructure must be flexible enough to accommodate the change. The wiring in metal-clad cables cannot be adjusted or augmented as the need arises; it must be removed and replaced. The wiring in conduits, however, can usually be upgraded or augmented at any time.

POWER SOURCE

Many schools, other than those in dense urban environments, are usually low-rise (1 to 3 story) buildings or campuses, spread out so that the distance from the incoming source of utility power to the most remote area is greater than 200 ft. This circumstance, coupled with the fact that virtually all schools that have air-conditioning use electricity as the energy source, leads us to consider three-phase 480/277 volts as the voltage for distribution of bulk electricity throughout a school. This means that large-loads mechanisms such as air-conditioning, elevators, pumps, and fans are powered at three-phase 480 volts. Fluorescent lighting systems can also take advantage of this plan, powered at single-phase 277 volts. Moreover, electrical closets local to the areas remote from the power source can contain transformers to step down the voltage to three-phase 208/120 volts for use mostly by 120-volt convenience outlets. Some schools still use 208/120 for the primary services if the higher voltage is not available at installation or the school started as a small structure.

EMERGENCY POWER

Unless a school building is a code-mandated "high-rise" (more than 75 ft above fire truck main access), the typical items required to be backed up by an on-site power source are exit signs and those light fixtures that lead people to exit the building in case of a power failure. Because these lights typically consume

only 0.5 watts per square foot of power, it is usually more cost-effective to provide them with local battery packs than to install an on-site diesel emergency generator.

LIGHTING SYSTEMS

Energy efficiency and visual comfort are the key words in lighting systems designs for schools. As discussed in chapter 13, a balance of direct and indirect illumination provides a classroom with sufficient light for children to perform paper-oriented tasks and computer operations. Care should be taken in the design stages of a school project so that maintenance personnel need only to stock a limited number of replacement lamp types. This measure helps to ensure timely replacement to maintain proper levels and quality of illumination.

FIRE SAFETY

Today's multiplexed, addressable fire detection and alarm systems simplify fire safety design tremendously. Classroom detectors, sprinkler-system tamper and flow switches, manual pull stations, air-handling duct detectors, and so forth, can all be looped together and then identified separately at the fire alarm control panel or remote annunciator location. This allows instant identification of the device that "called in" the alarm so that a response by staff and fire personnel can be appropriate. Alarm notification devices are now typically combination speaker/strobes. Not only alarm tones, but also voice announcements, can be transmitted to better manage the actions of people in the event of a fire. The strobe function allows visual notification of hearing-impaired people. The entire system must follow the guidelines of the Americans with Disabilities Act (ADA).

COMMUNICATIONS

Communications systems in schools include various types of voice, data, and video information. For example, voice systems include telephone, intercom, and public-address functions. Data systems include local-area networks (LAN), access to wide-area networks (WAN), time-of-day clocks, and class-change tones. Video systems include access to distance-learning video programs, cable TV, and in-room playback of recorded videocassettes.

Fortunately, today's technology allows for the integration of many of these systems. For example, a telephone PABX can allow the placing and receiving of outside telephone calls (with access restrictions to avoid unwarranted toll charges), room-to-room intercommunications, public address (PA) to various PA zones throughout the school complex (again, with access restrictions), as well as transmission of class-change tones. With appropriate interfaces to outside program source providers such as local cable television companies, satellite antennae, and local broadcast antennae, specific areas of the school can receive selective video and television programming. Media centers can connect to the WAN resources of the Internet, its World Wide Web, and other subscribed outside data services, and the information available can be shared in-house via LANs.

A structured backbone cabling system consisting of the proper infrastructure of fiber-optic and unshielded twisted-pair copper cabling, with appropriate electronic interface devices, can also integrate and simplify the installation of all these systems. For example, a typical classroom can have an intercom/telephone located at the teacher's desk and several data outlets strategically located in the room. This room can be reconfigured with the telephone at one of the data locations and conversion of the telephone outlet to data use by means of a simple "patch cord" change within the local telecommunications closet. Proper electronic equipment located in the telecom closets can allow any of the data outlets to be configured to one of the school's LANs or directly connected to a specific printer. Again, with proper electronics, the television located in the classroom can receive selected programming via its channel selector, or possibly even be configured as a remote monitor for the teacher's personal computer (PC).

SPACE REQUIREMENTS: RULES OF THUMB

The Electronics Industry Association/Telecommunications Industry Association (EIA/TIA) publishes standards that address the space requirements and configurations for equipment rooms, closets, and similar space. These standards also include environmental requirements (air-conditioning), as well as electrical power and grounding. The space standards should be applied judiciously, as they address "all-inclusive" equipment rooms and closets, and a particular school may not house all the components anticipated by the standards.

The electrical power systems discussed in this chapter can be housed in a series of electrical closets, placed strategically throughout the facility, and a centralized main distribution room. The closets can be located on every floor at every 15,000 sq ft or at a maximum horizontal spacing of 250 ft, whichever is less. They should each be a minimum of 8 ft by 10 ft to allow for wall-mounted panel boards and equipment, space for transformers, and adequate working clearances for installation and maintenance. The closets should be ventilated, taking into account the heat produced by the equipment located therein. The size of the main distribution equipment can vary greatly depending on a number of conditions—the incoming service voltage, capacity, branch circuit panel boards in the room, emergency system configuration, and so forth. It is always important, however, to consider the requirement for ventilation to dissipate the heat produced by the equipment.

CHAPTER 10

TECHNOLOGY AND SPECIAL EQUIPMENT

Twenty years ago a television set, a tape recorder, a film projector, and an overhead projector made up the typical electronic technology found in the average classroom. In every decade of the twentieth century a new technology was hailed as the harbinger of a revolution in teaching. As summarized in *Technology and the Future of Schooling* (Kerr 1996, pp. 2, 133), enormous expectations were rarely matched by results. In the 1920s film was expected to have a major impact; in the 1930s radio was expected "to bring the world into every classroom"; in the 1950s and 1960s the "new media" (television, super-8 film loops, language labs) and programmed instruction seemed to have potential; and in the 1970s there were "the novelties of distance learning and dial-access audio and video." All of these have had some impact, but it has been only in the last 10 to 15 years that "technology" has truly become a central issue in curriculum planning, facility design, and capital budgeting.

The number of computers and other new educational technologies has grown dramatically since the early 1980s. In 1983 the ratio of students to computers was 125:1, by 1990 it was 20:1, and by 1995 it was 9:1; since then the ratio has continued to decline (Kerr 1996, p. 52). The same trends exist for CD-ROMs (up from 7 percent access by students in 1991–92 to 37 percent by 1994–95), Internet connections (up from 35 percent in 1994 to 78 percent in 1997), schoolwide networks, closed-circuit TV, new media in the libraries, and other technology. The annual expenditure on school computers is now $5 billion (*New York Times*, May 9, 1999).

Any discussion of the role of technology in education is certain to be out of date by the time it is published. The potential for new technology is being explored in thousands of schools, and a flood of new tools, curricula, and concepts are being developed. Yet surrounding this excitement is a raging debate on the role and limits of technology in education. The debate is unlikely to end soon, but there appear to be several preliminary conclusions:

• The new technologies have created a wide variety of new educational tools, some of which are described later in this chapter.

"I believe that the motion picture is destined to revolutionize our education system." (Thomas Edison, 1922)

"The time may come when a portable radio receiver will be as common in a classroom as...the blackboard." (William Alexander, 1945)

"I was soon saying that, with the help of teaching machines and programmed instruction, students could learn twice as much in the same time and with the same effort as in a standard classroom." (B. F. Skinner, 1986)

- The new technologies are tools to help in teaching, but they are only tools.
- The cost of these tools competes with other educational budgets. In 1996 a task force recommended spending $11 billion on computers for schools in California—a state with chronic underfunding of its educational system. This proposed investment—if it is made at the expense of smaller class size, music and art, physical education and sports, expanded hours, higher teacher salaries, or better facilities—could clearly have a negative impact on the quality of education.
- The cost of technology has also increased the inequalities in facilities. As noted at a recent conference on the subject, "In one district, you can have multiple machines, an integrated curriculum and well-trained teachers. Step across a district line, and you have schools with one or two computers in an entire school" (School Districts Merge Studies and Technology," *New York Times,* May 9, 1999).

Nevertheless, computers and other new technologies have become an essential part of life in America. It is essential that more than half of all jobs in the United States require some use of computer skills. Although some of the required

skills can be learned quickly later in life, many can and should be learned in school. Thus computers and other technologies will have a major role in elementary and secondary education. Among the most important of these technologies—and their school design implications (in the year 2000 and beyond)—are the following:

- *Computer labs.* Most schools initially put most of their computers in a dedicated space or lab where computer skills could be taught and special computer-based projects could be carried out with the help of specially trained staff. The photo on page 143 illustrates a typical dedicated lab.
- *Computers in the classroom.* In recent years, as more computers, computer expertise, and computer-based curricula have become available, computers are moving into the classroom. In wealthier districts and private schools, new classrooms are being planned on the assumption that every student will eventually have a laptop, plus access to classroom computers linked to schoolwide networks and the Internet. This trend can have profound implications for seating design and the wiring of the classroom. In the future, wireless connections will reduce some of the impact, but hardwired connections are

Steven Jobs, one of the founders of Apple Computer, once stated, "What's wrong with education cannot be fixed with technology…No amount of technology will make a dent…. You're not going to solve the problems by putting all knowledge on CD-ROMs. We can put a Web site in every school— none of this is bad. It's bad only if it lulls us into thinking we are doing something to solve the problem with education." (*Wired*, February 1996)

◀ *Even with the steady increase in computer usage and literacy, there is a need for classrooms specially equipped to teach the proper use of the hardware and software. University of Connecticut, Stamford. Perkins Eastman Architects.*

likely to remain an important planning consideration. The illustrations on pages 142 and 143 show typical seating for a wired classroom.

- *Internet, local-area network (LAN), and wide-area network (WAN) connections.* School renovations, as well as new construction, now routinely include the provision of wiring and connections.

- *New educational software.* There is a rapidly growing library of software that replaces traditional teaching methods. These programs can simulate science experiments and create entirely new ways to teach geography and other subjects. This has the potential to change the future design of teaching labs and other special classrooms.

▼ *Wiring a classroom to accommodate computers at each desk often requires seating arrangements and furniture that can distribute the wiring from wall or floor connections. Or, as shown below, from a power source in the floor.*

• *Library as media center.* As noted in chapter 1, libraries are rapidly evolving. The school library still has books and story time, but now it must accommodate and manage a growing number of new media (Internet connections, videotapes, CD-ROMs, CDs, audiotapes, etc.). A major problem is that there is too much information. Part of the librarian's role is to teach information skills and to integrate content and skills in collaboration with the classroom teacher. Thus there is a need for more dedicated space for libraries, as well as rooms where these new media can be used.

• *Distance learning.* The concept of distance, or remote, learning and technology is still evolving. It is more

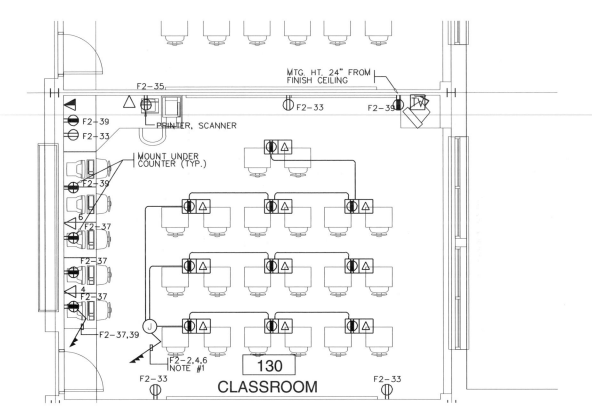

SCALE: 1/4" = 1'-0"

NOTE:

1. RUN POWER CABLES IN RAISED FLOOR TO NEAREST WALL AND, VIA 1"C, UP INTO HUNG CEILING TO RP–F2.

2. RUN DATA CABLES IN RAISED FLOOR TO NEAREST WALL AND, VIA CONDUIT, UP INTO HUNG CEILING TO TELECOM. CLOSET.

3. VOICE, DATA AND POWER FLOOR BOXES SHALL BE SUPPLIED BY RAISED FLOOR MANUFACTURER. WIRING SHALL BE BY ELECTRICAL CONTRACTOR.

common to find this for college-level courses, but a broader use in K–12 schools is inevitable.

• *Audiovisual equipment.* Overhead projectors, and even slide projectors, remain common audiovisual (AV) equipment in classrooms; but the computer—including Power Point and other programs and equipment—is replacing these traditional teaching tools.

• *Radio and television studios.* Radio and television have become part of both school activities and curricula in many districts. TV studios often require large rooms with high ceilings.

Undoubtedly the impact of media on school design will increase, and even the

▲ *Classrooms are being planned with one area permanently dedicated to computers linked to the Internet and the school's LAN. South Lawrence East School, Lawrence, Massachusetts. Earl R. Flansburgh & Associates, Inc.*

145

known changes will take years to implement throughout the United States. In implementing a technology plan schools face an array of issues:

- Decisions on what learning and administration functions will be served, what technologies will be provided, how many users the network must serve now and in the future, and how information will be secured.

- Location of new wiring. The U.S. General Accounting Office estimates that in 46 percent of schools the existing wiring is inadequate to support present technology. In addition, anticipated networks will require new wiring.

- Type of wiring (less costly copper vs. more expensive and flexible optical fiber vs. a combination).

- Decisions on where to locate wiring and how to facilitate future growth and change.

- Where laboratories and servers will be located.

- Selection of a strategy to maximize bandwidth and flexibility.

- How Internet access will be provided and how will it be screened.

- Establishing a policy on donated equipment (some free equipment is not worth having).

- Assuming and planning for the future, when there maybe an integrated communication system tying together telephones, intercoms, laser disks, alarms, bells, video, distance learning, etc.

CHAPTER 11
MATERIALS

INTRODUCTION

School buildings are among the public structures that are called upon to endure. Many schools in use today across the country are housed in buildings more than 50 years old. The need for these buildings to withstand decades of accommodating schoolchildren and various educational programs should be a major factor in the selection of materials. The materials used to construct a school building should be durable and maintainable. They should withstand years of use and abuse while continuing to provide an atmosphere conducive to learning.

COMMON MATERIAL SELECTIONS FOR PRIMARY SPACES

The decisions made regarding material selections, as well as the accessories to protect them, will possibly have the most profound effect on the physical environment and its familiarity to children. We often associate the most institutional and, unfortunately, intimidating settings with endless vinyl tile floors, painted concrete-block walls, cold fluorescent lighting, and numerous wall and corner protection accessories. Although these materials will last a long time, they convey a stronger sense of factory than of home. There are, however, many new products on the market that can provide the durability and maintainability needed without significant compromise of the environment. The following are the general material selection criteria used by experienced school designers for the major spaces in a school:

- *Walls.* The use of gypsum board for walls is more than likely, given today's budget considerations, but this material does not provide very suitable impact resistance. Highly susceptible to gouging, dents, and corner damage, standard gypsum products must be enhanced or protected. The use of new high-impact gypsum products now on the market, more commonly specified in public housing projects, or the addition of a "skim coat" of diamond-hard plaster to at least a height of 4 ft, can help to improve the durability of the walls. Painted or ground-face block is a common alternative.

- *Floors.* Consideration should be given to new carpet materials for classrooms and large play areas to both enhance acoustic quality and reduce injuries associated with slippery, harder surfaces. In many schools area rugs are used so that they can be moved, replaced, or quickly cleaned. Solution-dyed products with integral moisture backing should be specified to ensure color retention and easy cleanup of soils and spills. In areas used for artwork, toilet rooms, and wet or messy activities, the use of VCT or sheet-vinyl products, which provide long-term durability and maintainability as well as many aesthetic options, should be considered. Some products offer an attractive wood-flooring appearance with 6 ft wide sheets capable of welded seaming and flash cove base details for watertightness.

- *Ceilings.* Acoustics should be addressed for each area designed. The use of acoustic ceiling tile in most areas is important, and carpeting should be considered wherever possible. In areas with harder surfaces, such as large expanses of glass wall or hard tile flooring, acoustic tile ceilings will not be enough. Consideration should be given to the use of acoustic wall treatments such as fabric-wrapped panels. Care should be taken not to locate these panels in high-impact areas, which generally extend up to 4 ft above the floor.

- *Wall protection.* The protection of openings and corners, always a consideration, will ultimately help the facility maintain its appearance. The use of corner guards at key impact areas is recommended, and consideration should be given to recessed guards with carefully coordinated coloring, which helps them to blend with the interior design.

- *Trim and casework.* The use of natural wood to enhance the quality of a

space is often desirable and can provide a very durable low-maintenance alternative to painted trim and cabinets. Among the common woods used for their durability and affordability are maple and oak. Many manufacturers producing children's furnishings work in maple or other light woods, such as birch or beech. These woods are worth considering in determining the color and aesthetic for trim and casework. If painted cabinets are desired, factory polyester or vinyl paint coatings offer good durability as well as easy cleanup. Unfortunately, colors are often limited to white or almond. Countertops of plastic laminate are quite functional, but cabinet fronts, doors, and drawer fronts on lower cabinetry may peel and delaminate over time. Melamine materials should be used on concealed surfaces only.

The materials selected for a school building should support the educational programs and objectives of the client. The environment should be comfortable for the activities within the space, and the

STANDARD MATERIAL OPTIONS					
Interior Walls	**Floors**	**Ceilings**	**Roof**	**Structure**	**Exterior Walls**
Concrete block	Resilient tile	Acoustical tile	Membranes	Concrete block	Clay masonry
Gypsum board	Hard tile	Gypsum board	Built-up system	Concrete Poured	Cast/precast
Plaster	Carpet	Exposed structure	Shingles	Precast	Concrete block
Wood	Wood	Metal	Slate	Steel	Prefaced block
Metal	Sheet flooring	Wood	Metal	Stone	Stucco
Glass	Poured floors			Wood	Panel systems
Tile	Concrete				Stone
Partition	Terrazzo				Glass
Glass block	Stone				
	Cork				

materials chosen add to the comfort in the children's environment. For example, kindergarten children spend much of their day on the floor, working as groups or in centers, and require a soft play surface such as carpeting. In a high school science classroom, students work at a lab station with chemicals that could be damaging to certain materials. The lab space should have hard, smooth work surfaces and floor finishes that are easily cleaned and chemically resistant. See the table opposite for a summary of a number of standard material options.

DURABILITY AND MAINTENANCE

In a school building project, the architect is continually challenged to provide a durable building on a very tight budget, especially for public schools. It is critical that the budgeted or bonded taxpayer funds buy the most space or largest number of classrooms possible. To meet the demand of providing more square footage and program areas, a decision may be made to forgo the more expensive quality materials in favor of more building area. The architect should educate the client to the trade-offs associated with up-front versus life-cycle costs of the materials. The life-cycle cost includes the initial cost, maintenance cost, operating cost, and other costs over the useful life of the material. For example, a poured-in-place terrazzo floor may be less expensive than a vinyl tile floor when the cost is averaged over the life of the material. The vinyl tile floor, although less expensive initially, requires frequent waxing and polishing and is subject to damages that may require replacement of sections. The terrazzo floor requires

much less maintenance and is not subject to as much damage.

The client should understand the impact of material selections from the perspective of maintenance and replacement. The client will be responsible for maintaining the facility once constructed and thus should be directly involved in the selection of finish materials. This is also true for the structural and exterior construction materials. When asked to provide a brick aesthetic, the architect may investigate a brick veneer cavity wall with masonry unit backup, and a brick tile system backed up by metal studs. Both systems can provide the look the client has requested, but the full brick on masonry unit backup will outperform the brick tile system and require much less maintenance.

As mentioned earlier, it is important to balance material selection with available construction and maintenance funds. In a school building, durability is a major concern and should be a major focus in selection. Often, the more durable material is also more costly. The client may wish to pursue the more expensive material because it promises lower life-cycle cost or because a manufacturer provides a longer warranty period or additional warranty coverage.

The client should incorporate scheduled maintenance for the selected materials into the school staff's work plan. Maintenance has a direct effect on the longevity of a product. Because it is likely that difficult procedures will lead to a lack of maintenance for the product, the ease or difficulty of maintaining a material should be part of the decision to use it in the building. A sheet-flooring system that can be dry-mopped may be easier to maintain than vinyl composition tile that requires waxing and buffing several times throughout the year. Before a product is specified, the client should be made aware of the proper maintenance techniques, the expected life of the product, and any concerns about the performance of existing installations.

CODES

The codes governing the region where construction is to take place will play a role in the selection of materials. Most codes dictate a minimum construction type based on building occupancy. Typically, schools are more demanding construction types than other buildings and must meet more stringent regulations. A school must adhere to many fire code regulations, such as those involving limits on building area or area increases, fire separations, fire-rated construction, and so on. The fire rating requirements for walls, floors, roof, and vertical circulation paths may limit the materials available for construction. For example, the New York State Education Department requires that exit stairs be one-hour fire-rated construction, which can be provided with masonry construction or fire-rated gypsum board on metal studs. The fire code addresses finish materials by specifying a classification that is based primarily on the flame-spread rating of the material. Design loads mandated for different areas of the country will affect the materials considered for use as structural elements. Structural systems installed along the East Coast, for example, are required to meet high wind ratings because of the possibility of hurricanes. Possible requirements for long spans within a building also inform the structural framing system. Site conditions, soil type, and weather conditions all play a role in the selection of a structural system.

In addition to the building and fire codes, sanitation and health agency regulations affect material selection. There are some very specific requirements for food-preparation areas. These code requirements are intended to eliminate design elements that allow the growth of bacteria and other microscopic organisms by providing environments that can be disinfected. An example is the use of nonseamed stainless in commercial kitchens. Medical areas, such as the nurse's office in a school, also require materials that will minimize the spread of infection and disease from patient to patient. In these areas, finishes and furnishings must be disinfected. Thus, all applicable codes should be carefully reviewed during material selection to ensure compliance.

REGIONAL ISSUES

The availability of building materials in a region will affect construction in that region. For example, trees are rare in Southwest desert climates, and thus wood is not traditionally used in such areas as a major component in construction. Wood is, however, abundant and highly utilized for building in the Northwest. The level of local craftsmanship and skill with certain readily available materials should also be considered. When introducing a relatively new building system or material to an area, the architect should investigate the local resources for achieving a proper installation. Regional preferences in construction, as well as limits on available skills and materials, are common. Occupant heritage, immigrant cultures, economic circumstances, and many other factors, in addition to availability, influence the selection of materials. The traditional ways of building in a region may relate to or reflect the community's values and should be considered in design.

ENVIRONMENTAL CONSIDERATIONS

Materials should be selected to create a healthy, sustainable environment for all occupants. In new construction, selections should not contribute to the creation of the indoor air quality (IAQ) problems that currently plague many existing school buildings. Poor IAQ is a major contributing factor to "sick building syndrome" (SBS). The symptoms of SBS are flu-like, including headache; nausea; irritation of the eyes, nose, or throat; persistent coughing, wheezing, or upper respiratory complaints; hypersensitivity; and lethargy. These symptoms usually appear in a person one to two hours after occupying the building and disappear one to two hours after vacating the building. (See also chapter 6.)

The following are major causes of SBS:

- Outdoor chemical contaminants: motor vehicle exhausts, fumes from plumbing vents, and building exhausts brought inside via mechanical air-supply intakes or improperly located openings in the building

- Indoor chemical contaminants: adhesives, upholstery, carpeting, copy machines, manufactured wood products, cleaning agents, pesticides, tobacco smoke, and combustion products

- Biological contaminants: pollen, bacteria, viruses, molds

- Inadequate ventilation

Corrective measures for existing buildings that have poor IAQ and whose occupants show symptoms of SBS include the following:

- Increase ventilation of outside air

- Increase air changes to seven or more per hour

- Remove the source of the pollutant

- Thoroughly clean mechanical systems and ducts

- Provide air filtration

- Reduce excessive moisture

All building-design professionals should ensure that ventilation systems are properly designed to eliminate any possibility of biological growth, to change air frequently, and to provide noncontaminated fresh air intake. In addition, materials that do not add contaminants to the environment should be specified. Volatile organic compound (VOC)–containing materials are major contaminant sources that outgas once installed in a construction project. VOCs are found in adhesives, finishes such as paint and varnish, carpet and carpet padding, treated wood, some pressed composite wood products, some roofing materials, various insulation materials, and pesticides, among other products. Low- or non-VOC-containing materials should be specified. Water-based or natural finishes that do not contain formaldehyde, halogenated solvents, mercury, lead, or chromium are preferred. Earthen materials such as brick, stone, and natural wood should be used over chemical-containing materials. Several wood species have natural decay-resistance properties (e.g., cedar, redwood, black locust). Should any dangerous materials have to be used, care must be taken to contain them in the installation and keep them away from food-preparation areas and water supplies.

Most people now believe that designers should try to help maintain the ecological balance of the environment (see also chapter 6). The Earth's resources should be preserved, and the production of toxic products should be limited. The use of products containing recycled materials and the reuse of products such as doors and windows will aid in this effort. There are many alternatives to the chemically laden off-gassing materials in current use. However, these alternative materials are often more expensive and difficult to obtain. They are slowly becoming more available as they are specified for building projects. As demand increases, research and development is under way on a wide range of environmentally safe building materials.

CONSIDERATIONS IN MATERIAL SELECTION FOR SCHOOLS

The following lists contain considerations for the selection of interior materials, by area, within a school building project:

Administration

- Soft flooring for comfort and acoustics
- Acoustical barrier walls
- Appropriate lighting
- Cleanable surfaces in workrooms
- Ventilation for copying area

Offices

- Private, quiet environment
- Acoustical barrier walls for privacy

- Proper air change and ventilation
- Durability (but not as critical as in student environments)

Nurse's area

- Sanitary conditions
- Germ-resistant environment
- All areas easy to clean and disinfect
- Hard, nonporous flooring
- Smooth, cleanable surfaces
- Disinfectable sick cots
- Nonpollutant, nonallergenic environment
- Proper ventilation, humidity, and temperature levels
- Water-impervious materials

Library

- Quiet environment
- Nonglare, nonreflective surfaces for computer use
- Indirect lighting
- Comfortable for the age level of the students
- Controlled moisture and humidity levels

Classrooms

- Easily cleaned flooring
- Hard flooring, with a throw-rug option
- Environment conducive to concentration
- Glare from windows controlled
- Work surface/furnishing durability reflective of classroom function
- Durable storage areas (shelving)
- Water-resistant walls, cabinets, floors around sink and toilet areas

Kitchen

- Adherence to sanitation regulations
- Hard, nonporous, nonslip flooring
- Ability to withstand heavy daily cleaning with chemicals and disinfectant
- Seamless surfaces for food preparation and cooking
- Splash-guard surfaces at sink area
- Floor and wall surfaces resistant to oil and cooking residues
- Heat-resistant finishes
- Smooth surfaces to resist the growth of bacteria

Cafeteria

- Hard, nonporous flooring
- Smooth surfaces to resist the growth of bacteria
- Finishes that can be cleaned with disinfectants
- Hard, smooth wall surfaces for cleaning (at least as a wainscot)

Gymnasium

- Resilient floor surface that allows true bounce and spring action
- Hard, durable wall surfaces for ball play
- Padded wall sections located strategically for game play
- Noise reduction via acoustical block, ceiling treatments, etc.
- Durability of all products used: lights, scoreboard, doors, clocks, etc.
- Vandal-resistant materials

Locker rooms

- Nonporous, nonslip flooring
- Ability to withstand heavy cleaning and student abuse
- Water- and humidity-resistant materials
- Mildew-resistant curtains
- Vandal-resistant materials
- Proper ventilation at clothing and equipment storage areas
- Durable lockers and furnishings
- Moisture-resistant wall surfaces

Auditorium

- Ease of cleaning beneath the seating area
- Soft floor finish on walking surfaces to reduce noise
- Hard and soft wall surfaces placed to achieve the best acoustical properties
- Vandal-resistant materials
- Hard surface or cushioned seating, as defined by client
- Flame resistance of finishes and curtains
- Resilient stage flooring
- Dark stage walls

Technology

- Ergonomic considerations
- Nonglare or antiglare surfaces
- Static-resistant materials
- Quiet environment
- Ability to control exterior light

Science

- Chemical- and acid-resistant materials
- Hard, cleanable floor finish
- Proper ventilation for chemical and gas use

MATERIALS

- Water-resistant work surfaces, cabinetry, walls, and floors
- Chemical storage

Art
- Cleanable walls, floors, and ceilings (seamless preferred)

- Hard, smooth flooring
- Natural light
- Heavy-duty storage shelving
- Fire-resistant kiln area
- Water-resistant work surfaces, cabinetry, walls, and floors

CHAPTER 12

ACOUSTIC CONTROL

INTRODUCTION

The acoustical design of a space involves the attenuation of unwanted and disturbing sounds and the enhancement of desired sounds to the point at which they can be heard properly. Poor acoustical design in schools cause students to have trouble hearing and can thus hurt the learning process. The construction and mechanical systems of a building greatly affect its acoustics, which should therefore be a consideration as early as the schematic design phase. The best acoustic isolation occurs when isolation is not needed; in other words, when compatible adjacencies have been properly planned. With a clear understanding of acoustics, the architect can complete simple acoustic design alone, but in complex and critical cases should engage an acoustic consultant. It is almost impossible to fully attenuate noise, even with a double floor or double structure. With lack of proper acoustics in a classroom, reverberance can be so high that a teacher's speech can be distorted by the overlaying of reflected waves. This chapter outlines the areas of concern in the acoustics design of schools and suggests methods for creating effective acoustic spaces.

DEFINITIONS[1]

We are concerned here with the clarification of those definitions directly applicable to the acoustic design of a school. We assume that the reader is acquainted with the fundamentals or basic nature of acoustics, and thus these are not considered.

Sound is a wave, vibration, or change in pressure in an elastic medium, such as air, concrete, water, or glass. Note that sound can be defined as these disturbances themselves, or as the sensations they produce. We are concerned here with audible sound, or sound able to be heard by healthy ears within a detection range of 20 to 20,000 hertz (Hz). A sound radiates outward from its source until it strikes a room boundary or other surface, where it is partially absorbed, partially reflected, and partially transmitted to an adjoining space. Distance also attenuates sound intensity in large spaces.

Background Noise

Noise in a school can be generated inside or outside a space, by occupants, movement of furniture, HVAC systems, lighting systems, and ballasts, and can interfere with spoken messages; thus, louder speech is required. A range between two noise criteria (NC) curves has been developed to express typical background noise design criteria. The NC curves plot sound levels across eight standard frequencies at which sound levels in existing spaces can be tested.

---

[1]Definitions are derived from the following:

William J. McGuiness, Benjamin Stein, and John S. Reynolds, *Mechanical and Electrical Equipment for Buildings*, 6th ed. (New York: John Wiley & Sons, 1980).

Charles M. Salter, *Acoustics: Architecture, Engineering, the Environment* (San Francisco: William Stout Publishers, 1998).

Federal Register 36 CFR Chapter XI. "Architectural and Transportation Barriers Compliance Board: Petition for Rulemaking; Request for Information on Acoustics."

Definitions
- *Sound absorption* is the process of removing sound energy, or the ability of materials, objects, and structures (e.g., a room) to absorb energy.

- *Reverberation* is the persistence of sound after the cause of sound has stopped, or the ear's reaction to echoes in an enclosed space, giving an impression of "liveness" or "deadness." Reverberation is a mixture of previous and more recent sounds, and its converse is articulation. An articulate environment allows sound events to be kept separate and is more suited to speech. A more reverberant environment should be designed for music.

- *Noise criteria (NC) curves* are a set of spectral curves used to obtain a single-number rating describing the "noisiness" of environments for a variety of uses, and generally used to describe the maximum allowable continuous background noise. NC curves plot sound levels across the frequencies between 63 and 8,000 Hz, the speech-perception range. The NC curve of a room is the lowest curve that is not exceeded by sound levels measured at each frequency. NC criteria are often expressed as a range in specifying acceptable background noise levels. Equivalent (dBA) values typically exceed NC values by 8 to 10 units. NC is typically used to rate the relative loudness of ventilation systems.

- *Room criteria (RC) curves* were developed for background noise from heating, ventilation, and air-conditioning (HVAC) systems. NC curves are adjusted at very low and very high frequencies to prevent annoying mechanical sounds.

- *Noise reduction (NR)* is defined either as the reduction in sound-pressure level caused by making some alteration to a sound source, or as the difference in sound-pressure level between two adjacent rooms caused by the transmission loss of the intervening wall (in other words, the difference in background sound level between a source on one side of a wall and a receiver on the other).

- *Noise reduction coefficient (NRC)* is a single-number rating of the sound absorption of a material, equal to the arithmetic mean of the sound-absorption coefficients in the 250, 500, 1,000, and 2,000 Hz octave frequency bands rounded to the nearest multiple of 0.05.

- *Sound transmission loss (STL)* is the decrease or attenuation in sound energy of airborne sound as it passes through a building construction. Generally, STL increases with frequency.

- *Sound transmission class (STC)* is a single-number rating of a wall or other assembly, describing the sound-insulating properties in the 100 to 4 kilohertz (kHz) range, primarily for assessing speech transmission through a structure.

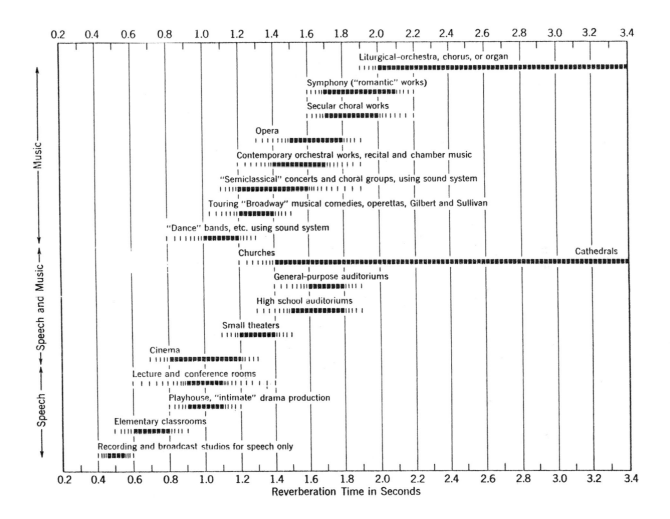

Reverberation Time in Seconds

▲ Optimum reverberation (500–1,000 Hz) for auditoriums and similar facilities. Source: Stein and Reynolds 2000, p. 1537.

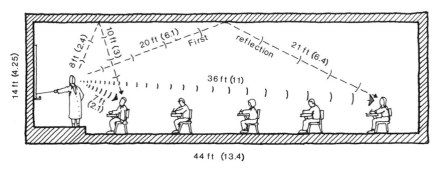

▲ Sound paths in a typical medium-size lecture room. The maximum path-length difference between direct and first reflection: 11 ft. Source: Stein and Reynolds 2000, p. 1536.

SUGGESTED NOISE-CRITERIA RANGES FOR STEADY BACKGROUND NOISE	
Type of Space	NC Curve
Large auditoriums, large drama theaters	20–25
Small auditoriums, small theaters, music rehearsal rooms, large meeting and conference rooms (for good listening conditions)	25–30
Classrooms, libraries, private or semiprivate offices, small conference rooms (for good listening conditions)	30–35
Cafeterias, reception areas (for moderately good listening conditions)	35–50
Laboratory work spaces, lobbies, drafting and engineering rooms	40–45

Source: Adapted from McGuiness, Stein, and Reynolds 1992.

ACOUSTICAL PERFORMANCE: MATERIALS AND SPATIAL PROPORTIONS

Three main criteria determine how effectively a student can hear and understand in a given space, and designers should consider these criteria from the preliminary design phase onward to ensure effective speech reception within a space:

1. Distance of the student from the signal or source, and the effects of interference or loud background noise on the signal

2. The level of background noise from HVAC and lighting systems, or from sounds generated within or outside the room

3. The effects of reverberance

Designers can control background noise levels and reverberance, and thereby ensure good speech intelligibility. Typically, in terms of placement of acoustic control on the walls, floors, or ceilings, the surface of a room that is closest to all of the occupants all of the time is the surface that should be acoustically treated. In other words, where the length or width of a room is greater than the height of the ceiling, it is the ceiling that should be "softened" because it is the surface closest to most of the room's occupants.

It is equally acceptable to "soften" the floor by installing a carpet, but in terms of cost and maintenance, an acoustical tile ceiling with an NRC of at least 0.7 is often more practical in meeting the room's acoustical needs. With such a ceiling, there should be no need for additional control in a room during normal use. (Plaster ceilings should not be used in classrooms.)

Walls in a classroom need not be treated unless the ceiling is unusually high and this height approaches the horizontal dimensions of the room.

Except in auditoriums, room dimensions are more important for audiovisual equipment than for acoustical applications. Most classrooms still work without audiovisual equipment other than basic VCR, TV, and overhead projector. Teledistancing/ distance learning is typically available only in specially equipped classrooms. Audiovisual technology in every classroom is not yet the trend in school design.

RECOMMENDED SOUND TRANSMISSION CLASSES (STC) FOR PARTITIONS IN NORMAL SCHOOL BUILDINGS			
Wall, Partition, or Panel Between		Sound-Isolation Requirement (Background Level in Room Being Considered)	
Room	Adjacent Areas	Quiet	Normal
Classroom	Adjacent classrooms	STC 42	STC 40
	Laboratories	STC 42	STC 40
	Corridors or public areas	STC 40	STC 38
	Kitchen and dining areas	STC 50	STC 47
	Shops	STC 50	STC 47
	Recreation areas	STC 45	STC 42
	Music rooms*	STC 55	STC 50
	Mechanical equipment rooms	STC 50	STC 45
	Toilet areas	STC 45	STC 42
Large music or drama area	Adjacent music or drama rooms*	STC 50	STC 45
	Corridors or public areas	STC 45	STC 42
	Practice rooms*	STC 50	STC 45
	Shops	STC 50	STC 45
	Recreational areas	STC 50	STC 45
	Laboratories	STC 45	STC 42
	Toilet areas	STC 45	STC 42
	Mechanical equipment rooms	STC 50	STC 48
	Exterior of building	STC 45	STC 42
Music practice room	Adjacent practice rooms*	STC 55	STC 50
	Corridors and public areas	STC 45	STC 42
Counseling offices	Adjacent offices	STC 50	STC 45
	General office areas	STC 48	STC 45
	Corridors or lobbies	STC 45	STC 42
	Toilet areas	STC 50	STC 47

*Requires decoupled construction such as double walls and floor, or a room within a room.
Sources: Adapted from McGuiness, Stein, and Reynolds 1992; and McGuiness and Reynolds 1980.

DESIGN GUIDES
Acoustic problems differ by room function.

Classrooms
Typically, classroom acoustic design is achieved readily through the location of sound-absorbing materials or treatments to reduce noise levels; by ensuring adequate privacy between adjacent spaces; and by controlling the noise of the mechanical systems. Classroom areas average 650 to 900 sq ft, with 10 ft high ceilings. Sound absorption is most easily provided by acoustic ceiling tiles with an NRC of 0.7. Alternatively, walls and floors may be treated. Full-height partitions should isolate and prevent disturbance from adjacent areas. The noise-reduction characteristics of any air-

ACOUSTIC CONTROL

▶ *Untreated space. In much of room (a) reverberant sound is the greatest part of received sound. Wall and ceiling absorption in room (b) eliminates most of these reflections. Source: Stein and Reynolds 2000, p. 1524.*

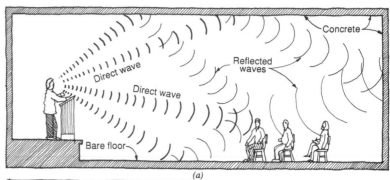

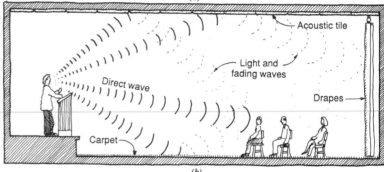

▼ *Section and plan of an auditorium with surface treatments. These control reflections and reverberation. Source: Stein and Reynolds 2000, p. 1544.*

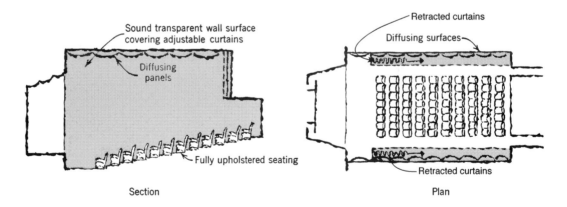

Section

Plan

transfer ducts should be as good as those of the walls or doors they are penetrating.

In the design and construction of a school, the budget is usually low, so it is unrealistic to expect optimal NC ratings. Speech must be clearly heard, and the proper acoustic design for a classroom is a balance or compromise between the need for some reflection to achieve correct levels and absorption to maintain clarity and intelligibility. The optimum reverberation time for speech in a classroom with a volume of 5,300 cu ft is 0.35 seconds, and in general a good figure for lecture environments is 0.35 to 0.4 seconds. A quiet classroom would have a background noise of NC-35; background noise in a normal classroom would be NC-40.

The following are guidelines for acoustic designs of classrooms:

- Minimize external noise.
- Where possible, locate classrooms away from noisy spaces such as gymnasiums and mechanical rooms.
- Design and specify adequate acoustic isolation in partitions, ceilings, windows, and doors.
- In certain cases it may be necessary to line ventilation ducts or to specify heavy, gasketed doors to lessen unwanted noise from outside.
- Unwanted sounds from inside a room—for example, from noisy light fixtures, HVAC systems, or furniture, and from the students themselves—may be attenuated by applying additional acoustic material, preferably high on the walls.
- There are no strict rules for room shapes and proportions, but to avoid the flutter of sound that can be caused by parallel side walls, furnishings or wall finishes can be used to break up direct sound waves.

Music Practice Rooms

Music rooms and suites require special isolation. For example, if a violin practice room is adjacent to a trumpet practice room, then, even with an STC of 55, the trumpet will be heard in the adjacent room. A much higher STC is required, implying special construction. Generally music rooms require decoupled construction: double walls and floor, or a room within a room.

Sound waves produced by music have a dynamic range and a tendency to excite the room construction into vibrating motion. To prevent excitation between both similar and dissimilar uses, decoupled construction should be used. This construction can be prefabricated, in the form of units installed in an existing space, or built with general construction methods, depending on the size of the room. For smaller music rooms, it may be practical to install prefabricated units, but for larger general practice rooms prefabrication cost becomes prohibitive.

For construction reasons, there are benefits to aligning smaller music practice rooms. In this case, and in the case of larger practice rooms, it may be advisable to place these near mechanical rooms, gymnasiums, or circulation zones rather than near classrooms or other teaching spaces.

Auditoriums

School auditoriums are, almost without exception, designated for multipurpose use. The spectrum of sound in these spaces ranges from speech at one end to music at the other. Because the installation of variable acoustics is very expensive, auditoriums should generally be designed to the middle of the spectrum with a reverberation time between the optimal time for speech and for music. Various factors, including the volume of the room, affect the reverberation time. Elimination of extraneous noise and careful planning of the mechanical systems serving the space are important to the acoustic design.

When the reverberation time of a room has been established, acoustic materials should be placed in such a way that as

ACOUSTIC CONTROL

▶ *Use of ray diagrams shown in section through a typical lecture room. Source: Stein and Reynolds 2000, p. 1542.*

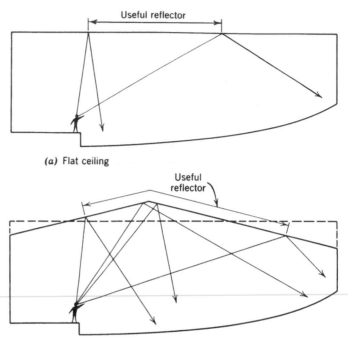

(a) Flat ceiling

(b) Two panel ceiling increases useful reflecting area

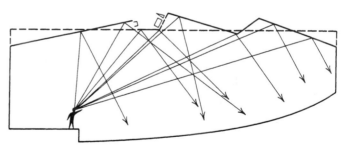

(c) Multifaceted ceiling incorporates lights and loudspeakers

the proper reverberation time is achieved, there are reflecting surfaces to help project sound and absorbing surfaces to prevent sound reflections. In an auditorium it is best to avoid placing absorptive surfaces in the ceiling or walls close to the stage; these surfaces should, rather, occur on the rear wall facing the stage. Inasmuch as suspended acoustic clouds are impractical in schools because of maintenance requirements and common room volumes, ceilings finished with a hard or smooth material may be used as reflectors. If needed, depending on the volume of the auditorium, soft absorptive surfaces can be placed on the

IMPROVEMENTS IN SW RATING OF STUD[a] PARTITIONS

Description	STC
Basic Partition—single-wood studs, 16 in. on centers. ½-in. gypsum board each side, air cavity	35
Add to Basic Partition:	
Double gypsum board, one side	+2
Double gypsum board, both sides	+4
Single-thickness absorbent material in air cavity	±3
Double-thickness insulation	+6
Resilient channel supports for gypsum board	+5
Staggered studs	+9
Double studs	+13

[a]When using two improvements, add additional +2. When using three improvements, add additional +3.

Example: Improvements to 35 STC basic partition:

Staggered wood studs	+9
Double gypsum board, one side	+2
Single insulation	+3
Adder	+3
Total	+17
Total STC	35 +17 = 52

For application to metal-stud partitions, use adders as above except begin with STC = 40 for 3⅝ in. basic partition. Source: Adapted from Stein and Reynolds 2000.

side walls toward the rear of the room. Ceiling and side walls provide diffusion, and at the front of the auditorium they distribute sound to the audience. The reflective surfaces of ceilings and walls should be close enough to the performers to minimize delays between natural and reflected sound. Upholstered chairs are advisable, as they offer similar absorption characteristics for the audience that will occupy the space. Curtains can be used, where affordable, to achieve varying reverberation times, depending on the desired activity or function of the room. The use of circular spaces and curved side walls should be avoided, because such walls focus the sound waves rather than provide even reflection.

Air-handling systems serving auditoriums require special design with low-pressure fans, slower-than-average air velocities (less than 1,000 ft per minute), and grilles and diffusers sized at maximum NC20, based on design air quantities.

Sound systems, incorporating microphones, loudspeakers, and control locations, are required in almost all auditoriums and should be part of the design of the space from the start.

Gymnasiums

Gymnasiums are often problem areas where acoustics are concerned, even when these spaces have been acoustically treated. Physical activity generates high noise levels that make communication difficult. (Some spaces have been noted in which the reverberance levels were so high that the instructor had to teach a physical education class in the hallway before sending the students back into the gym for the "physical" aspect of the class.) Although the acoustical design of gymnasiums is not nearly as critical as that of auditoriums, these spaces nevertheless require reasonable reverberation control. For practical reasons related to its use, the floor and walls of a gym must be hard, so the only surface that remains available for acoustical treatment is the ceiling. In most cases a gymnasium has a long-span roof structure, often with exposed trusses or beams, and acoustical material can be applied to the underside of the slab above. To afford adequate absorption to a lower frequency range, this material should be a minimum of 2 in. thick with an NRC of 0.7.

However, where a sound-amplification system is used, sound-absorbing wall treatment or devices may be required. Gymnasiums are sometimes used as auditoriums. In such cases, loudspeaker placement requires careful consideration, and it may be advisable to have flexibility in loudspeaker switching.

A gymnasium should never be located above any sensitive spaces, including classrooms. It is feasible, however, to place sensitive spaces above a gymnasium, inasmuch as the separating slab has a high STC and acoustic control is thus manageable. In addition, sensitive spaces should not be placed next to a gymnasium; instead, use mechanical space or a circulation zone as a buffer.

Laboratories

Fume hoods in chemistry and biology laboratories generate noise, because extraction is usually done by remote high-pressure fans. A hood has a pressure valve controlling the extracted air. This valve has to dissipate pressure, thereby generating noise. Thus, in selecting fume hood exhausts, the design team should review the acoustical performance and NC level of the equipment based on the pressure and air quantities to be controlled, and make sure that the NC level is no greater than 45 to 50 (a 10 decibel (dB) excedence over the ambient-noise level).

Dining Areas

Cafeteria and lunchroom activities produce fairly high noise levels, so these should be separated from kitchens and serving areas. Sound-absorbing material, such as acoustic tile, should be applied to walls and ceilings, and, ideally, the space should be carpeted. The minimum NRC should be 0.8.

Shops

Tools and equipment in the metal, woodworking, and scenery shops of schools generate very high levels of airborne and structure-borne noise. These areas should thus be carefully located in the initial planning of the building, preferably with an adjacency or combination of noisy areas, and should have ceiling and wall treatments with a minimum NRC of 0.75.

Swimming Pools

High humidity usually causes deterioration of the absorptive materials in the often unruly acoustic environments of school swimming pools. Special sound-absorbing and moisture-resistant materials, or combinations of materials, may have to be used to limit noise levels.

Mechanical Systems and Mechanical Rooms

Mechanical rooms with classrooms or other acoustically sensitive rooms located above or below, need a minimum structural density in the floor slab so that the slab may act as a barrier to airborne sound and be sufficiently rigid to act as a stable platform for rotating equipment. Typically, the design team should look for 75 to 100 psf concrete to obtain a good shell in which to specify resilient mountings for the equipment. If the foundation is not sound, it has a tendency to resonate and the decoupling provided by the mountings will be less efficient than theoretical predictions. Lightweight, flexible structures degrade isolation efficiencies of resilient mountings.

With proper planning, almost anything can be programmed over a mechanical space without designing an expensive, acoustically isolated structure. However, whenever practicable, direct adjacencies should be avoided. Mechanical rooms generate low-frequency sound; therefore, masonry is the better partitioning material inasmuch as it provides basic mass to absorb low-frequency waves. For speech privacy, on the other hand, masonry construction is not desirable, because the human voice lies midrange in the spectrum; drywall construction attenuates this sound effectively.

HEARING IMPAIRMENT AND ADA REQUIREMENTS

The Americans with Disabilities Act Accessibility Guidelines (ADAAG)[2] state that in certain assembly areas where audible communications are integral to the use of the space,[3] there must be a permanently installed assistive listening system in the following situations:

- If they accommodate at least 50 persons, or if they have audio-amplification systems

- If they have fixed seating

A permanently installed assistive listening system, or an adequate number of electrical outlets or other supplementary wiring necessary to support a portable assistive listening system, must be provided for other assembly areas.
The number of receivers that must be provided should be equal a minimum of 4 percent of the total number of seats, but in no case should there be fewer than two receivers.

These regulations apply to new construction of classrooms seating at least 50 students or classrooms with fixed seating and audio-amplification systems. Sounds are usually broadcast by the assistive listening system through infrared or FM signals transmitted from the speaker's microphone to listeners with special receivers and headsets. Such systems aid communication between teacher and student, but not between the students themselves.

A drawback of assistive listening systems is that they may be severely compromised by a reverberant noisy environment,

---

[2]Federal Register 36 CFR Part 1191 4.1.3. 19(b).
[3]For example, lecture and concert halls, playhouses, movie theaters, and meeting rooms.

where unwanted sounds are picked up by the microphone and transmitted to the listener, often impeding hearing ability. Design teams should thus take special care to prevent highly reverberant environments.

The ADAAG is looking into the acoustical performance of classrooms as it relates to hearing-impaired persons and will attempt to develop acoustical guidelines for educational facilities. Published in the *Federal Register*, June 1, 1998, 36 CFR Chapter XI, the Architectural and Transportation Barriers Compliance Board's "Petition for Rulemaking: Request for Information on Acoustics" is highly recommended reading material.[4]

---

[4] The Web site may be accessed at *http://www.access-board.gov/rules/acoustics.htm.*

CHAPTER 13
LIGHTING DESIGN

INTRODUCTION

The lighting system is a critical factor in the design of a school, both in terms of its impact on energy costs and its effect on the health, performance, and stress levels of students. It is vital that lighting and daylighting systems be carefully considered and that any value-engineering decisions take into account both first costs and long-term and maintenance costs, as well as the impact of any decision on the user. Inadequate lighting, glare, or conflicting lighting levels will cause eyestrain and make it hard for students to concentrate.

Classroom lighting requirements involve the illumination of the room, not just the desk, where light seems to be needed most. Classroom lighting is a diverse issue, inasmuch as classrooms are often used for different kinds of teaching and various types of classes, which may mean different lighting needs from day to day or from year to year. Thus the approach must be one whereby all problems are solved and all levels provided for without resulting in an over- or underlit space.[1] This approach is especially important in elementary schools and kindergartens, where many activities can occur in a space at once, as compared with high schools and colleges, where the tasks tend to be more specific. There is no single solution or simple guideline for classroom lighting. A lighting method that perfectly illuminates a classroom with a 10 ft ceiling may not work in a room with a 9 ft ceiling.

Note that there is a vast difference between quantity and quality of light. The illumination of a classroom to 50 foot-candles, the generally accepted level, is often considered adequate, but no attention may be given to the way in which this illumination is achieved. The result can be a poorly lit space, even though the lighting level seems to be correct.

LIGHT LEVELS, LIGHT REFLECTANCE VALUES, AND GLARE

Research and experience point to the desirability of uniform brightness ratios in the field of vision and an average light reflectance value (LRV) of 50 to 60 percent in school environments. LRVs of surfaces and materials are shown in the table at the top of page 169. The maximum

---

Lighting can make a classroom come alive…Lighting must also contribute to the mood for learning…It must be a stimulant. Bland, coldly uniform, "scientifically planned" lighting usually has the opposite effect: it bores and depresses…The classroom can have lighting that changes, that is a shifting interplay of opposites—warm and cool, light and shadow, soft and hard, level light and accent light. (Perkins 1957, p. 37)

---

[1] Many new classrooms are overilluminated, with high glare, and older classrooms often have inefficient lighting systems.

Definitions
- *Candlepower:* The unit of luminous intensity is the candlepower, abbreviated to cp. A wax candle has a luminous intensity in the horizontal direction of about 1 candlepower.
- *Lumen:* A candle radiates light equally in all directions. One lumen (lm) is the amount of luminous energy (flux) emanating from 1 sq ft of the surface of a transparent sphere with a radius of 1 ft surrounding a candle.
- *Footcandle:* An illumination of one footcandle (fc) is produced when 1 lumen of luminous energy falls on 1 sq ft of area.
- *Illumination:* This can be expressed as the density of luminous energy, expressed in lumens per unit area, or footcandles. Measurements of illumination levels can be made with footcandle meters.
- *Luminance/Brightness:* The luminous flux, or light, emitted, transmitted, or reflected from a surface. Luminance affects the acuity with which we see objects, and, generally, visual performance increases with object brightness. The object's background, it should be noted, is important, and introduces the notion of contrast.
- *Contrast:* The contrast or luminance ratio between an object and its surroundings is important in creating and maintaining visual comfort. Depending on the task being performed, luminance ratios should decrease as luminance levels increase.
- *Light reflectance value* (LRV): The measurement of a material's ability to reflect light. The LRV of a material is used to establish the brightness ratio or luminance ratio of a room. Thus, it is important that the reflectances of the major surfaces in a room be considered and controlled.
- *Brightness ratios:* Although visual performance increases with contrast, the difference between the average luminance and that of the visual field or task should, conversely, be low. In other words, although contrast may be recommended in the *object* of view, it is detrimental to the *field* of view.

brightness difference should not exceed 3 to 1.

Younger students require lower light levels—about 30 to 35 footcandles—than older students, for whom more detailed reading, requiring about 50 footcandles, must be accommodated. The bottom table at right shows recommended minimum illumination levels in schools.

A chemistry lab may need as much as 100 footcandles illumination on the benches, but not throughout the space, and the higher level on the benches may be achieved through tasklighting.

LIGHT REFLECTANCE VALUES (LRVs) OF SURFACES AND MATERIALS	
Surface or Material	LRV(%)
Furniture	40–50
Equipment	40–50
Doors and door frames	40–50
Floors	20–30
Walls	50–55
Teaching walls	45–50
Accent walls	45–50
Ceilings	90–100
Average for typical classroom	40–60

Source: Adapted from William C. Brubaker, *Planning and Designing Schools* (New York: McGraw-Hill, 1998).

RECOMMENDED MINIMUM ILLUMINATION LEVELS IN SCHOOLS	
Tasks	Footcandles
Reading printed material	30
Reading pencil writing	70
Reading spirit duplicated material:	
Good copy	30
Bad copy	100
Classrooms	
General	20–50
Chalkboards (supplementary illumination)	150
Drafting rooms	100
Laboratories	50–100
Lecture rooms	
General	70
Special exhibits and demonstrations	100–200
Auditoriums	10–20
Lip-reading classes	150
Shops	100
Sewing rooms	150
Sight-saving classes	150
Study halls	70
Social activity	5–10
Toilets and washrooms	20–50
Corridors and stairs	20–50

Figures are taken from Table 18.4 in McGuinness, Stein, and Reynolds 1980, and are based on IES standards and recommendations for maximum performance; and Gary J. Gordon, and James L Nuckolls, *Interior Lighting for Designers*, 3d ed. (New York: John Wiley & Sons, 1995).

RECOMMENDED LUMINANCE RATIOS	
1 to ⅓	Between task and adjacent surroundings
1 to ⅒	Between task and more remote darker surfaces
1 to 10	Between task and more remote lighter surfaces
20 to 1	Between luminaires (or fenestration) and adjacent surfaces
40 to 1	Anywhere within the normal field of view

Source: Adapted from McGuinness, Stein, and Reynolds 1980.

▼ The diagram shows direct and reflected glare light paths, with direct glare strongest in a head-up position, and reflected glare at a reading position. Glare can be controlled when lighting design takes into consideration room size, surface finishes, size and placement of light sources (including windows), and luminance ratios. Source: Stein and Reynolds 2000, p. 1084.

In a teaching/lecturing type of class, it is important to reduce contrast for students looking up at the teacher and down at their books; a light balance is needed so that the students' eyes are not strained through constant adjusting. All surfaces should be lit.

The architect should ensure that desks, walls, blackboards, and screens are adequately lit. A brightness ratio of 5 to 1 ensures visual comfort and minimizes strain. From normal viewpoints, brightness ratios between areas of appreciable size should be restricted to the approximate values shown in the table above so that a comfortable brightness balance is reached.

Glare, an effect of extreme contrast or luminance, can be disturbing and frustrating to students. If light is coming from the wrong direction because of too much luminance, there will be glare. To limit glare, the designer can either limit the amount of light emitted toward the eye of the observer or increase the area from which light is emitted (i.e., increase the number of fixtures). The careful location of light fixtures is also vital in the prevention of glare. In terms of the overall design of a space, one should remember that too many light fixtures that are poorly located can create "clutter" in the field of vision, which can be equated to static or noise in acoustic design. Reflected glare, which is as distracting as direct glare, results when there is too much uncontrolled luminance reflected by

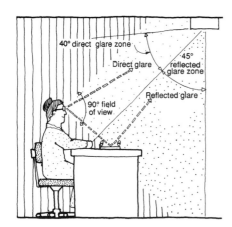

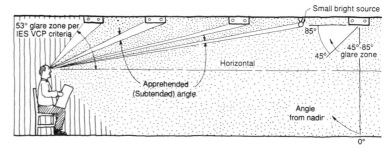

▲ Size, luminance, and location in the field of view determine the glare afforded by a fixture. The diagram shows how, due to the apprehended solid angles of source, the glare from a small source, through luminance, is less objectionable than a source on a dark background. For this reason ceilings and upper walls should be light-colored to reduce glare. Source: Stein and Reynolds 2000, p. 1085.

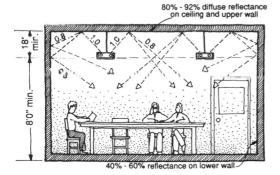

▲ *The diagrams show how reflected glare is reduced as the number of light fixtures is increased and luminance decreased, with an all-luminous ceiling producing the least glare. Source: Stein and Reynolds 2000, p. 1096.*

◀ *Indirect fixtures directly illuminate ceilings and upper walls, which become secondary sources to illuminate the spaces below. A largely uniform brightness can be produced with good indirect lighting design. Source: Stein and Reynolds 2000, p. 1215.*

surfaces or objects. The designer should beware of reflected glare from desk surfaces and, especially, computer screens. Direct and indirect glare are most easily avoided by indirect lighting systems.

There is no formula governing light fixture choice: this should be a function of what the architectural design, the LRV, and the brightness ratio of the spaces must be. Direct/indirect lighting is more comfortable with adequate ceiling heights (9 ft to 9½ ft).

The color of the walls is part of the lighting design. A colored accent wall in a classroom can help to relieve eyestrain and glare and to focus attention. Colors in the cool range, such as soft greens and blues, are usually best, although it must be noted that choice of color depends on

the type of school environment. For example, in elementary schools, bright, warm colors are often used to inspire students.

Sophisticated audiovisual presentations have become more prevalent with advances in technology, especially in more affluent schools. Here the architect may have to introduce multilevel switching and dimming, whereby, for example, three or four rows of lights may be operated individually to set the required light levels. In all likelihood, the cost of school construction is such that this level of sophistication will never be sufficiently affordable to become the norm, but will be achieved primarily in specialized rooms. Nevertheless, audiovisual teaching methods and the use of computers will become the norm for learning.

ELECTRIC LIGHTING SYSTEMS

The most common electric lighting system is a two-by-four fluorescent lamp lay-in troffer. This is appropriate where students read books at their desks, but does not take into account multipurpose use or the increasing presence of computers in the classroom. Computers have introduced new lighting needs for which traditional prismatic lenses, although cost-effective, are not adequate.

Parabolic louvers can create a shielding zone to reduce glare and provide pleasant lighting levels. The disadvantages are that louvers add to the cost of a troffer and may cast shadows on walls, creating a dark ceiling zone even though the work surfaces are adequately illuminated.

Increasingly often, indirect lighting systems are being used in computer labs and classrooms, where it is important that glare and reflection on the computer screen be avoided. Indirect lighting systems use ceilings, and sometimes walls, to reflect light and illuminate a space softly and evenly. Users of such a space tend to have less eyestrain, headaches, and visual fatigue than users of the aforementioned systems. Effective indirect lighting provides little contrast and no bright spots; thus, the fixtures typically must be suspended at least 18 in. from the ceiling and spaced in rows approximately 10 ft apart.[2] The ceiling height may need to be raised to maintain 8 ft between the bottom of the fixture and the floor. Indirect lighting is usually more expensive, in terms of first cost, than the described earlier. However, spaces that are indirectly lit appear brighter owing to the elimination of

shadows, and thus less lighting is needed. In fact, directly lit classrooms require illumination of 50 to 100 footcandles, as compared with 35 footcandles for indirectly lit spaces. The resultant energy savings usually compensates over time for the higher initial fixture cost.

The advantages and disadvantages of different lighting systems are described in the opposite table.

WINDOWS AND DAYLIGHTING

Windows bring air and light into a room and connect the room with the world outside. They introduce different ventilation and lighting requirements for a school, and the choice of a window system has an impact on both the owner and the user. The issue of windows in classrooms has been much debated, ranging from the introduction of windowless classrooms at one time in the State of Florida, to laws in New York State that require 50 percent of a window wall to be glazed. In some schools, windows are targets for vandalism and crime, and it has been argued that views to the outdoors are distracting to students. However, a report in the *Archives of Internal Medicine* advocates the compulsory use of windows as a necessary relief. The report states that the type of distraction caused by windows is "soft," and that without windows students become even more focused on doodling in their books and can less easily refocus their attention on the teacher.

Windows and daylight in a space can have the following effects:

---

[2] This spacing depends on the suspension length. For example, a row spacing of 12 ft is acceptable with a 24 in. suspension length. Some features are effective when mounted less than 12 in. from the ceiling.

LIGHTING SYSTEMS COMPARISON					
	Prismatic Lenses	**Parabolic Louvers**	**Indirect Lighting**	**Windows**	**Skylights**
Lens	A12, A19	3 in. deep, RP-24	None	Glass	Acrylic
Advantages	A12: Low cost A19: Slightly less glare and more comfort than with A12 lenses	3 in. deep: Reduces glare RP-24: Eliminates glare	Excellent visual comfort, especially in computer spaces	View, daylight	Daylight, color quality, savings, high light levels
Disadvantages	A12: High glare, low comfort A19: Slightly higher cost Both: Not recommended for computer rooms	3 in. deep: Cost RP-24: High cost	Cost	Vandalism	First cost, potential leaks resulting from penetration of roof membrane, limitations on control of light levels
Application	A12: Low budget, no computers A19: Small budget, no computers	Computer spaces, low-ceiling aesthetics	Computer spaces, high ceilings	Classrooms and offices	Classrooms, media centers, gymnasiums, and offices

Source: Adapted from table in CEFPI Issuetrak: "Electric Lighting and Daylighting in Schools."

- Daylighting introduces high contrasts, and north- and south-facing rooms have different lighting requirements. Northern Hemisphere south-facing windows can be designed with *brise-soleils*, "eyebrows" or shades against the summer sun, and winter sun can be used to advantage (e.g., for solar warming). West-facing windows should be avoided where feasible.

- In a classroom supplied with 60 footcandles of electric light, sunlight may introduce 8,000 to 10,000 footcandles and, hence, a large contrast.

- Daylighting can be used to control lighting costs through the careful design of the electric lighting system.

- Daylighting usually introduces the need for shading devices, inasmuch as too much sunlight can cause glare and heat up a room.

- Energy loss or heat gain through windows can be minimized by the orientation of classrooms in the plan, by the efficient design of the windows themselves, and by the use shading devices.

- Vandalism can be countered by the organization of the plan around a courtyard or easily monitored areas, and by the use of skylights, which also provide good light levels.

- Interior windows are an excellent means of invigorating the design of a school, making visual links to different activities and displaying the educational process and its programs while, at the same time, transmitting light. At times, the use of glass block is an appropriate device for lighting an interior space while maintaining its privacy, as is the use of skylights.

DESIGN GUIDES

School, commercial, office and institutional buildings, in many ways, have similar lighting requirements. However, school construction, renovation, and operating/maintenance budgets and allowances are nearly always small, and, thus, equipment, including lighting, must be:

- As maintenance-free as possible
- Very energy efficient
- Long-lasting
- Tough and relatively damage-proof

In choosing light fixtures, the following guidelines should be noted.

In general

- Daylight is the most efficient light source.
- Fixtures and/or their ballasts may generate noise.
- To reduce maintenance, long-life lamps and fixtures are important. In corridors and less accessible or high-ceilinged spaces, extended-life fluorescent lamps are longer lasting and require less frequent changing.
- Light fixtures are cleaned infrequently, which affects light levels. Generally, the design and selection of fixtures should be based on the assumption that maintenance will be infrequent.

Classrooms

- Surface reflectance is important: see the illustration below for recommendations.

▶ *Classroom lighting: The image shows a computer model of a 24 ft x 28 ft classroom with 16 4-ft luminaires in a 14 ft x 22 ft perimeter layout, suspended 18 in. from the ceiling and 9 ft above the floor. Average horizontal luminance on the desks is 74 fc; average vertical luminance on the chalkboard is 39 fc. Source: Stein and Reynolds 2000, p. 1300.*

- Compare life-cycle costs of different lighting systems.
- Compare life-cycle costs with first costs.
- Maximize daylighting.
- Multiple lighting levels may be required for varying teaching applications, and this is achieved economically by multiple switching and multilevel ballasts.
- For direct-indirect and direct fixtures, use standard fluorescent cool and warm white lamps.
- Incandescent lamps are not advisable.

Auditoriums and multipurpose spaces
- Flexible, dimmable lighting is recommended.
- Incandescent lamps are preferred.
- Additional fluorescent or high-intensity discharge (HID) fixtures may be required to supplement light levels for writing and study tasks.
- Long-life lamps are advisable because of the relatively inaccessible higher ceilings.
- Install lights on steps or tiers for safety.
- Locate noisy ballasts carefully.

Gymnasiums
- Use tough, well-protected fixtures that can be relamped from the floor with a pole.
- Provide multilevel switching to allow multipurpose use of the space.
- Take into account the accumulation of dirt.

Lecture Halls
- Lighting is similar to that of classrooms.

▲ Here, a multipurpose space, doubling as a dining area and assembly room, uses high-intensity, indirect tungsten-halogen units located at the concrete beam junctures. Source: Stein and Reynolds 2000, p. 1303.

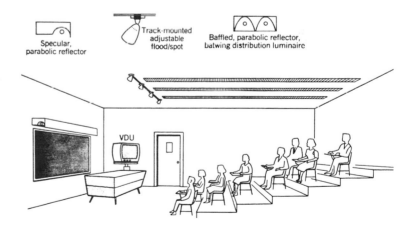

▲ Typical lecture-room lighting utilizes 45-degree cutoff baffled parabolic reflector troffers for minimum direct and reflected glare, adjustable track lights for demonstration table illumination, and an asymmetric reflector for chalkboard lighting. The large visual display unit in the room will not have veiling reflections with the illustrated lighting arrangement. Source: Stein and Reynolds 2000, p. 1304.

LIGHTING DESIGN

▶ *This photograph of an exhibition room demonstrates good and bad lighting techniques. High windows give excellent daylight penetration. The art display is perfectly highlighted by track lighting, but the tracks should be carefully positioned to prevent glare and shadows, especially when the ceiling is lower than 10 ft high. Also, here the incandescent downlights for general lighting are used excessively and unattractively. Source: Stein and Reynolds 2000, p. 1302.*

- Use switching and multilevel ballasts to achieve three-level fluorescent lighting.
- Locate clearly labeled light switches at the entrance and at the front of the room. Label switch cover plates so that users know which lights the switches control.
- Locate a row of adjustable fixtures to light the front of the room.
- Chalkboards and markerboards may be lit with fluorescent fixtures.
- Control the entry of light from outside the room, and use narrow vision panels in doors.
- In large lecture halls, spotlights are recommended to light the speaker/ teacher during a film or slide presentation.
- In applications where a chalkboard and a screen are used concurrently, separate lights may be needed.
- If possible, locate doors so that light from outside the room does not fall on and wash out the screen when a door is opened during a class or lecture.

Art Rooms

- Skylights or north-facing windows are recommended.
- Constant-color daylight.
- For artificial lighting, use deluxe fluorescent tubes.
- Provide tasklighting, adjustable by students.
- Use spotlights for certain focused, detailed applications.
- Provide track-mounted incandescent lights, adjustable wall-washing fixtures, or color-corrected fluorescent fixtures for display of artwork.

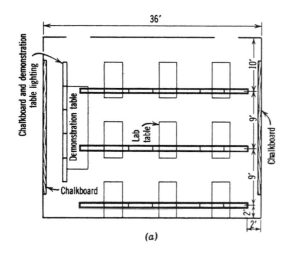

(a)

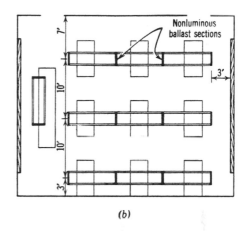

(b)

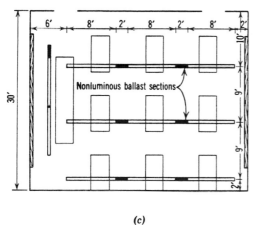

(c)

◄ *Laboratory lighting schemes. Running lights across tables or in aisles is preferable to the transverse direction from the aspect of reflected glare. (a) Pendant direct-indirect units. (b) and (c) variations of the single, semidirect HO design. The relatively high noise level of ballasts is generally not objectionable in labs, although quiet electronic ballasts are recommended for their acoustic and energy characteristics. Source: Stein and Reynolds 2000, p. 1304.*

▼ *Library stack lighting is best accomplished by fixtures with lenses specifically designed for the purpose. Fixtures with baffles and plastic diffusers generally do not give adequate vertical surface illumination. Source: Stein and Reynolds 2000, p. 1305.*

Laboratories

- Lighting approaches should take into account fixed, dark-colored benches and shiny surfaces.
- Locate fixtures parallel to and slightly behind benches.
- Indirect lighting is preferable here for diffusion on vertical surfaces.

Libraries

- Lighting should accommodate the various activities and areas that typically make up a library, primarily the reading room(s) and stacks.

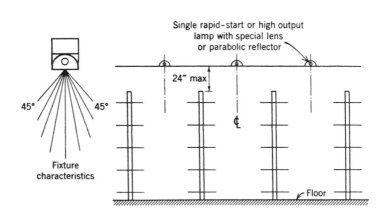

LIGHTING DESIGN

▶ *Lighting of school corridors. High reflectance walls, floor, and ceiling improve utilization of light and increase the feeling of cheerfulness. The lighting technique illustrated is appropriate for school corridors. The rows of luminaires at each side wall illuminate bulletin boards, special displays, and the faces of interiors of lockers more efficiently than do units centered in the ceiling. Source: Stein and Reynolds 2000, p. 1306.*

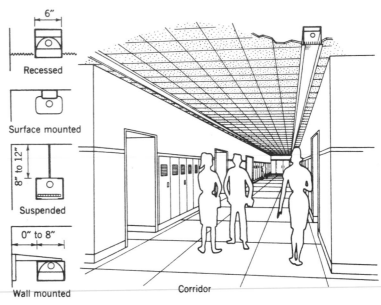

▼ *In this cafeteria, soft, even, glare-free light from cove lighting in a pyramidal coffer is of sufficient intensity to permit the cafeteria to double as a work/study and meeting space. Source: Stein and Reynolds 2000, p. 1303.*

Wall lighting with single lamp units

- Reading rooms may be lit with the use of general lighting, such as fluorescent or HID sources,[3] or lower-level general lighting reinforced by fluorescent tasklighting at the carrels or tables. Beware of noisy ballasts.

- For the stacks, specially designed fluorescent fixtures, mounted between and 2 ft above the shelving, are available to light the vertical surfaces.

- Work and checkout areas require lighting similar to that of the reading room, with higher lighting levels.

- Direct-indirect lighting is recommended for computer areas.

---

[3]Ceiling heights should be a minimum of 10 ft when HID fixtures, such as metal halide or deluxe mercury, are used.

CHAPTER 14
INTERIORS ISSUES

Each student should feel that he or she has "a home within the school." To create such a comfort level, the scale of the building and the daily inhabitant space must be based on the respective ages of the student population. The kindergarten classroom is larger than other classrooms in square footage, but should have a more intimate feel for a group of smaller children. The square-footage requirements are driven by the need of the students to move around, developing motor skills, as discussed in chapter 1.

At the youngest ages, it is critical that students do not feel overwhelmed or out of place. The designer must be aware of the scale of the children to appropriately size the width of corridors, the height of the ceiling, the furnishings, and the toilet facilities. This is particularly important in developing a classroom in which the children spend most of their day. They should feel a sense of ownership and be able to easily distinguish this space from other classrooms. If color, graphic patterns, and special materials are strategically applied along the corridors and public areas, the children are able to quickly orient themselves and find the classroom. Within the room, each student should have an area of personal space. The cubicles for personal storage have traditionally served the smaller student, and individual desks or lockers have been used as the child grows older. A variety of areas should be offered within the classrooms, so that the child can engage in group activity or move away for individual quiet study.

All support areas of the classroom should be sized to be accessible to the age group of the students served. Among the

▲ Nooks and other spaces scaled for children can enhance the interior environment. Tenderloin Community School, San Francisco, California. EHDD Architects. (Photograph by Ethan Kaplan; courtesy of Esto Photographics.)

components to be considered are the following:

- Toilet facilities—sink height, fixture size and height, height of dispensers, etc.
- Depth of counter and sinks within the classroom
- Water fountains
- Cubicles
- Door handles
- Light switches

▶ *Storage and display are particularly important in the interior design of classrooms for younger grades. If these needs are not addressed, classrooms become cluttered and visually chaotic.*

The ergonomic diagram shown on page 188 aid in determining the appropriate height for placement of equipment.

Provisions for handicapped access and wheelchair clearances to meet the Americans with Disabilities (ADA) height regulations, which tend to be higher than necessary for general students, must be balanced with the lower heights required for younger student populations.

Child comfort is most critical in those areas within the building where children spend most of the day. The public and primarily adult-use areas, such as administration, should be sized to support adult users. Adjustments should be made to certain items, such as the reception desk, nurse's station, and guidance office, that will be serving children. For example, a section of the reception desk may be at lower height to allow young children visual contact with the receptionist. Areas of larger square footage, like the cafeteria, library, and gymnasium, and those spaces students encounter directly, such as computer stations or food-service counters, should be sized for their use.

For small children, it is important that the spaces not be physically or emotionally overwhelming, but approachable and friendly. Areas regularly occupied by each child daily should be grouped into smaller subunits. For example, a child should not have to travel far from the home-base classroom to special classes like art and music. In a large school, this may mean the creation of mini-schools to serve a number of home-base classrooms. This type of educational program is seen in the house concept discussed in chapter 1, in the section on middle schools.

As the students grow, the scale of the support areas gradually begins to conform to the adult dimensions and the spaces are adjusted to support the movement of students from classroom to classroom.

The corridors widen, students' personal space becoming part of the public corridor areas, typically in banks of lockers. The general classrooms become more standardized in their layout. The classrooms must now support a specific academic subject such as language, math, science, or art.

The home-base classroom is no longer the venue for most of the day. The middle school students' home-base area is now often the house to which they are assigned. The house is a cluster of classrooms containing all the major subjects a student will explore in a given day. Typically, it is an arrangement of classrooms, one for each subject—science, math, English, social studies. This area supports the students' main class subjects and serves as a home base. The lockers in the corridor should be clustered within the house. Corridors should be wide enough to allow simultaneous student traffic and locker access. Each house should have its own identity within the overall school. Color coding and the use of particular materials can create an identity for a house.

At the high school level, students are typically more mobile within the building. Travel from class to class occurs over a large area of the school. Students' contacts increase, and the building should provide opportunities for impromptu meetings along the travel paths. "A good school building is like a good house—or a hotel for kids and teachers—in that it has a variety of spaces that provide a variety of

▲ For older students, each one's personal space is his or her locker. Lockers are a common interior design element along the major corridors. Dr. Freddie Thomas Learning Center, Rochester, New York. SWBR Architects.

▶ In the upper grades more adult design elements are appropriate. Brunswick High School library, Brunswick, Maine. Harriman Associates.

▲ Natural light is an important feature of a good educational environment. Library at Longmeadow Center Elementary School, Longmeadow, Massachusetts. Tappé Associates, Inc. (Photograph by Steve Rosenthal.)

will have to be identified and approved by the client early in the design process. A multipurpose space is less common in a high school building, but it does occur and must therefore be designed for multiple uses. Again, emphasis is shifted from the individual classroom to the more public areas like the auditorium, gymnasium, and library. These spaces should be accessible, functional, and comfortable for visitors as well as students and staff.

Combinations of materials that create a strong design statement can provide a visually interesting environment for the students. The textures, both physical and visual, of the interior should be age appropriate. For younger students, a simple graphic or material pattern that is easily understood and relates to their travel through the building is preferred. As the student population ages, many more mature schemes can be pursued that lend a level of complexity and texture to the space. The weaving of natural light into the design texture of the building can support the students' daily enjoyment of the spaces. Natural light should be

opportunities for interaction" (Strickland 1994). The interiors are more focused on the public space and contacts outside the classrooms, and the classrooms become more subject-specific spaces.

Although the house or mini-school concept has been used on very large high school campuses, the buildings are traditionally laid out with departmental foci like science, social studies, and math, surrounding the shared areas at the building's core. Each classroom is designed for a specific activity, which can be as technically complex as a science laboratory or as simple as a lecture hall. Therefore, the exact needs of the spaces

used creatively in all areas of the school building. Although mandated by many codes for instruction rooms, its use as an aid in defining space should not be limited to classrooms. A beam of natural light falling into a corridor or cutting across a main lobby space has a dramatic effect on all occupants of the space. It can allow occupants to understand their relationship to the exterior at any given point within the building and can aid in their orientation. The appropriate use of natural lighting for the function of a space, which can reduce the use of electricity, can also provide a very pleasing working environment that may reduce

student and staff stress levels. The architect's main task is to provide space for the education of children, but by bringing creativity to the project in the combination of interior materials, finishes, and natural elements, he or she may have a positive effect on the daily lives of all the occupants.

FLEXIBILITY

The increase in multiple-use spaces leads in turn to the specification of more generic products for interiors. Finishes, furnishings, and treatments have become defined by the compromises between the functions for which a space is used. All aspects of design are affected when functions are combined, such as a gymnasium combined with an auditorium to form a gymatorium. The furnishings become more standardized and generic, as do the walls, floors, lighting, acoustics, heating, and ventilation. All design considerations for interiors must be planned to support the compromise decisions reached with the client.

Partition walls and demountable walls can also be used. Two traditional classrooms can be opened up to each other to provide large group instruction and team teaching. The furnishings for these areas should be considered part of the individual classrooms and should coordinate with the overall space whenever the spaces are combined.

The more multiple uses within a space, the more generic the interiors and design; thus, materials and finishes used must be more basic. The following materials and furnishings are used widely for multipurpose rooms:

• Vinyl composition tile flooring

• Tight level-loop carpeting

> Today's classroom design is based on other principles, most basic of which is flexibility—flexibility to keep pace with changing concepts of education's role in society, and of the teacher's role in the learning process. Also, the classroom must reflect the teaching methods of the school; it must be an efficient tool and a suitable atmosphere for education, regardless of the educational approaches used. (Perkins 1957, p. 22)

- Neutral painted walls
- Heavy-duty, durable vinyl wall coverings
- Separate table and chair combinations
- General area lighting

Storage for furnishings and teaching materials is also very important to maintain the flexibility of the space. It is difficult to accomplish a group dance or demonstration with nonfolding tables cluttering a room where storage is not provided.

FURNISHINGS

In selecting furniture for schools, the age of the users must be kept in mind. The age of the children being served has traditionally been considered in selecting the appropriate height and size of furnishings, but the durability of construction and materials can also weigh heavily in age appropriateness. The age and activity level of the student population should inform the selection of furniture materials. For example, an art class in an elementary school will require chair materials that allow for easy cleanup, whereas a computer class in a high school may have upholstered computer chairs.

Small children require small-scale desks, chairs, counters, and other furnishings. Chairs should be made of spill-resistant materials such as plastics and should be light enough for children to maneuver. Work surfaces should be of durable, wipe-off materials that hide scarring and resist scratches. With small children's tendency to encounter germs, the ability to disinfect all pieces should be considered. Many new products, such as some plastics, are being developed to actually resist the growth of bacteria and germs.

As the children age, the focus of furniture selection shifts to durability under abusive conditions. Although adult-dimensioned furnishings may be appropriate, the strength and life cycle of the pieces become critical. Schools want to purchase furnishings that will last a long time and can be used over many school terms, so as to improve their value. The pieces should be of such quality as to endure. Furnishings with warranties are preferred. The furnishings provided in the more private areas of the schools (e.g., classrooms) should be functional, durable, cleanable, and comfortable. The more public realm of a school should be comfortable for visitors and parents. For example, the furnishings in an administration reception area may be upholstered, cushioned, sofa-type furnishings, whereas classroom chairs may be high-density plastic on chrome structures.

The furnishings that are provided within individual program areas should support the learning objectives of the space. The art room and science laboratories may need stand-up work areas at counters that support large projects, and a music room may need only a chair and a music stand for each student. Furnishings should allow some flexibility in space arrangement, except in areas of extremely specific functions, such as a computer-based distance learning center in a high school, where the incorporation of technology will dictate the selection of furniture. Many school settings have ambiguous functions and are used for a variety of purposes. With the increase of multiple-use areas and multipurpose rooms, the flexible use of the space is increased but the exact function for which furnishing must be provided is less obvious to the designer. When faced with this circumstance, the client must come to a compromise among the various uses. A cafetorium may be furnished with stacking chairs and foldable roll-away tables. When the space is in cafeteria mode, the chairs are set up around the tables; when it is an auditorium, the same chairs are placed in rows for audience members and the tables are rolled away to storage.

In all the practical, functional, and flexible uses of furnishings, the designer should not underestimate the value and strength of furniture in making or upsetting an aesthetic statement. Furniture that fits the user group, the intended use, and the aesthetic scheme of the building can add visual pleasure to the lives of its occupants and visitors.

◀ *Furnishings must be durable, flexible, and scaled to the children. Tenderloin Community School, San Francisco, California. EHDD Architects. (Photograph by Ethan Kaplan.)*

There are a number of questions to consider in selecting furnishings:

Curriculum perspective

- Will the subject be taught to an entire class at once, to student teams, or both?

- What books and learning materials will the students require as they work at their desks, tables, or computers?

- How frequently and to what extent will the class work require reconfiguration of the furniture plan?

- How may the computers be used?

Building interface perspective

- How are the electrical power and computer cabling distributed in the classroom, and what will be required in the future?

- How can power and cabling be connected or rerouted and still allow for furniture reconfiguration?

- How is wire management addressed? Should it be part of the building design or the furniture design?

- Where might the computers be located?

General perspective

- Are materials durable, safe, and maintenance-free?

- What is the best way to accommodate a broad range of student sizes? Should adjustments in table height require the efforts of maintenance personnel?

- How will storage of students' books and materials be accommodated?

TECHNOLOGY

The influence of information technology pervades the design of today's schools, especially in the interior spaces. The variety of applications of computers in educational programs does not allow development of a definite set of design guidelines. The system needs constant adjustment as educational foci and teaching styles change. Certain basic issues should be considered where computers are being used regardless of the scale of the space, whether it is an individual classroom with a few stations or a computer learning laboratory for an entire class.

The following are some design considerations for the reduction of glare in computer environments:

- Even illumination, without hot spots or glare, should he provided.

- Natural light should be diffused with blinds, louvers, or roof overhangs.

- The room and its furnishings should be arranged to reduce the effects of glare.

- Finishes within the space should absorb rather than reflect light.

In an area dedicated to computer use, the floor treatment and construction may be vital. Although a hard-surface tile floor is not recommended because it may produce a glare, carpeting can cause static electricity build up in a dry atmosphere, which can be harmful to the sensitive electronics of a computer. Several manufacturers have developed carpeting systems that reduce or eliminate static buildup. Another flooring system often used in computer areas that require the option for frequent rearrangement of workstations is an elevated sectional computer floor. This system provides several inches of height between the permanent subfloor of a room and the finished walking surface, where computer

◄ The increasing use of computers made it necessary to design new furniture, lighting, and static-free flooring. Longmeadow Center Elementary School, Longmeadow, Massachusetts. Tappé Associates, Inc. (Photograph by Steve Rosenthal.)

wiring can run unrestricted by furnishings. This is perhaps the most aesthetically pleasing (and costly) installation for computer wiring inasmuch as all runs are out of sight of the users. Other options, wall circuit systems and wiring drops from the ceiling, are more visually invasive and limit the room's flexibility but often cost less.

ERGONOMICS

A student should feel comfortable while in school no matter what the task undertaken. In discussing computer use in any environment, ergonomics should not be overlooked. Furnishings should have the ability to adjust to a broad range of motion typical to the age group being served. For example, schoolchildren in kindergarten through third grade

should not be using chairs designed for older children. The basic rules of computer use apply to children, as well as adults, and should be part of computer education. The relationship of the keyboard to the hands and the angles of the wrist to the elbow and to the shoulder remain the same but are applied on a much smaller scale.

Work surfaces for computers available to schools vary in design. In selecting tables or desks for computers, the exact use is critical. A setup for word processing will vary drastically from one used for music exploration or computer drafting. It is mainly the use of the computer, combined with the instruction method that will inform the selection of furnishings. Any special needs should be documented with the client, solutions should be developed, and appropriate

▶ Ergonomics has become an important issue in the design of new school furniture.

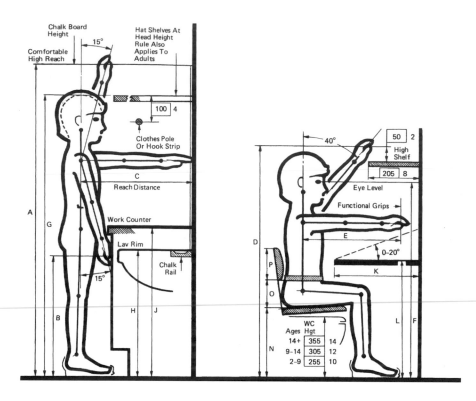

furnishings and equipment specified. Several issues are critical in the selection of furniture for use with computers:

- Keyboard height

- Monitor positioning in relation to the keyboard and the viewer

- Depth of the workstation to accommodate the monitor and work surface

- Size of the user group

- Specific tasks for which the computer will be used

- Selection of comfortable, adjustable, rolling chairs with sturdy backs

- Flexibility of furniture arrangement

- Instructional style of the teachers

The wiring layout for computer technology is critical to locating the hub and head in rooms that will service the entire facility. The type of system to be installed defines the location of these rooms. In general, hub locations should be centrally located in areas of easy access by technicians. Wiring should be run in accessible locations for easy rerouting and servicing. Many schools have utilized a wiring trough or raceway hung from the structure above finished ceilings to condense computer cabling.

With computer labs a standard part of today's schools, there is a move to incorporate stations within all classrooms and curricula. One of the major decisions to be made by a district is the commitment to a set number of stations per classroom. The number of computers spread throughout the campus will affect the overall network and system designs.

The policy adopted by the school system as to technology on its campuses will be the architect's guide in determining the best means of addressing technology in the interiors.

SECURITY

The safety of children within the traditional haven of the schoolyard has come into question in recent years, so administration, faculty, and parents have become more focused on security.

Security measures installed on the interior of a school must be a planned part of every building, but security truly begins at the perimeter of the school site. The site should be laid out to ensure lines of sight across main parking and play areas. Bright lighting and video camera recordings allow observation of the site, and directional signage and short direct access roads and sidewalks point the visitor to the main entry. A single point of entry for visitors allows visual control by limiting unobserved access to any other areas of the building. Some schools have installed metal detection systems and professional security staff at the entries. Part-time or full-time security personnel have become standard for many campuses, and office space should be provided for them. This area can be located within the administration suite, or perhaps in a more remote area of the campus in a larger facility to increase coverage of the areas more distant from the main entrance.

An addition to the possible threat from strangers, security concerns often arise within a building because of the actions of students. Student access to weapons, although illegal, and their ability to use them in acting out their disturbances has made the high school experience one of

fear for many young people. In the 1997–98 school year, 40 school-related deaths occurred nationwide, most at the hand of student peers ("News: School Shooting," *Education Weekly*, April 28, 1999).

Measures used to control such threats include the following:

• Video surveillance

• Metal detectors

• Search of person

• Search of property

Enacting these measures may limit the freedom or personal privacy of students. Many school systems choose a balance between such drastic, visible measures and more passive controls. The following is a list of passive measures to consider in the early phases of the design process:

• Ensure clear sight lines throughout the campus.

• Position administration adjacent to the front entrance.

• Position areas frequented by staff throughout the building.

• Provide reasons for staff to be seen in the corridors.

• Eliminate secluded areas.

• Provide side corridors with plenty of areas for student flow.

• Provide a system of communication between administration and all other areas.

• Design open, visible, bright areas.

In addition to those in the preceding list, there are more intrusive measures:

• Addition of security staff

• Closed-circuit television surveillance

• Metal detection

▶ Security features can be built in without being intrusive, as is the case when the grills recessed in the ceilings of this school are open. Middle school prototype, Broward County, Florida. STH Architectural Group.

- Alarm systems
- Interior physical barriers such as gates and bars
- Theft-detection systems
- Keypad or coded-locking access system

A balance of the various approaches should be reached that fits the school system. The client should be comfortable with the level of security for the educational programs, as well as the protection of persons and property.

CODES

The regulatory agencies and the codes they enforce are intended to "protect human health, safety, and welfare" and help provide safe environments for all. The most consistent standard nationally is the Americans with Disabilities Act (ADA) of 1990, as discussed in chapter 5. Consistent with the passing of this legislation, there has been a movement toward universal design. Universal design provides equal access to all spaces regardless of an individual's abilities. For example, a designer would not design a set of stairs with a ramp off to the side when the ramp could be centrally located and serve all people. Schools must integrate disabled students into the mainstream student population. Several school systems still function under particular requirements for dedicated special education classrooms or suites that segregate various groups, even though research has shown that many disabled students learn best when they are among age-appropriate nondisabled peers (Rydeen 1999).

Integration is a question of educational program; however, several items should be considered in providing access without barriers. The regulations set forth by the ADA must be met as part of the design.

Following is a brief list of measures that may be incorporated:

- Accessible parking areas adjacent to the entry
- Automatic entry doors with accessible vestibule areas
- Centralized vertical circulation
- Graphics with information given in large print and braille
- Wider classroom wing corridors to accommodate various user groups
- Adjustable furnishings and work surfaces to accommodate wheelchairs

Design decisions influence accessibility. An open classroom arrangement allows flexibility and keeps students with disabilities from appearing different from others. Furnishings that adjust for wheelchair and regular use are recommended. The traditional classroom of 750 to 900 sq ft may not be adequate to provide accessible space for the instruction of disabled students. All marker boards and bulletin boards should be located within the reach of all students. Lighting for various activities, including those of children on the floor, in entry areas, and other spaces, should be carefully considered. Subdued lighting should be provided for areas where the students may be situated on the floor. Barriers to universal design in schools include the following:

- Education specifications typically establish minimum space sizes too small to adequately support the participation of disabled students.
- Many existing sites are not large enough to accommodate the requirements.

◀ *Barrier-free design often involves incorporating ramps into a school's circulation. Carrie Ricker Middle School, Litchfield, Maine. Harriman Associates.*

▸ Although designing to accommodate people with various physical disabilities is important, the dimensions for chair-bound students and staff are often the most determinant factors in ADA compliance.

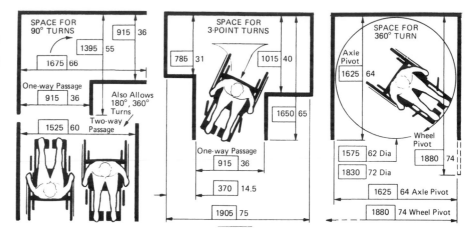

Code requirements have a serious impact on the design of interiors. They mandate highly fire-resistant construction and allow only materials that support minimal flame spread. Although the codes in effect from state to state may vary slightly, the safety levels required in all school construction are strict. A thorough code review should be undertaken, beginning in the schematic design phase, with reviews at every interval of the design that follows. In design development and through creation of the construction documents, the interior finishes, materials, and furnishings should be reviewed periodically as the design progresses. Code requirements affecting interiors address the following:

- Means of egress, path of travel, and size requirements.
- Natural lighting
- Areas of refuge
- Area allowances within a single fire zone
- Area increases to existing buildings
- Fire-wall separations and their construction
- Fire-rated construction
- Flame spread regulations

The design will have to include fire extinguishers at regular intervals and may have to incorporate a sprinkler system. The construction of fire walls, separations and enclosures for vertical circulation will affect material selections as the design develops. Some materials that have particularly high fire-resistant traits are concrete and brick masonry, rated gypsum wallboard, and concrete.

CHAPTER 15
WAYFINDING

Wayfinding refers to the way people orient themselves in a given environment and eventually find their destination. The ability to orient oneself is based on many pieces of information—visual clues, memories, knowledge of a place—and the ability to reason. Environmental psychology terms the ability to acquire, code, store, recall, and decode information about the physical environment "cognitive mapping." Cognitive maps are psychological impressions or representations of individuals' ability to understand space and the organizing elements by which they orient themselves. "Most of the research on questions of orientation has focused on the city level, but the findings have been generalized to buildings" (Lang 1987). Successful wayfinding is the ability to naturally orient oneself in the environment and to easily locate a destination without experiencing stress.

The work of Kevin Lynch, presented in *The Image of the City* (1960), was based on studies that found three analysis components of environmental imaging:

- *Identity* or objects in background

- *Structure* or objects in relationship to each other

- *Meaning* or personal, societal, or figurative belief

Lynch focused on the identity and structure of spaces to discern what makes cities imageable or known. He notes:

[Imageability is]... that quality of a physical object which gives it a high probability of evoking a strong image in any given observer. It is that shape, color or arrangement which facilitates the making of a vividly identified, powerfully structured, highly useful mental image of the environment. It might also be called legibility.

A highly imageable space has components that relate in a well-structured manner. The way a space is mapped for an individual varies, depending on the person. There are certain images and visual clues that are perceived similarly by groups of people

▼ Landmark elements such as chimneys, cupolas, and towers are often used to establish a school's image. Troy High School, Troy, Michigan. Perkins & Will Architects.

Clear paths—often using natural light—should form the major circulation system. Left: Perry Community Education Village, Perry, Ohio. Perkins & Will Architects (photograph by Hedrich/Blessing). Right: Trent Elementary School, Spokane, Washington. ASLC Architects.

who share similar backgrounds, activities, or routines, and recurrent features in their environment. For example, a group of schoolchildren may be of a similar age, share the learning and play activities of a school, and be aware of the physical features of the school building. The image and understanding of any environment is enriched by continual use. Lynch's research resulted in the identification of five categories of elements that people use to map an environment:

- Paths = channels of movement
- Edges = boundaries that break or contain or run parallel to the forms
- Districts = areas of recognizable identity

- Nodes = places of intense activity
- Landmarks = points of reference that are visually distinguishable

Cognitive maps usually combine several of the elements listed. These elements are not formed simply in floor or site plan, but the three-dimensional characteristics of a space, the material choices, the colors, and the lighting can all impact the formation of edges, districts, or nodes.

The five categories can relate directly to the layout of a school campus. The paths or circulation corridors should be planned to provide clear, direct access to all major areas or districts within the school. Performing-arts wings and central administration suites are examples of

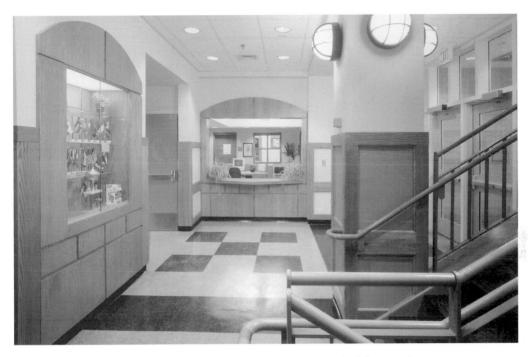

▲ At key intersections and centers of activity the design should clearly define a node as a visual reference point. Agassiz Elementary School, Cambridge, Massachusetts. HMFH Architects. (Photograph by Wayne Soverns Jr.)

districts. Where the boundaries of the districts meet, an edge may be formed, giving a child a clear sense of having exited one area and entered another. A node may occur at an intersection of activities or along paths where activity is concentrated. Landmarks may be used by the designer to mark entrances or points of interest. For example, the traditional clock tower over a school's main entry serves as a major reference point and object of visual orientation for the students and the community.

In the 1970s, Donald Appleyard (1970) explored the differences in individual's cognitive map forms and, in particular, the distinction between path-oriented and spatial styles of mapping. Almost 70 percent of the research subjects drew maps that were sequential images or series of events. This result indicates that the path is the dominating organizational element for the majority of people. Within a school building, the paths or corridors to and from different activities should be clearly planned and understandable. It may help to link functionally related or sequentially visited spaces with color-coded corridors from the origin points to the destinations.

The process of learning involves an increase in perception of detail as a person develops. The following reference system, proposed by Gary Moore (1976),

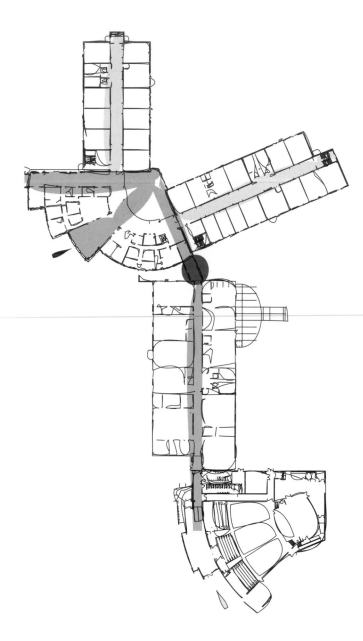

▲ The Northside High School, by Smith Sinnett Associates, illustrates a clear path and node plan.

2. Several different possibilities of fixed reference systems organized around various fixed, concrete elements or places in the environment

3. An abstract or coordinated reference system organized in terms of abstract geometric patterns including in special cases the cardinal directions (north, south, east, and west).

As adults, people tend to rely on maps, diagrams, and more highly abstract information for orientation and finding their way within a new area. As indicated in item 3 of the preceding list, an adult who is visiting an unfamiliar city will use a city map to reach a destination. Adults navigate wide-reaching, complex environments on a daily basis, whereas children's environments are more limited in overall range and tend to be perceived on the basis of reference points. The adolescent child's orientation system (item 2) may be based on a local hang-out, the path of travel between home and school, local landmarks within the community, and similar points of reference.

The designer of learning environments for small children should be aware that children are naturally oriented in relation to their own positions, as in item 1. Children see the world always in relation to themselves. For example, an especially enjoyable piece of equipment at the playground and its relationship to the toilet facility a child uses while at the playground may be the elements by which he or she organizes and understands that environment. A child's cognitive map will likely include detailed aspects of a space with which he or she is directly involved. Details of the play area within the classroom, shown on a child's drawn map, may include the floor material, number of toys, type of light,

relates the phases of development to the progress of perception from early childhood to the adult years:

1. An egocentric reference system; that is, one organized around the child's own position and actions in space

◀ *Clear main circulation paths, such as the one at Hamilton Southeastern High School, Fishers, Indiana, can be dynamic streets where students can interact between classes. Fanning/Howey Associates. (Photograph by Emery Photography.)*

◀ *Design team should remember that for smaller children, landmarks are often near the floor. Lego Child Care Center, Enfield, Connecticut. Jeter, Cook, and Jepson Architects. (Photograph by Wheeler Photographics.)*

▶ *At the detail level, signage is an essential part of wayfinding. The Dalton School, New York, New York. Helpern Architects. (Photograph by Durston Sailor.)*

type of furniture, number of children playing in the space, and so forth. The social and natural elements of an environment are far more important in a child's world than built structures. Therefore, the school design should incorporate detailed elements at the child's level, in areas where children are active, and with which they can identify.

Signage is an important part of directing people through a space. Building signage can include building identification, building layout illustration, directional signs, and place signs. A clearly designed signage package should be part of every school building design. The following are important considerations in developing signs for schools:

• Color coding can be used to identify district areas or paths of travel.

• Signs for small children should incorporate graphics as well as text identification.

- The text and graphics should be appropriately scaled to the age of the user groups.

- A clear, sequential numbering system should be developed.

- Signs should be legible, direct to the point, and visible at reasonable distances.

- Signs should be designed and placed consistently throughout the facility.

- The overuse of signage and cluttered signage, which becomes ineffective, should be avoided.

- Signs should be placed strategically at decision-making areas.

In addition to signage, visual clues can be utilized to help orient the user. Architectural elements like lobbies, stairs, elevators, and areas of special use, such as a gymnasium, can create a framework into which users can place themselves. The following interior treatments typically used for aesthetic effect can also assist the designer in creating a highly understandable environment:

- Change of wall color, type, or texture

- Change in flooring

- Use of lighting to highlight or minimize areas

- Change of ceiling treatments

- Furniture arrangement or type

The extent of wayfinding clues incorporated in the environment should vary from public to private spaces. Public areas require more information to be presented to aid visitors in locating their destinations. As the spaces become more private, fewer clues will be needed because of the occupants' knowledge of the environment. This is mainly true of older student populations and staff;

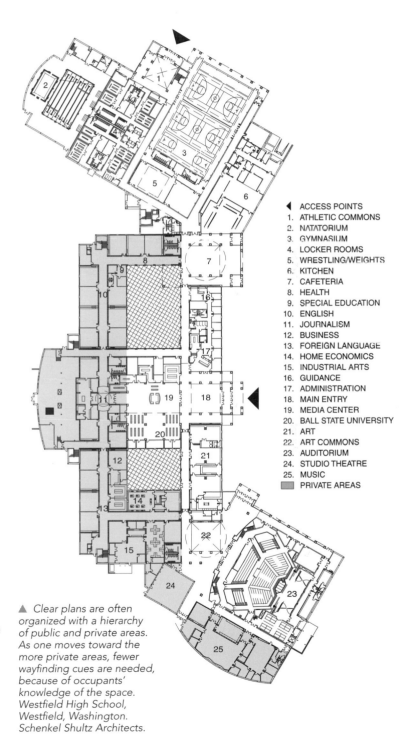

▲ Clear plans are often organized with a hierarchy of public and private areas. As one moves toward the more private areas, fewer wayfinding cues are needed, because of occupants' knowledge of the space. Westfield High School, Westfield, Washington. Schenkel Shultz Architects.

◀ ACCESS POINTS
1. ATHLETIC COMMONS
2. NATATORIUM
3. GYMNASIUM
4. LOCKER ROOMS
5. WRESTLING/WEIGHTS
6. KITCHEN
7. CAFETERIA
8. HEALTH
9. SPECIAL EDUCATION
10. ENGLISH
11. JOURNALISM
12. BUSINESS
13. FOREIGN LANGUAGE
14. HOME ECONOMICS
15. INDUSTRIAL ARTS
16. GUIDANCE
17. ADMINISTRATION
18. MAIN ENTRY
19. MEDIA CENTER
20. BALL STATE UNIVERSITY
21. ART
22. ART COMMONS
23. AUDITORIUM
24. STUDIO THEATRE
25. MUSIC
▨ PRIVATE AREAS

however, the youngest students at the elementary level will benefit from the inclusion of color coding or graphic representations along travel routes to and from the classrooms and most private instructional areas. The functional areas within a school building are listed here in order of most public to most private:

1. Site areas:
   Parking
   Drop-off drives
   Bus loading areas
   Sidewalks
2. Main entry
3. Administration area
4. Main public spaces:
   Gymnasium, accessed from the exterior and the interior
   Auditorium, accessed from the exterior and the interior
   Cafeteria, accessed from the interior
   Media center or library, accessed from the interior
5. Speciality education areas:
   Art
   Music
   Science
6. Dedicated instructional areas:
   Classrooms
   Houses (clustered classrooms around a home base).

CHAPTER 16

RENOVATION

As Lawrence Perkins liked to note, "Buildings do not fall down; they are torn down" (Perkins 1957, p. 62). But because it is neither necessary nor realistic to replace the existing stock of tens of thousands of school buildings, most school building programs will involve renovations, restorations, additions, or adaptive reuse of existing buildings.

INTRODUCTION

A 1995 U.S. General Accounting Office (GAO) report, presented to the United States Congress, estimated that it would require $112 billion to repair or upgrade the nation's school facilities simply to establish good overall conditions. This report found that about two-thirds of America's schools reported being in overall adequate condition; however, the remaining one third housed more than 14 million children.

The renovation needs of most schools districts have grown steadily in recent decades for a number of reasons (see table below):

- Growth in enrollment
- Changes in class size, curricula
- Implementation of technology, including additional electrical capacity
- Energy conversation measures
- Adjusting to new legal requirements and mandates—the Americans with Disabilities Act (ADA), English as a Second Language (ESL), mandatory preschool, women's athletic programs, etc.
- Removal of hazardous materials—asbestos, lead paint, etc.
- Improved security
- Correction of deferred maintenance
- Expiration of the useful life of a school building or its systems

TYPES OF RETROFITS PERFORMED			
	Elementary (percent)	Middle (percent)	High (percent)
ADA compliance	32	60	46
Carpeting	39	45	29
Electric	54	75	55
Flooring	39	65	46
Heating, ventilation, and air-conditioning (HVAC)	57	80	68
Indoor air quality	25	45	29
Lighting	57	60	55
Painting/interior trim	48	70	57
Plumbing	38	50	43
Roofing	41	30	38
Security/life safety	30	25	27
Technology infrastructure	48	40	45
Windows/doors	39	65	41

Source: Agron 1999.

EDUCATION CONSTRUCTION EXPENDITURES, 1989–1998	
Year	Expenditures (billions)
1989	$ 9.277
1990	9.665
1991	10.699
1992	10.731
1993	10.778
1994	10.687
1995	10.417
1996	10.964
1997	12.394
1998	17.095

Source: Agron 1999.

- Converting underutilized areas to effective program use

- Reducing inequalities between schools in the same district

- Implementation of air-conditioning to permit more community and year-round use

The poor conditions described by Kozol (and) many others are not limited to poor inner-city neighborhoods of the country, nor are they limited to urban schools. These conditions also exist in middle-class and wealthy suburbs. It was estimated that almost 60 percent of school districts reported at least one school building needing major repair or replacements of major building features.

Estimates show that school construction and renovation projects steadily increased over the last decade. (see table above). In 1998 approximately one-half of all construction dollars were spent for new school construction, and the remaining half were split equally between additions and renovations to existing schools.

TO BUILD NEW OR TO RENOVATE?

Many school buildings have already had numerous additions, and there comes a point at which a site will not allow for any more building. The age of the original building and its additions is one of the deciding factors as to which direction the school district should take. In many cases, when additions were designed, the electric and mechanical systems, fire alarm systems, plumbing, and structural systems of the new construction were not made compatible with the original existing systems, either because of the age of existing systems or because it was less expensive to provide different systems for the addition. Adding onto existing systems can be quite expensive; moreover, many manufacturers no longer make parts and pieces for replacement in older systems, and it is thus impossible to upgrade them.

Is it better to renovate an existing building or to build a new one? Note the figures given in the following tables. However, this question is not simply answered by computing the cost of renovations, the expected building life, and the expected future renovation needs versus the cost of a new building. Many factors must be considered. The initial approach should include a thorough inspection of existing building systems and components to compile lists of

PROJECTED CONSTRUCTION, 1999–2001	
Type	Cost
New	$21,562,379
Additions	12,638,033
Modernizations	12,238,469

Source: Agron 1999.

COST BREAKDOWN FOR NEW SCHOOLS

	Percentage of Total Costs		
	Elementary	Middle	High
Site purchase	3.4	2.9	5.9
Site development	5.9	6.4	6.2
Construction	75.4	75.8	75.3
Furnishings/equipment	6.5	8.2	5.5
Fees	8.8	6.7	7.1

Source. Agron 1999.

TYPES OF TECHNOLOGY RETROFIT

	Percentage of Total		
	Elementary	Middle	High
Category 5	59	75	72
Fiber-optic	52	38	68
Twisted pair	7	38	16
Other	11	1	4

Source: Agron 1999.

strengths and weaknesses in regard to adaptability for immediate use and for anticipated future use:

- *General building appearance.* Is the building attractive and appealing, or is a lot of work needed to make it acceptable?

- *Building site location.* Is the building located in an area where the school district must accommodate increased enrollments, or will added capacity distort neighborhood school boundaries?

- *Building age and construction characteristics of the era when it was built.* Is the building in disrepair because of design and construction flaws, expiration of the normal life of existing systems, or lack of maintenance?

- *Building structural systems and adaptability to new functions and building requirements.* Does the structure permit adaptation, or will it seriously complicate or compromise renovation?

◀ *Scarsdale High School, Scarsdale, New York, created a safe student drop-off and pickup area as part of a general upgrade of the school site. Peter Gisolfi Associates, architects and landscape architects. (Photograph by Norman McGrath.)*

RENOVATION

▶ *Some districts have made efforts to upgrade a utilitarian exterior with a modest set of exterior changes, as at the Trent Elementary School, Spokane, Washington. ALSC Architects.* ▼

- *Accessibility to disabled persons.* Is the building easily adapted to accommodate ramps, elevators, accessible bathrooms, etc., or will it be hard to adapt?

- *Life safety code deficiencies.* Are the existing deficiencies easily remedied, or will large amounts of money have to be spent to bring the building up to today's codes (e.g., exiting stairs, corridors, fire alarm systems, etc.)

- *Energy usage.* What is the general energy performance condition of building components (e.g., does it have single-pane windows, uninsulated walls, uninsulated roof construction, etc.)?

- *Capacity of existing electrical systems.* Can the electrical systems be upgraded to accommodate increased demand resulting from computer usage, increased classroom needs for electricity, more air-conditioning, new codes and regulations, etc.?

- *Capacity of existing HVAC equipment.* What is the expected life of the existing equipment, and can it be upgraded to accommodate demand resulting from computer usage, new codes and regulations, increased use of school facilities not limited to the academic year, etc.?

- *Adaptability of existing conditions to accommodate security measures required today.* Is the existing facility configured, or can it be reconfigured, in such a way as to facilitate security measures to protect students, faculty, staff, and the building itself?

• *Hazardous materials required to be removed from facility.* Does the facility contain unencapsulated asbestos that would have to be removed in to a renovation project?

The accumulated weight of the answers to these questions can—at times—make new construction more attractive than renovation.

There are, of course, those building assets that must be taken into consideration that do not necessarily appear in a monetary assessment: unusual spaces with high ceilings, unique plaster work and woodworking, tall windows, durable terrazzo flooring, hardwood flooring, brick and stone detailing, and the like. These features would most likely not be affordable in new construction considered by school districts today.

The age of a building is not the only consideration for replacement. School buildings constructed in the early 1900s were built to have a life span of 50 to 100 years. They generally have high ceilings,

wide corridors, and large gymnasiums and auditoriums. These features may enable new computer cabling and HVAC ductwork to be more easily accommodated in older buildings than in schools designed at the middle of the century. Many schools built during the 1950s and 1960s were constructed with "modern" materials: single-story steel structures, metal-framed single-pane windows, flat built-up roofs, and brick veneers with concrete masonry unit interior walls. During this time energy conservation was not a priority; therefore, many buildings were not well insulated and contained a great amount of uninsulated glass.

Schools built during the 1970s typically incorporated systems with life spans of only 20 to 30 years. Many of these schools, built quickly and cheaply, continue to cause maintenance problems for school districts. During the oil embargo of the 1970s, energy consumption and alternative energy sources became a focus of the nation.

◄ *The Scarsdale, New York, school system initially used unattractive brown replacement windows in the older Georgian and Collegiate Gothic style schools and, because of community reaction, replaced them several years later with more architecturally appropriate units with superior energy conservation and operating characteristics. Peter Gisolfi Associates. (Photograph by Norman McGrath.)*

COST OF RENOVATION VERSUS NEW CONSTRUCTION			
	Elementary	Middle	High
Costs for Retrofits			
Average size (sq ft)	49,000	46,761	23,000
Cost/sq ft	$22	$13	$33
Cost/student	$1,076	$1,281	$1,208
Total cost	$736,000	$710,000	$762,500
Costs for New Construction			
Cost/sq ft	$114.29	$118.81	$123.08
Cost/student	$13,322	$16,325	$18,750
Sq ft/student	105	143	167
Median no. pupils	600	788	950
Median size (sq ft)	71,000	113,750	160,000
No. classrooms	30	40	57
Total cost	$7,645,303	$12,690,637	$20,734,816

Source: Agron 1999.

Many school districts began replacing windows with less glazing and more insulated panels. A more radical approach by some school districts was to eliminate windows and skylights throughout each school building. At that time, this seemed like a logical response to the energy crisis. But, as we look back, we realize the full impact: decreased light transmission into interior spaces, as well as exteriors, making schools appear to be grim internalized "jails." Students' concentration, performance, and attendance all are believed to increase when they have access to sunlight.

Significant advances in window and skylight design have prompted many schools in recent years to include window replacement in their major construction projects to return their school buildings to the original aesthetics while gaining better insulating values. Many of the windows being removed today were installed in the past 25 years.

During the 1950s and 1960s student enrollment peaked. The 1970s marked the beginning of a 13-year decline in public school enrollment from a high of 46 million in 1971 to 39.2 million in 1984. A steady increase began at about 1985 as the baby-boomers of the 1950s and 1960s sent their children off to school. The U.S. Department of Education estimated that 46.8 million students walked through the doors of public schools in the fall of 1998. Projections indicate that by the year 2006 public school attendance will reach 48.4 million, an all-time high.

In response to these projections, school districts are looking for unused or underutilized spaces in existing facilities to alleviate the overcrowding that already exists. One school system found space for special education classrooms by completely gutting and renovating unused elementary school boys' and girls' locker rooms and shower facilities. This saved the district the time and money that would have been spent in building an addition to the school. Another school district was considering the necessity to build a larger gymnasium and locker room facilities at its high school to accommodate increased enrollments. The design team proposed to renovate the existing gymnasium and locker rooms to create a much-needed auditorium and music classroom/practice room suite.

Older buildings that have gymnasiums or auditoriums with high ceilings, but are too small to accommodate the school population, have the potential to be converted to other uses through the insertion of second level within the existing building volume. The second district may thus save the cost of building exterior walls and a new roofing system.

However, this approach must be analyzed carefully. Inserting a new structure and new mechanical and electrical systems may be far more costly than building new.

Often, additions are the only solution, but in some cases—particularly in older school buildings—there are underutilized or unused spaces that can be converted to academic use. One school system that was studied found spaces for several programs in the existing elementary schools by reclaiming basement areas that could—with some regrading—be opened to the outdoors.

One of the goals of any renovation or adaptive reuse should be to minimize the serious results of deferred maintenance and any physical inequalities between the older and the newer buildings in a school system. Unfortunately, this goal is missed in too many school systems.

The example given in the sidebar below is not an isolated or unusual situation in many school systems, nor does it describe a problem found only in older, urban areas. Poor school facilities are a major problem across the country, and it presents one of the greatest design and construction challenges.

If maintained properly, many of the systems in a school building can be made to last for decades. If not maintained, many of the systems will deteriorate quickly to a point that the building is no longer a safe or appropriate environment for children. Jonathan Kozol writes in *Savage Inequalities* that even though the deterioration is well known and widely documented, many districts continue to defer the necessary funding because there are demands of higher priority on limited resources. "A year later, when I visit Morris High, most of these conditions are unchanged. Water still cascades down the stairs [when it rains]. Plaster is still falling from the walls. Female students tell me that they shower after school to wash the plaster from their hair.... A plaque in the principal's office tells a visitor that this is the oldest high school in the Bronx" (Kozol 1991, pp. 99–100).

In order to find Public School 261 in District 10, a visitor is told to look for a mortician's office...The school is next door, in a former roller-skating rink. No sign identifies the building as a school...The school's "capacity" is 900 but there are 1,300 children here...Two first grade classes share a single room without a window, divided only by a blackboard. Four kindergartens and a sixth grade class of Spanish-speaking children have been packed into a single room in which, again, there is no window. A second grade bilingual class of 37 children has its own room, but again there is no window...I ask... "Do the children ever comment on the building?" "They don't say," [the teacher], answers, "but they know...All these children see TV...they know what suburban schools are like. Then they look around them at their school... They understand." (Kozol 1991, pp. 83–88)

Removal of Hazardous Materials

The design team must know how to deal with the presence of hazardous materials. Not long ago the primary issue was asbestos, and a large part of many renovation budgets was devoted to removing all asbestos—even asbestos floor tile—when lower-cost options might have been appropriate. Asbestos can be found in many materials, including floor tile and mastics (typically found in 9 in. x 9 in. floor tile, but very possible to find in 12 in. x 12 in. floor tile produced during the same era), transite building panels (used for fire separations in some cases as well as for exterior building cladding), piping insulation (typically found, but not limited to, plumbing piping and boiler breeching), and plaster walls and ceilings.

More recently, analyses of sites for the possibility of contamination by leaking underground oil tanks, lead paint, polychlorinated biphenyls (PCBs), and other hazards have become routine parts of the renovation process. If existing fuel storage tanks are not up to code, they should have been removed or closed in place by December 23, 1998, as mandated by the Environmental Protection Agency (EPA).

The presence of hazardous materials can greatly increase the cost of a reconstruction project and must be included in the designer's analysis and findings. However, if an existing building containing hazardous materials is demolished to make way for a new building, the hazardous materials will

▲ At the Hastings, New York, Middle/High School, a number of spaces were recaptured, including this cafeteria space. Peter Gisolfi Associates. (Photograph by Norman McGrath.) ▶

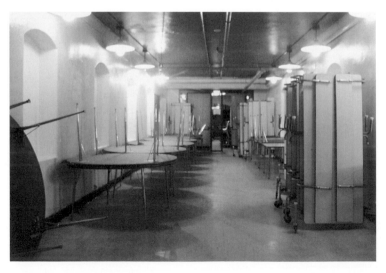

◀ *At the Scarsdale High School, Scarsdale, New York, all of the older schools were renovated to remove unattractive renovations and restore the original design character. Peter Gisolfi Associates. (Photographs by Norman McGrath.)*

have to be removed under the guidelines applicable to any other hazardous materials removal project.

Technology Upgrades

Rapid changes in technology and how schools use this technology have also put a heavy burden on school districts to provide their children with the best the world has to offer. Many schools in the United States were built before the current technological boom and are not easily adaptable to support the necessary equipment required for today's computers (computer wiring, computer cabinets, Internet exchangers) electrical loads, heating and ventilation requirements, and so on. (See chapter 10 for a more extensive discussion.)

ADA

See chapter 5 for a discussion of requirement of the Americans with Disabilities Act (ADA).

Other Issues in Renovation

The design team working on an existing facility faces special challenges. Diagnostic skills are needed to identify hidden conditions in determining whether repair or replacement is required. Analyses of the remaining useful life of such basic systems as the roof, piping for water and heating, boilers, and windows are a common design team task. Special techniques have been developed for many of these analyses, but others rely on such basic approaches as the cutting of sample pipe sections to measure the extent of corrosion. Window-by-window surveys are often required to identify rot, broken counterweights, and cracked panes.

The design team must also have knowledge of the building systems, materials, and techniques commonly found in older schools—plaster and clay tile walls, slate roofing, terrazzo floors, typical asbestos-containing materials, old electrical and HVAC systems, and large

▲ At the Hastings, New York, Middle/High School a sensitive renovation recreated an attractive lobby Peter Gisolfi Associates. (Photographs by Norman McGrath.)

wood windows. Many of these are no longer commonly used in new designs, but they often raise important issues in additions and renovations. Thanks to the preservation movement, there are now reference materials available on most historic building materials and systems.

Knowledge of historic preservation has become a major consideration for the designer. Maintaining the unique character of their building or buildings, which are often the architectural centerpieces of their neighborhoods, is important to many communities and schools.

Design teams have also had to learn how to help sell unattractive bond issues. A difficult obstacle for a school district to overcome is how to explain to the public the millions to be spent to repair or replace roof systems or HVAC systems, remediate hazardous materials such as asbestos, upgrade old and deteriorating piping, or upgrade electrical systems to support increased demands. These are the areas of the school system that the public rarely observes and of which it has little knowledge. Renovations to existing classrooms, libraries, and toilet facilities; building additions; and new schools are things that the public can see, which helps them to understand where their money is being spent.

Design and construction teams have had to learn how to schedule renovations around breaks in the school year. The careful management of key milestones (drawing completion, bidding, approvals, construction start, etc.) is a critical skill. Most projects—or at least, their disruptive phases—must be completed before school begins again.

CHAPTER 17
INTERNATIONAL DESIGN OPPORTUNITIES

In the elementary school in the mountain community of Pachali, Guatemala, where I was helping teach in 1965, the major issue for the facility was whether the community could afford to bring an electric line to the school to power a lightbulb. A lightbulb would make it possible to have evening classes for the children and adults whose work schedules made daytime classes infeasible. In large parts of the world, the problems of educational facilities are just this basic.

As a result, school design in other countries has not traditionally been a major involvement for North American design professionals. There is the occasional "American school" on a foreign military base or for a large expatriate community in some countries, but the architects of most developed countries are able to meet the design needs of programs equivalent to K-12 programs in their own countries.

At times, North American design professionals are advisers for very specialized schools or for large-scale school building programs financed internationally or by a particularly progressive government. Overall, however, international design assignments are few and far between.

Where there is such an assignment, the major issues tend to be the following:

- The school design should be adapted to make maximum use of local construction traditions, site features, building materials, and design concepts.

- Marketing and servicing overseas projects is expensive, and schools are often too small to justify the time, expense, and risk. Most experienced international design professionals receive up-front payments before they start on an international assignment.

- Documentation standards are often very different. In some countries, projects are implemented by large design/build organizations after the architect completes the equivalent of design development. In other countries, the design team is expected to do more than is common in North America, including creation of the equivalent of shop drawings.

- It is often advisable to work with a local design team to deal with the problems of language, local codes, documentation standards, and so forth. Every country is different in this regard.

- Even with a local associate, any good design professional will have to provide staff in the field to ensure continuity of the design concepts during implementation.

For all these reasons, school design in other countries is probably not a major issue for North American design professionals at this time.

CHAPTER 18
OPERATION AND MAINTENANCE

INTRODUCTION

A well-designed school will withstand the impacts and abuse to be expected from its students. The building should be easy to operate and maintain by its caretakers and ultimately preserve the financial investment made by the community that authorized its construction. Operations and maintenance issues are different for new construction and existing buildings. This chapter considers both.

NEW SCHOOL CONSTRUCTION

A new school assignment is an ideal opportunity for an owner and a design team to develop a building that is operations and maintenance friendly. The design of the building should be tailored to the requirements of its educational program, consider the ability of its caretaker, and be easy to operate and maintain. Common sense is usually the best tool for making design decisions that create a school that is easy to operate and maintain. Locating primary mechanical equipment and controls for ease of access, positioning janitor's closets and equipment near the locations where they will be used, and sensitivity to the ability of the caretaker of the building—all contribute to the ease of operation and maintenance of the school. The architect should consider the following factors related to operations and maintenance:

- The design team's responsibility to advise the community on the best life-cycle strategy for any school construction program
- Utilities available to the site
- Sophistication of the building's caretakers
- Durability of building products and equipment
- Special considerations for specific program areas

One of the challenges of new school design for the design team is to balance the client's desire to keep first (construction) costs low against the desired longevity and durability of the resultant building. The architect's responsibility is to offer the community a building that will stand up to the punishment unique to school building. Throughout the twentieth century, a large percentage of schools used masonry materials for the exterior, as well as masonry, glazed tile, hardwood trim, plaster, and other durable materials for major interior corridors and common areas. The use of robust materials continues to offer the soundest approach for school design today.

The availability of and access to utilities at the site is an important factor in new school design. Early in the design process the architect must verify the potential infrastructure for heating fuel, electrical service, and water source that will serve the facility. The nature of the utilities that will enter the building and their access paths have a direct impact on the location and sizes of primary and secondary mechanical rooms in the building. By identifying potential fuel sources one can begin to narrow the choices of possible mechanical systems.

It is critical for the architect to understand the client's ability to maintain the building and operate the proposed systems. The skills of a school's staff vary greatly from district to district. The size of the caretaking staff can range from a single custodian to a team of custodial and facility management people. The size of the staff is, of course, no indicator of its sophistication. For example, the most technically advanced mechanical building management system (BMS) is worthless if the school's personnel are not qualified to operate and maintain the system.

Likewise, extravagant and/or delicate landscaping is not appropriate if the caretakers are not accustomed or willing to meet the higher level of maintenance required.

The durability of building products and equipment is directly related to the expenditure of maintenance staff hours and the subsequent life-cycle costs of the building's systems. The architect must specify building products that anticipate vandalism, graffiti, and heavy use. The building design should make supervision as easy as possible for the adults who will work in the building. Such a plan includes simple sight lines and provides adult use areas throughout the building—staff meeting rooms and educational resource areas. Sound location of staff use areas (i.e., closer to the classrooms) can reduce adults' travel time to these spaces and ensure that an adult is always present in every area of the school. This arrangement can increase adult supervision and reduce vandalism and abuse of the school.

It is common for corridor and classroom partition walls to be built of painted concrete block or glazed masonry units. Because gypsum surfaces are easily scarred, these more durable walls have proven to be easier to maintain. Similarly, terrazzo flooring products have historically provided an attractive and durable floor surface in areas of heavy traffic. Owing to their cost, however, these products have virtually disappeared from new school construction in recent decades. Alternate products such as vinyl composition tile, epoxy tile, and the much more durable media carpet fibers, where appropriate, are typically used today.

As indicated earlier, a new school will be operations and maintenance friendly if the design team carefully considers its plan and selection of building systems and finishes. The table at right highlights special considerations for specific program areas.

EXISTING SCHOOL BUILDINGS

Renovation of an existing school typically involves the correction of existing maintenance and operations problems. For obvious reasons, school districts generally tend to invest most of their financial resources in teaching staff and educational materials (books, technology, athletic equipment, etc.) The physical condition of the school is typically ignored until a problem occurs. Student overcrowding, a leak in the roof, and continuous shorting-out of the electrical power system are examples of such problems. Operations and maintenance considerations for new buildings, as discussed earlier, should be applied in renovations of existing buildings whenever possible. The architect should consider the following additional factors as they relate to operations and maintenance of an existing school:

- The condition of the mechanical, electrical, and plumbing systems

- Energy conservation through replacement and upgrade of systems

- Sophistication of the building's caretakers

- Typical points of failure

- Identification and mitigation of toxic substances

DESIGN CONSIDERATIONS FOR PROGRAM AREAS

Space	Floor Finish	Electrical Power/ Communications Requirements	Special Mechanical Requirements*	Comments
General Classroom	VCT	Con.+ Comp.+ group Comm.	C	Plan for a minimum of a five-computer cluster in each classroom; special storage is required.
Computer Center	VCT/Carpet (special type for computer room)	Con.+ Comp.+ Comm.	Cooling for special equipment load	Floor power/communications boxes and linear wall distribution systems maximize computer location options; floor outlets in VCT can obstruct polishing/waxing equipment.
Cafeteria	VCT	Con.	Ventilation	Ease of floor cleaning/disinfecting critical; adjacency to loading dock needed.
Kitchen	Quarry Tile	Con.+ special equipment	FP/ventilation/Ref.	Direct access to loading dock is critical; ease of cleaning/disinfecting required; kitchen use has high impact on floor/walls/ceiling.
Auditorium/ Performance Space	VCT/carpet	Con.+ special equipment + Comm.	Ventilation/air-conditioning "quiet" system	Special acoustical requirements flat floor increases flexible use; adjacency to main entrance and proximity to loading dock are suggested.
Science Laboratories	VCT	Con.+ special equipment + Comm.+ Comp.	FP/special ventilation/ natural gas	Instructional lab vs. combination instructional space and lab area, special storage required.
Art Classroom	VCT	Con.+ special equipment+ Comm.+ Comp.	Ventilation	Special FP and Mech. Requirements for kiln room, special storage requirements; proximity to loading dock is suggested.
Music Classroom	Wood / VCT	Con.+ special equipment+ Comm.+ Comp.	"Quiet" system	Special acoustical requirements, furniture systems risers (for choral/orchestral practice) increase space flexibility; special storage requirements; close proximity to auditorium is suggested.
Gymnasium	Wood (special systems)	Con.+ special equipment+ Comm.+ Comp.	Ventilation	Special storage requirements.
Locker Room	Ceramic tile (floor and walls)	Con.	Ventilation	Ease of cleaning/disinfecting critical; simple sight lines—avoid plan layouts with hidden corners; special storage requirements.
Multipurpose Meeting Room	Carpet/VCT	Con.+ special equipment+ Comm.+ Comp.	"Quiet" system	Consider furniture type and impact on floor finish; acoustical equipment; furniture storage adjacency to main entrance, proximity to loading dock is suggested.

Legend:
Con.   Convenience outlets
Comm.   Communications (network tie-in)
Comp.   Computer station(s)

FP   Fire-protection system
Mech.   Mechanical system
Ref.   Refrigeration/freezer
VCT   Vinyl composition tile

Source: Perkins Eastman Architects.

EXPECTED LIFE OF MAJOR SYSTEMS		
System	Expected Life Recommended If Properly Maintained	Recommended Inspection/Maintenance Cycle
EXTERIOR ENVELOPE		
Foundation		
Block	Indefinite	3 years
Concrete	Indefinite	5 years
Structure		
Steel	Indefinite	7 years
Concrete	Indefinite	5 years
Masonry Bearing Wall	Indefinite	5 years
Wood	Indefinite	3 years
Exterior Wall		
Masonry	Indefinite	3 years
Stucco	40 years	2 years
Painted Wood	30 years	Annually
EIFS	20 years	Annually
Brick Joints	10 years	3 years
Windows		
Aluminum/Steel Windows— Long-Life Finish	40 years 5-year warranty	Annually, including weather stops, glass, and hardware lubricator
Aluminum/Steel Windows— (Field) Painted Finish	40 years 2 to 5-year warranty	Annually, including weather stops, glass, and hardware lubricator
Wood Windows	40 years	Annually, including weather stops, glass, and hardware lubricator
Brick/Window joints	10 years	Annually
Roof		
Slate Shingles	Indefinite	Annually
Copper Roofing	50 years	Annually
Fiberglass Shingle	25–40 years	Annually
Asphalt or Wood Shingle	20–25 years	Annually
Built-up	20+ years*	Twice yearly—spring and fall, always after a major storm
Single-Ply	20+ years**	Twice yearly—spring and fall, always after a major storm
Spray-Foam System	15–20 years	Annually (typically for repair/restoration)
BUILDING SYSTEMS		
Mechanical		
Boilers	25–40 years	Annually
Piping	20–50 years	Annually (depends on material)
Duct Work	20–50 years	Annually
Electrical	15–20 years	Annually (limited by technical upgrades)
Plumbing	20–50 years	Annually
Fire Protection	15–30 years	Annually

*10-, 15-, or 20-year warranty with 2-year installers' warranty. **10- or 15-year warranty with 2-year installers' warranty.

Source: Perkins Eastman Architects.

The architect's design team must survey the school's mechanical, electrical, plumbing, and fire-protection systems. Part of the conditions assessment phase must include estimates of the remaining life of existing equipment. This phase should also include detailed interviews of the caretaker(s), teaching staff (user group), and administration of the school. These interviews can identify problems that are unique to the particular school building and that recur throughout the school year.

A study of the existing mechanical and electrical systems and the building envelope (windows and typical wall/roof section) can suggest upgrades of the systems through more efficient energy use. The design team will have to compare first costs with savings in utility costs through the payback period. Another area of study includes the building's heating system. Again, the design professional will be asked to determine the cost of a system upgrade in contrast to future utility cost savings (see chapter 6 for additional discussion).

Typical points of failure in the exterior envelope include brick joints, brick/window joints, and roofing materials. These three areas are among the most neglected in school buildings throughout the country. The table at left touches on these and other issues and outlines good practice methods associated with each.

An addition or major renovation to an existing school offers the architect an opportunity to understand the caretakers' ability to maintain and operate the building, to become acquainted with the strengths and weaknesses of both the caretakers' abilities and the existing building systems. Such a study often indicates that the best course of action is to extend the existing building systems to the new construction. Fuel availability, system performance, and level of maintenance are historic facts; an addition can be an opportunity to correct existing undesirable conditions. There are no rules of thumb in this area; careful consideration of each facility and its caretaker group is the key.

Identification and mitigation of toxic substances is critical to both the project budget and the schedule. It is essential that a qualified environmental engineer completes thorough tests of an existing school as early as possible in the design process. Only the written reporting of a qualified engineer should be relied upon for determinations in this area. If left undetected until late in the design or construction process, the presence of asbestos or other toxic substances can undermine the construction budget and cause serious delays in the schedule. It can also undermine the architect's credibility with the school board and the community.

CHAPTER 19
COST ISSUES

INTRODUCTION

Cost management is one of the most complex tasks facing a school's owner and design team. No single chapter can provide a comprehensive review of this topic, but there are several guidelines that are relevant to the effective cost management of a school building program. Specifically, this chapter includes an outline of the basic steps in a cost-management program, an introduction to the relative costs of typical school building choices, a review of some of the nonquantitative factors that can affect the cost of a project, a discussion of value engineering and life-cycle costing, and a review of the general sources of cost information.

MANAGEMENT

An effective cost-management approach includes setting a realistic budget; developing regular, careful cost estimates; and making adjustments to fit the design to the budget.

As school building programs have become more complex and expensive, there has been increased emphasis on a comprehensive, professional effort to manage costs. In summary, the key components of a cost-management program are the following:

1. Retain a design team, professional cost estimator, or a construction manager with proven cost-estimating and cost-management capabilities. Some schools retain all three, but at the very least the project team must have one member who can objectively and accurately analyze the cost impact of the thousands of program and design choices that will be made.

2. Start the budgeting process during the initial program phase. As stated in chapter 3, one of the most common errors is to start a project with an unrealistic budget. An experienced team should be able to translate a space program and evaluation of building conditions into a realistic budget.

3. Prepare detailed cost estimates at at least four points in the design process:

- The end of schematic design
- The end of design development
- The midpoint of the construction document phase
- The end of the construction document phase

These estimates should be more than one-page calculations based on past experience and square-foot cost data. Most experienced teams try to quantify the building components in increasing detail as the design progresses, apply accurate unit prices to each component, and add in appropriate contingencies for what is not yet designed and the inevitable extras that occur in most construction programs.

The earlier estimates tend to be more useful, as they can be used to adjust the design to bring the building program back within budget. The greater detail of the later estimates, however, also helps to identify potential budget problems, facilitates final design choices, and provides information useful in making decisions to keep the project within budget. The detailed estimates also help in the analysis of construction bids or contractor proposals to identify possible problems such as inadequate builder interest or a misunderstanding of the contract documents.

4. Make cost a factor in evaluating major design decisions. Most sophisticated owners and teams evaluate both the first cost and, as discussed later in this chapter, the life-cycle cost inherent in a design decision.

5. Using value engineering techniques to achieve the proper balance between cost and quality. Value engineering is often misused as a synonym for cost cutting. Instead, it should be used to describe efforts to achieve the same program quality and design goals for the originally determined budget or even less cost.

RELATIVE COSTS

Costs are always a function of local factors (local labor and material costs, contractor availability and interest, building systems required by local climate or site conditions, etc.), as well as regional and national factors. As a result, new schools today can cost less than $100 per square foot in a particular community and more than $200 per square foot in some high-cost urban areas.

In communities of all types, however, the choice of building systems and materials, as well as issues inherent in the site, can have a significant impact on the cost. The following table provides a partial comparison, illustrating the relative costs of a number of common choices. This information should be used with great caution, because costs vary significantly over time and between locations. Moreover, the choices listed are far from comprehensive.

OTHER FACTORS THAT CAN AFFECT COSTS

Exact-quantity takeoffs and careful unit pricing do not always ensure an accurate construction cost estimate. Care in both

areas is essential, but there are many other factors that have significant effects on the final cost of a construction project.

Some of these factors—for example, the accuracy of the contractors' own estimators—defy prediction. Others, however, can be analyzed and, to some extent, quantified. Therefore, qualitative and quantitative analyses of local construction markets are important elements of cost-management programs. The adjustment factors that can be found in the published services such as R.S. Means and *Engineering News–Record* magazine, provide a general guide, but they are inadequate by themselves. Analyses of these factors do not adhere to a standard format, because each project differs from all others. However, the following are among the general areas covered:

1. Local geographical, sociological, and economic factors

2. Contractors' interest in and capabilities for the job

3. Labor availability and cost

4. Availability of materials

5. Other factors relating to the owner and the designer

Local Construction Industry Issues

The first set of factors, including population density, proximity to urban centers, and accessibility via major traffic routes, can readily indicate potential problems. The capabilities of the construction industry in a smaller town can be strained by the requirements of a large project, so the estimator should take note of the work experience and size of local contractors' firms and labor pools.

COST COMPARISON FOR MAJOR BUILDING SYSTEMS				
	Structural System	Architectural System	Plumbing System	HVAC System	Electrical System
Simple Cost	• Unclassified earth excavation, minimal elevation deviations • Stockpiling of excavated material on-site • Balanced cut and fill • Uniform spread footings • Continuous wall footings, nonstepped • Concrete-block or poured-concrete foundation walls • Wood frame or roof truss (if permitted by code) • Block wall and simple joint roof framing	• Simple shaped building with minimal architectural features • Exterior brick or block with stock window shapes, some stonework or precast trim low ratio of windows • Unplastered block or drywall partitions in most areas • Resilient tile floors, VCT predominantly used • Painted exposed ceilings in most areas • Suspended ceilings with 2 x 4 acoust. tile in corridors and offices • Flat roofs with parapets • Simple waterproofing requirements • Vitreous spray or epoxy enamel in lieu of ceramic tile, minimal use of vitreous materials except for floors in wet areas • Simple program requirements • Low ratio of interior work • Hollow metal doors and bucks at normal heights • Simple stair exiting and fire-protection requirements • Minimum provision for future flexibility • Miminum circulation space, double-loaded corridors	• Gravity-type sanitary and storm systems using extra-heavy cast-iron pipe and fittings • Domestic hot and return water systems utilizing submerged tankless coils in boiler • Gas distribution for gas unit heaters, rooftop cooling and heating units, and boilers • Austere fixtures • Economical toilet layouts (i.e., typical in-line facilities) • Fire standpipe system, if required • Insulation for mains, risers, water lines, and horizontal storm drains in finished areas • Fire sprinkler system	• Low-pressure, one-pipe system • Two-pipe circulating hot-water system • Ventilation of interior areas (toilets) • Self-contained, low-pressure heating and air-conditioning systems, all air • Forced-air heat only • Self-contained boiler rooms • Limited insulation of piping and supply duct work	• One main distribution panel (wall mounted) serving simple 120/208V • Feeders: runs feeding one or more panels at a time • Lighting fixtures: fluorescent fixtures mainly in continuous rows; few incandescent fixtures • Branch circuit work, use of one light switch per average room, minimal outlets • Motor work: individually mounted starters furnished by others • Fire-alarm system: master control board with stations and gongs at stairs and exits; noncoded, nonzoned • Sound system: master amplifiers with microphone and page common to all speakers • Inexpensive clocks, not connected to central system • Emergency lighting: wall-mounted battery units with headlamps

Source: Bradford Perkins, Perkins Eastman Architects 1999.

continued

COST COMPARISON FOR MAJOR BUILDING SYSTEMS *(continued)*				
	Structural System	**Architectural System**	**Plumbing System**	**HVAC System**	**Electrical System**

	Structural System	Architectural System	Plumbing System	HVAC System	Electrical System
Average Cost	• Unclassified earth excavation, some variance of grade elevations • Stockpiling of excavated materials on-site • Balanced cut and fill • Spread footings of generally uniform dimensions with some oddities • Continuous wall footings, with stepped requirement • Poured-concrete foundation walls • Concrete slab on grade • Some interior foundation wall requirements • Usually uniform bay size layouts for structural system, including variances for special conditions • Reinforced-concrete frame and arches • Structural steel frame, masonry or spray-on fire protection • Simple-use precast concrete or architectural cast concrete members for structural purposes • Generally more complicated building shape with breaks, corners, and cantilevers requiring an experienced contractor • Masonry bearing wall and plank structure • Simple structural steel frame, metal deck/concrete or plank deck	• More complex shaped building expressing architectural features • Exterior glass brick, architectural concrete, larger ratio of windows, special size windows, moderate use of stonework, cast stone and other special exterior materials • Unplastered block partitions utilizing expressive bonds; use of more expensive interior finishes, especially in public areas • Resilient tile floors, VCT or similar products, predominantly used; some use of carpeting or other more costly finishes • Greater requirement for hung ceilings; simple suspension system and economic use of acoustical tile • Flat roofs with some setbacks on different levels • More complex waterproofing requirements • Greater use of vitreous materials on walls and floors in wet areas • More complex program requirements, modular design • Greater density of interior work • Solid-wood doors and metal bucks; heights may vary according to need and location • Greater fire-protection and exiting requirements	• Includes "simple" category plumbing, plus the following items • Sump and ejector pump systems • Hot-water generator • Domestic water-pressure system • Emergency generator—gas connections • Standard fixtures • Kitchen work • Tempered water for showers	• Includes "simple" category HVAC, plus the following items • Central station heating and air-conditioning (single zone) • Feeders: runs feeding one or more panels at a time • Multizone heating and air-conditioning systems with reheat coils • Fan coil perimeter system, two- or four-pipe • Unit ventilator system, two- or four-pipe • Kitchen and "simple" science room exhaust • Mechanical equipment rooms, including converters, chillers • Acoustic lining • Automatic sprinkler system (fire prevention) • Pneumatic controls, electric-electronic controls • Basic rooftop heating/cooling/ventilation equipment limited ducted distribution	• Service and panels: one main distribution board (freestanding) serving light and power panels; simple 120/208V service • Feeders: runs feeding one or more panels at a time • Lighting fixtures: basic 2 x 4, 1 x 4, or 2 x 2 fluorescent fixtures, mainly in continuous rows; few incandescent fixtures; speciality lighting where necessary, plus some architectual lighting for aesthetic purposes • Branch circuit work, two or more light switches for each major room control-ling different rows of fixtures, use of three-way switching; more generous employ-ment of receptacles—both duplex and special • Motor work: motor control center furnished by electrical contractor • Fire-alarm system: master control board with stations and gongs at stairs and exits, plus zoning and coding of fire signal; use of some heat and smoke detectors • Sound system: master amplifiers with microphone and page common to all speakers • Clock and program system; master-control cabinet plus devices in major rooms and halls • Television system: cable or antenna amplifier and receiving outlets throughout building

COST COMPARISON FOR MAJOR BUILDING SYSTEMS *(continued)*				
	Structural System	Architectural System	Plumbing System	HVAC System	Electrical System
Average Cost (continued)		• Modest provisions for flexibility • More circulation space requirements • Greater need for mechanical equipment space • Modest use of varied materials for interior finishes • Limited use of moveable partitions			• Emergency lighting system: emergency generator and auto transfer switch feeding one emergency panel • Basic wiring for computer lab and some other technology
Above Normal Cost	• Classified earth excavation such as hardpan, clay, boulders, rocks, etc. • Great variations in grade • Dewatering problems • Required bracing, shoring, etc. • Unbalanced cut and fill resulting in need for borrowed or exported material • Foundation complications requiring spread footings of varying sizes and shapes; special foundations, such as piles • Grade beam requirements more often than typical; continuous wall footings and foundation walls • Structural slab not on grade • Interior requirements for foundation walls and footings • Varying bay sizes • Complicated reinforcing concrete-frame and slab; structural steel frame encased in concrete fireproofing • Detailed precast concrete, architectural concrete, or cast stone details	• Complex building shape requiring architectural treatments such as frequent overhangs, setbacks, multilevels, etc. • Exterior walls expressing and accentuating architectural aesthetics, utilizing stonework, complex precast or architectural concrete units, special window shapes and details, high ratio of glasswork, high-quality windows with long-life finishes and Low e glass, greater use of metal alloys for trim and decorative purposes • Plastered interior partitions, greater use of vinyl wall • Greater use of vinyl tile floors and architecturally expressive finishes • Greater use of hung ceilings with Sheetrock or high-quality 2 x 2 acousti-cal tile in most areas • Multilevel roofs, setbacks, pent-houses, promenade decks, etc. • Complex damp- and waterproofing requirements	• Includes "simple" and "average" categories of plumbing, plus the following items • Galvanized steel or cast iron above grade for sanitary and storm systems • Foundation drainage, if required • Preheater for domestic hot water • Water treatment, if required • Gas piping for laboratories • Acid-neutralizing system for labs • Gas systems for labs • Emergency showers and eye-washing facilities • Deionized and distilled water systems for labs • Heavy kitchen work • Fire pump and jockey pump • Insulation of all domestic water piping and all horizontal storm piping • Luxury fixtures	• Can include "simple" and "average" categories of plumbing, plus the following items • Variable air volume system with mixing boxes or terminal reheats • Induction system • Fume hood exhaust • Dust-collection system • Thermal wheel heat exchange • Heat reclamation • High-pressure steam, with PRV stations • Radiant ceilings and floors • Heat pumps • Steam humidification • Snow-removal systems • Water treatment systems • Boiler feed system • CO_2 fire prevention system • Remote power plant installation • Central station, computerized monitoring for automatic temperature controls • Sound attenuation systems • Design requirements for future expansion	• Service panels: 480/177V service into building, one or more freestanding main distribution board 480/120–208V transformers, subdistribution panels, light and power panels • Feeders: multiple sets of feeders between main distribution boards and from main distribution boards to subdistribution panels; single feeder runs from subdistribution panels to light and power panels; possible use of bus duct for main feeders • Lighting fixtures: low-glare and up/down fluorescent fixtrues; some incandescent fixtures and specialty lighting where necessary, plus some architectural lighting for aesthetic purposes; high-intensity lighting for special areas • Branch circuit work: two or more light switches per major room, controlling different rows of fixtures; use of three-way switching; more generous employment of receptacles—both duplex and special • Motor work: motor control centers, plus intricate interlocking and control devices; fan shutdown coupled with fire-alarm system

continued

	Structural System	Architectural System	Plumbing System	HVAC System	Electrical System
COST COMPARISON FOR MAJOR BUILDING SYSTEMS *(continued)*					
Above Normal Cost (continued)	• Generally complicated structure shape requiring unique structural design solution, or considerations requiring high-caliber contractor • Design for future expansion	• Ceramic tile or glazed block used on floors and walls in wet areas • Complex program requirements for multipurpose occupancy • High-density requirements for interior work; single-loaded enclosed corridors • Expensive fire-protection requirements, substantial exiting needs • Large circulation and public areas • Large mechanical equipment space • Expensive vertical and horizontal transportation equipment • Large degree of flexibility inherent in layout and design to accomodate future changes and requirements for mechanical and electrical trades • Use of large moveable partitions		• Design for a high degree of flexibility	• Fire-alarm system coded and supervised fire-alarm system plus complete smoke detection, heat detection and sprinkler alarm systems; fan shutdown facilities coupled to motor control centers • Sound system: master system plus subsystems in other facilities, interconnected for selective paging • Clock and program system: master control cabinet, plus devices in major rooms and halls • Television systems: cable and/or antennas, amplifiers and receiving outlets throughout building, plus program originating and sending facilities; possible television studio • Emergency lighting system: emergency generator, plus complete system of feeders and panels to all areas • Telephone system with features (voice mail, etc.): complete system of feeder, conduits, terminal cabinets, and outlets • Stage lighting: theatrical stage lighting with complete dimming facilities • Intercom telephone system: automatic exchange plus handsets • Lightning protection • Laboratory work: special lab panels with contactors, wiremold raceway with multivoltage receptacles, lab bench wiring, explosion-proof areas • Surveillance and security systems: all exterior and stair doors, plus door to special rooms, wired to central security console; possible closed-circuit television hookup included • LAN and WAN wiring as well as wiring all classrooms for computers and Internet • Design for future expansion • Design characteristics reflecting high degree of flexibility

The character of a town can also have an effect on costs. In some towns outside urban areas, for example, the construction industry can depend heavily on one owner for work. Therefore, local work must be suited to this employer's construction program. In other areas, the presence of organized crime and other circumstances can, unfortunately, determine the number and interest of bidders in some trades.

General market information, such as that described, rarely provides the detail necessary for either design decisions or final cost estimates, but it does indicate where further research is necessary. It is the research on local contractors, labor, material, and owner/architect factors that can and should shape the final plans.

Lack of Bidder Interest Raises Costs

The interest and capabilities of a contractor are often major cost considerations. It is not uncommon for there to be substantial cost overruns, owing largely to lack of interest and competition. In one such case, only two firms were willing to bid on a New York City educational project that would last four years, and neither was willing to take it without premiums that approached 100 percent. In years when there is a great amount of private-sector work, it may take creative bid packaging and bidder solicitation to attract adequate interest.

During a recession "negative escalation" can be experienced on projects in many regions. Bid prices actually stabilize or go down as contractors and labor just try to stay employed. When the economy recovers, however, both contractors and labor are often quick to reestablish their normal markups, overtime requirements, and other costs. It is not uncommon for

costs to jump rapidly, to amounts far greater than can be accounted for by normal increases in labor and material costs, when a local construction market gets busy.

Interest is only one of the two important considerations in selecting a contractor; the other is capability. In small cities and rural areas, local contractors may not be able to build a complex project efficiently. An inexperienced contractor facing a complex project or unusual materials and details usually adds a significant premium to his bid—if he bids at all. What usually happens is that outside contractors have to be encouraged to bid inasmuch as they have to expect problems in working in a new area with a limited labor and subcontractor pool, and large outside contractors add premiums as well.

On a smaller scale, many contractors add a premium for handling new materials or unfamiliar details. For example, architectural concrete, complex brick patterns, the newer curtain walls, radiant heating systems, and many other materials, systems, or details may be beyond the capabilities of the local construction industry.

Checklist of Key Questions

Unfortunately, there is no central source for the information needed to select a contractor. However, by calling Associated General Contractors (AGC) chapters, local contractors, and other industry sources, it is usually possible to obtain partial answers to the following key questions on the subject of contractor interest and capabilities:

• How many contractors in the area work in a given category of construction?

- How many bids does a project of a given size normally receive?
- Is there so much directly competing work in the area that there is a reduction in the number of potential bidders?
- Is the seasonal factor in this area any more pronounced than normal for the construction industry as a whole?
- Are there ways of stimulating contractor interest?
- What is the prevailing contractor attitude toward unusual design or site location?
- Are local contractors familiar with unusual materials or details that may be employed on the project?
- Is there likely to be any reduction in the number of bids or bid premiums resulting from minority hiring or training requirements?
- Are local contractors finding construction loans unusually difficult to obtain?

Labor Shortage May Restrict Design Options

A major factor in contractor interest and capability is, of course, the local labor force. A cost estimator must know the local wage rates and be aware of any shortages in critical trades, the prevailing premiums necessary to obtain local labor or induce migration, the trade jurisdictions, and any other factors that can have cost ramifications.

Shortages can be an important factor. An architect recently designing a project in upstate New York was informed of a shortage of carpenters. This helped him during schematic design as he realized that several design options, such as a

poured-in-place concrete structure, were foreclosed. In other areas, a shortage of masons has made precast and other exterior materials more attractive.

Local work practices are also important. In many areas prefabricated components, such as prehung doors, are disassembled and then reassembled on-site because of local union rules. In other areas, union locals prevent the use of any materials manufactured by nonunion labor.

Strikes are a similar risk and another unknown cost for the contractor to estimate. Therefore, it is important to check on the expiration date of existing contracts, the likelihood of strikes, the size of the increases likely to be negotiated in the next contract, and related factors.

Information on these and other labor-related cost factors can be supplied by local contractors and construction trade associations, minority group representatives, and other related sources. The following questions should be asked:

- Are the jurisdictions of unusual size?
- Are there any jurisdictional disputes that may affect the project?
- Are there significant variations in labor supply owing to seasonal factors?
- Are there extreme shortages in any trades, and if so, will they result in premiums and/or delays in construction schedules?
- What inducements are required to encourage labor to come to the area?
- What is the impact of training programs, and what is the availability of minority workers if the contractors are expected to meet minority hiring targets?
- What are the basic and fringe rates for each trade?

- When do local contracts expire, what increases are scheduled in existing contracts, and what percentages are predicted for the next contract?

- Is local labor cooperative or belligerent, and what is its level of interest in the project?

Materials are usually a lesser problem than either contractors or labor, but on some projects material supply and cost volatility can be critical. Too often designs include materials that are either unavailable locally or unfamiliar to local contractors. In some cases too many projects are competing for the same material. Where any of these situations occurs, it is worth devoting part of the market study effort to this subject. Among the basic questions to ask are the following:

- Are any of the critical materials unusual or difficult to obtain?

- How far is the project site from the nearest major source of the materials incorporated in the design?

- Are there other projects in the area that may compete directly for the same materials?

- Are there complications—shipping limitations, delays, etc.—in supply because if unusual materials, shortages, or lack of capacity?

- Which materials are on national rather than local price scales? Are any local materials unusually expensive or inexpensive?

The last area, and most difficult to research for a full market study, includes owner/designer factors. There are a few good clients who actually attract additional bidders or an unusually large number of bidders for their projects.

Most owner/architect cost factors are negative, however. Some subcontractor associations have told public clients that

their members have added premiums to their bids on the clients projects to account for slow payments, onerous contracts, and/or excessive paperwork.

Some architects, unfortunately, have also been known to cause contractors to add premiums. Their consistently incomplete construction documents, disruptive actions during the construction phase, and unnecessarily complex designs are among the most common reasons. Therefore, an increasing number of construction market studies are including such questions as the following:

- Do the owner's administrative, contract, payment, or inspection procedures cause significant problems for the contractor?

- Does the architect have a reputation for causing problems or providing inadequate construction documents?

- Are there problems that the owner or architect can help mitigate?

If a market study reveals serious problems in any of these areas, it is possible to save more money by concentrating on overcoming adverse market conditions than by refining costly segments of the design. The difference between an efficient and inefficient design may be less than 15 percent, whereas market conditions can add far more than that amount in premiums.

Adverse market conditions can usually be overcome. Split contracts, expedited payment procedures, careful selection of local materials, aggressive bidder solicitation, contractor orientation meetings, and careful timing of bids and other techniques are being used with increasing frequency to solve market problems. The first step, however, is to identify the problems.

VALUE ENGINEERING AND LIFE-CYCLE COST ANALYSIS

As noted earlier, value engineering is often confused with cost cutting. The term was originated, however, to describe a technique used to seek design options that achieve the original design objectives at a lower cost. Some school systems even use a formal process to develop and evaluate value engineering ideas. At the very least, most owners expect to see construction and operating cost comparisons of the major building system alternatives.

In a sophisticated value engineering effort, cost is defined not only as construction cost but also as life-cycle cost. Experienced owners and design professionals know that a building's design has a significant impact on its operating cost and its life-cycle cost. What has been less well understood is how and where to apply this concept in the design process. Unfortunately, the rhetoric of life-cycle cost analysis is more advanced than its application.

Some owners and design professionals have ignored this critical design parameter in favor of an overriding concern with construction cost control. Construction cost is certainly a critical factor, but life-cycle cost is an increasingly important design consideration.

The following examples are well known in school design:

• Should the school use low-maintenance finishes or lower first-cost finishes, such as paint, that require regular maintenance?

▶ The ability of the project team to reduce cost is highest during the early phases, when plans and programs are easier to modify.

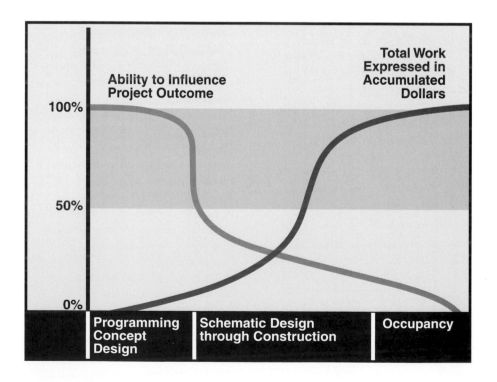

- Should the school install long-life light fixtures that have a higher first cost and bulb replacement cost in order to gain the benefits of the lower energy usage, reduced maintenance load, and lesser heat gain impact on the air-conditioning?
- Will a central mechanical system (vs. a decentralized system of package units) justify a higher first cost with lower replacement, energy, and other costs?
- Should the school use more expensive aluminum windows with a baked-on long-life finish or less expensive wood windows that require periodic painting?
- Should the school system build a new, more efficient building or renovate an inefficient older building?
- Will proposed energy conservation measures, such as new windows or added insulation, be justified by their lower operating costs?

In response to these questions, a systematic life-cycle analysis can help identify the most appropriate design solution. Most such questions can be analyzed relatively simply, but others require an analysis of several or all of the following factors:

- *Capital investment costs*—often called "first costs": cost of construction, furnishings, equipment, design fees, and other related items

- *Financing costs*—the costs of construction or long-term financing
- *Staff costs*—costs associated with operating and maintaining the facility
- *Building operating costs*—the cost of energy and other related expenses
- *Maintaining costs*—the cost of custodial care and repair, annual maintenance contracts, and salaries of maintenance personnel
- *Alteration costs*—the costs related to interim changes required because flexibility or additional capacity was not built in
- *Replacement costs*—the costs of replacing systems or building components that have a shorter life than other available choices

It is typical to create a spreadsheet that compares key choices, such as those listed earlier, over time. Costs that occur after the first year are discounted by the cost of money to the school system to take into account the fact that costs incurred in future years have less financial impact than costs in the first year.

Cost management has become a central issue on every school project, and increasingly complex. To be effective, a design team must be able to manage all aspects of this task.

CHAPTER 20
FINANCING

PUBLIC SCHOOL FINANCING

Most school building programs are financed with bond issues voted on by the residents of the school district. Private schools have to raise money from alumni and other private sources, special schools may be funded with state aid, and some others may draw upon still other sources; but the vast majority of programs that cannot be funded from the annual operating budget must go to public vote. Every year billions of dollars of school bond issues are on the ballot, and the majority pass. However, the failure of a bond issue, which is not uncommon, inevitably has serious negative consequences for the school district. This chapter outlines the basic issues involved in public financing of school construction, as well as the process used by many districts to gain the necessary public support for passage. A good source on the many steps—and legal issues—related to the public funding of school construction is *Planning and Financing School Improvement and Construction Projects*, published by the National Organization on Legal Problems of Education and the American Bar Association, Topeka (Bittle 1996), hereafter referred to as the NOLPE monograph. Some of the major points made in this monograph, as well as in other sources, are the following:

1. *Legal constraints.* There are a number of laws that govern the public financing of schools. Districts typically retain legal counsel to see that they stay within these laws. For example:

   • Any irregularity in the notices and procedures—such as an incomplete environmental assessment or an inaccurate public notice describing the purpose of the bond issue—can void a referendum.

   • A school district typically cannot do indirectly what cannot be done directly. As the NOLPE monograph (p. 7) notes, "A lease with an option to purchase was held [by the courts to be] beyond the authority granted by statute."

   • There are strict rules governing any interest earned on bond proceeds prior to their use to fund construction and equipment.

   • In some states, a school district cannot promote a "yes" vote; it can only provide information. In such cases it must rely on a citizens committee or other groups to be the advocates.

   • Most districts must operate within debt limits established by law.

2. *Determination of need.* As discussed throughout this book, the financing process should begin with a careful analysis of the district's needs as well as a detailed estimate of the probable costs. This estimate should include adequate contingencies to cover the expansion of scope inherent in the implementation phases that follow the bond issue.

3. *Financial feasibility.* The school district typically retains bond counsel and a financial consultant. The financial consultant will help determine the financial feasibility of a bond issue and will compile the financial data, projections, and related calculations needed to structure the bond issue. This consultant also develops the information that must be disclosed to potential purchasers of the bonds.

4. *Fees.* Part of the budgeting process should be a calculation of the various fees—for an architect, engineer, special consultant, bond counsel, financial consultant, investment banker, and so forth—that must be covered by the bond proceeds. Establishment of the design team fee has historically been guided by state or local fee schedules developed by the American Institute of Architects (AIA), the school district, or another entity. However, many of the school district schedules are too rigid to recognize the inherent differences between projects (see also "Educational Specifications, Programming, and Predesign" in chapter 3). Therefore, most experienced design teams calculate the time (and thus the cost) it will take to

▼ *The creation of the consensus needed for a successful bond issue is typically created with significant input from many groups.*

provide both the prebond services and the services following passage.

As noted in the NOLPE monograph referred to earlier: "Bond counsel will ordinarily work for a fixed or hourly fee for work during the planning and election process.... Financial consultants generally charge a fee at the time the bonds are issued. Bond counsel and financial consultant fees are generally based on the completion of the project, the complexity of the financing, and the amount of bonds to be issued" (p. 6).

5. *Managing a successful bond-issue referendum.* As typical bond-issue size and antitax sentiment have grown, most districts must carefully plan the campaign for a successful referendum. According to DLR Group Educational Facilities

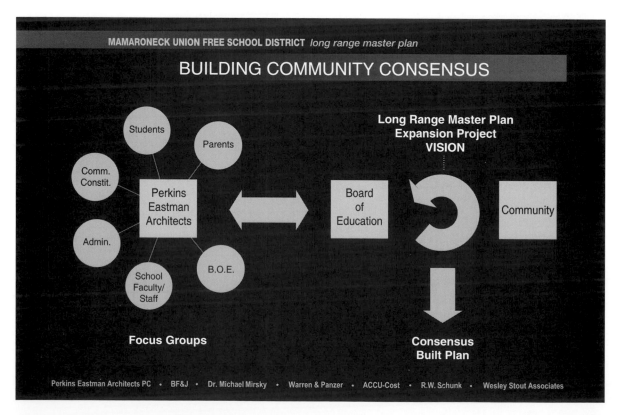

MAMARONECK UNION FREE SCHOOL DISTRICT *long range master plan*

BUILDING COMMUNITY CONSENSUS

Students

Parents

Comm. Constit.

Perkins Eastman Architects

Admin.

School Faculty/ Staff

B.O.E.

Board of Education

Community

Long Range Master Plan Expansion Project VISION

Focus Groups

Consensus Built Plan

Perkins Eastman Architects PC • BF&J • Dr. Michael Mirsky • Warren & Panzer • ACCU-Cost • R.W. Schunk • Wesley Stout Associates

Consultants, the basic precepts of a successful bond issue include the following:

- A unified school board
- A campaign that is citizen-led and staff supported
- Knowledge of what the community wants and expects from its facilities and curriculum
- A completed facilities study, clearly showing the need for improvements with all options studied and documented
- Informed district employees, who know the election issues and know how they can help
- A public relations plan that includes a free flow of information to the public about the need and costs associated with the improvements.
- A publicity plan that continually reminds the voters that the election is about educating students, who are the benefactors of the bond passage

DLR goes on to note, "It's extremely rare to ignore these tools and still win." Therefore, most districts do the required initial planning and then involve one or more citizens committees that include respected leaders in the community to help achieve a positive vote. It is not uncommon to have several committees working in a coordinated fashion toward this end.

Among the most common committees formed to analyze and promote a potential bond issue are the following:

- A steering committee to coordinate the several committees. This committee may also be responsible for obtaining endorsements from organizations within the district and for identifying and getting out the vote by probable "yes" voters.
- A facilities committee to help analyze and confirm the need and the options.
- A publicity committee to disperse accurate information about the need, the proposed solution, and the bond issue.
- Special subcommittees, such as a senior citizens committee, to deal with the special concerns of particular groups of potential voters. For example, senior citizens, who do not have children in the schools also tend to have a high voter turnout and are naturally concerned about the impact of the bond issue on their fixed incomes. They can often make or break a bond issue.

6. *Getting out the vote.* The final step is to get out the vote. The "no" voters are often more motivated, but it is usually apathy or confusion among the "yes" voters that dooms most unsuccessful bond issues. Thus, it is important not only to establish a strong prereferendum education and public relations effort but also to make sure an informed, supportive public goes to the polls and votes.

PRIVATE SCHOOL FINANCING

The financing of private schools must follow a process similar to that used in a well-planned public school bond referendum:

- *A clear definition of need*—The process should begin with a careful definition of the school's need.
- *Educating the school's constituency*— There must be a broad-based educational program for the school's consistency (primarily the alumni and families of the students).

- *The leaders must lead*—The school's leadership (the board, the head of the school, and the individuals responsible for fund-raising) must take the lead in the fund-raising effort.

- *Professional planning*—The fund-raising effort should be planned and coordinated by a professional, either an outside consultant or an experienced person on the school staff.

Along with following these steps, however, there are a number of recommendations that many professional fund-raisers believe should be observed in a capital campaign:

- *Analysis of fund-raising potential.* There should be a careful analysis of the real fund-raising potential of the school's consistency. Setting an unrealistically high target can doom a program before it starts. In addition, asking a potential donor for an unrealistically large amount makes refusal likely.

- *Advance pledges.* Many campaigns try to obtain pledges for a third or more of the target from key donors before the campaign officially starts. These initial donations give the campaign credibility and momentum.

- *Board support.* Unified support—including financial support—from the school's board is essential. Donors expect to see that the school's leadership is committed to the campaign.

- *Donor recognition and naming opportunities.* Many campaigns provide a list of naming opportunities to potential donors as a reward, recognition, and/or incentive for their gifts. The pricing of these opportunities—such as a name on the building or a room or other element within the building, such as a seat in an auditorium—should be carefully structured. In campaigns in which the naming opportunities are a major incentive, the most attractive items should be priced high enough to cover the elements no one wants to fund, such as roof replacement, asbestos abatement, or a new boiler.

- *Recognition of smaller donors.* Some schools have used creative ideas to attract smaller donors, with incentives such as brick pavers on which donors names are engraved, or computerized lists of donors that can be called up on a touch-screen monitor, among others.

- *Multiyear pledges.* Many campaigns receive gift pledges that are paid off over several years. If the pledges are in writing and creditworthy, they become security for interim financing that allows the project to proceed. (Private schools can also borrow if tuition or endowment income is sufficient to cover the debt service.)

- *Follow-up.* Proper follow-up with, and treatment of, donors—no matter how small their contributions—is important to maintain goodwill and the potential for future donations.

Virtually all schools find the prospect of raising the money necessary for a building program a daunting task. With careful planning and implementation, however, thousands of public and private school building programs are successfully funded each year.

BIBLIOGRAPHY AND REFERENCES

General

Agron, Joe. 1999. "25th Annual Construction Report." *American School and University,* May.

The American Architect. 1915. *Modern School Houses Part II: Illustrating and Describing Recent Examples of School House Design Executed in the United States.* New York: The American Architect.

Appleyard, Donald. 1969. "Why Buildings Are Known." *Environment and Behavior* 1 (no. 3):131–156.

———. 1970. "Styles and Methods of Structuring a City," *Environment and Behavior* 2 (no. 3):100–107.

Biehle, James T. "Renovate or Replace: Deciding the Fate of Your School." *E Architect.* Available on the Internet: http://www.e-architect.com/pia.cae.renovate_cae.asp

Bittle, Edgar H., ed. 1996. *Planning and Financing School Improvement and Construction Projects.* Topeka, Kan.: National Organization on Legal Problems of Education and American Bar Association.

Bliss, Lynne. 1996. "Six Keys to the Twenty-Second-Century High School." *School Planning and Management,* May. Available on the Internet: http://www.spmmag.com/articles/may_1996/article010.html

Bloom, Benjamin S. 1956. *Taxonomy of Educational Objectives Ltd.* New York: Longmans, Green and Co.

Brubacker, C. William. 1998. *Planning and Designing Schools.* New York: McGraw-Hill.

Chuang, Jeffrey. 1997. "Classroom Cacophony." *The Dallas Morning News,* June 30. Available on the Internet: http://www.dallasnews.com/

Conant, James B. 1959. *The American High School Today.* New York: McGraw-Hill.

Deasy, C. M. 1985. *Designing Places for People: A Handbook on Human Behavior for Architects, Designers and Facility Managers.* New York: Whitney Library of Design.

Dorn, Michael. 1998. "Make School Safety a Priority." *School Planning and Management,* October. Available on the Internet: http://www.spmmag.com/articles/1098_6.html

Dryden, Ken. 1995. *In School.* Toronto: McClellend & Stewart.

Edwards, Carolyn P., George Forman, and Lella Gandini. eds. 1993. *The Hundred Languages of Children: The Reggio Emilia Approach to Early Education.* Norwood, N.J.: Ablex.

Erb, Tom. 1996. "'School' No Longer Means What You Thought." *Middle School Journal* 27 (March).

Fickes, Michael. 1998. "The Security Factor in School Renovations." *School Planning and Management,* February. Available on the Internet: http://www.spmmag.com/articles/Feb_98/security.html

Gordon, Gary J., and James L. Nuckolls. 1995. *Interior Lighting for Designers.* 3rd ed. New York: John Wiley & Sons.

Graves, Ben E., and Clifford A. Pearson, eds. 1993. *Schools Ways: The Planning and Design of America's Schools.* New York: McGraw-Hill, Inc.

Jackson, Lisa. 1997. "Learning from Your Mistakes." *School Planning and Management,* October. Available of the Internet: http://www.spmmag.com/articles/may_1996/article010.html

———. 1998. "Right Sizing for Tikes." *School Planning and Management,* May. Available on the Internet: http://www.spmmag.com/articles/may_1998/tykes.html

Kerr, Stephen T. 1996. *Technology and the Future of Schooling.* Chicago: University of Chicago Press.

Kozol, Jonathan. 1991. *Savage Inequalities: Children in America's Schools.* New York: Crown.

Lackney, Jeffrey A. 1998. "Changing Patterns in Educational Facilities." *DesignShare Planning News.* Available on the Internet: http://www.designshare.com/

Lang, Jon. 1987. *Creating Architectural Theory: The Role of Behavioral Sciences in Design.* New York: Van Nostrand Reinhold.

Lawton, Millicent. 1999. "School Design Can Say a Lot About Teaching and Learning." *Harvard Education Letter,* January-February.

The Little Institute for School Facilities Research. 1997. *The School Technology Primer: A Non-Technical Guide to Understanding School Technology.* Wilkesboro, N.C.: The Little Institute for School Facilities Research.

Lynch, Kevin. 1960. *The Image of the City.* Cambridge: MIT Press.

McGuinness, William J., Benjamin Stein, and John S. Reynolds. 1980. *Mechanical and Electrical Equipment for Buildings.* 6th ed. New York: John Wiley & Sons.

McQuade, Walter, ed. *Schoolhouse.* 1958. New York: Simon Schuster.

Moore, Gary T. 1976. "The Development of Environmental Knowing: An overview of an Interactional-Constructivist Theory and Some Data on Within-Individual Development Variations." In *Psychology and the Built Environment,* ed. Davi Canter and Terrence Lee. London: Architectural Press.

National Middle School Association. Summary 3. "Number of Middle School Students."

———. Summary 8. "Grade 5 in Middle School."

National Organization on Legal Problems of Education. *Planning and Financing School Improvement and Construction Projects.*

"News: School Shooting." *Education Week* 18 (no. 33):17.

Nixon, Charles W. 1998. "Today's Schools, Tomorrow's Classrooms." *School Planning and Management,* November.

Packard, Robert T., and Stephen A. Kliment, eds. 1989. *Ramsey/Sleeper Architectural Graphic Standards: Student Edition Abridged from the Seventh Edition.* New York: John Wiley & Sons.

Perkins, Lawrence B. 1957. *Workplace for Learning.* New York: Reinhold.

Perkins, Lawrence B., and Walter D. Cocking. 1949. *Schools.* New York: Reinhold.

Porter, Jessica. 1995. "State-of-the-Art School Seeks to Take a Bite Out of Crime." *Education Week,* Sept. 6.

Powderly, H. Evan. *A User's Guide for the H.C. Crittenden Middle School.* Armonk, N.Y.

Salter, Charles M. 1998. *Acoustics: Architecture, Engineering, The Environment.* San Francisco: William Stout Publishers.

Seyffer, Charles. 1999. "Clearing the Air About IAQ." *School Planning and Management,* February. Available on the Internet: http://www.spmmag.com/articles/Feb99/articles0179.html

Shen, Fred. 1999. Personal interview conducted with principal of Shen Milsom & Wilke, Inc., New York, New York, consultants in telecommunications, acoustics and audiovisual systems.

Stein, Benjamin, and John S. Reynolds. 1992. *Mechanical and Electrical Equipment for Buildings.* 8th ed. New York: John Wiley & Sons.

———. 2000. *Mechanical and Electrical Equipment for Buildings.* 9th ed. New York: John Wiley & Sons.

Strickland, R. 1994. "Designing the New American School: Schools for an Urban Neighborhood." *Teachers College Record* 96:32-57.

Thompson, Thomas, and Ellen Sears. 1999. Personal interview conducted with principals of Thomas Thompson Lighting Design, New York, New York.

"Tools for Schools." 1998. *American School and University,* May.

Wood, George H. 1992. *Schools That Work.* New York: Dutton.

Standards and Codes

Americans with Disabilities Act Accessibility Guidelines for Buildings and Facilities. 1994. 59 Fed. Reg. 31,676.

American National Standards Institute. Published standards. www.ansi.org

American Society of Heating, Refrigerating, and Air-Conditioning Engineers. 1999. Published standards.

Barrier-free Design: Selected Federal Laws and ADA Accessibility Guidelines. New York: Eastern Paralyzed Veterans Association, 1996.

Building Officials and Code Administrators International Code. Published standards. www.bocai.org

Building Officials and Code Administrators International, Inc. *The BOCA National Building Code/1993.* Illinois: Building Officials and Code Administrators International, Inc, 1993.

Department of Justice. *Code of Federal Regulations: 28 CFR Part 36.* Department of Justice, July 1, 1994.

Federal Register 36 CFR Chapter XI. Architectural and Transportation Barriers Compliance Board: Petition for Rulemaking; Request for Information on Acoustics. Also available on the Internet: http://www.access-board.gov/rules/acoustic.htm

"Indoor Air Quality Rules." *American School and University,* May 1998.

National Association for the Education of Young Children. Published accreditation standards. Washington: NAEYC.

National Conference of States on Building Codes and Standards, Inc. *Directory of Building and Codes Regulations.* www.ncsbcs.org

New York State Education Department. *Directory of Building Codes and Regulations.*

U.S. Department of Education, Office of Civil Rights. *Compliance with the Americans with Disabilities Act: A Self-Evaluation Guide for Public Elementary and Secondary Schools.*

See also the state standards for, for example, California, Florida, and Virginia, which are available through the state departments of education at Sacramento, Tallahassee, and Richmond.

Websites

American Council on Education: http://www.accnet.edu/

The American Montessori Society (AMS): http://www.amshq.org

American Vocational Association: http://www/avaonline.org

Arc of the United States: http:/thearc.org/welcome.html

Association for Childhood Education International: http://www.udel.edu/bateman/acei/

CEFPI: http://www.cefpi.com/index.html

Council for American Private Education: http://www.capenet.org/

Council on Education Facility Planners International: http://www.cefpi.com/cefpi/index.html

Architectural Lighting Magazine: http://www.lightforum.com/links/index.html

Education Week Links: http://www.edweek.org./context/orgs

Energy Efficiency and Renewable Energy Network: http://www.eren.doe.gov/AB/

Energy Efficient Portable Classrooms for Florida: http://www.fsec.ucf.edu/~bdac/SSPROJECT/SSproj.htm

Environmental Design Collaborative: http://www.cstone.net/edc/index1.htm

ERIC: www.accesseric.org:81/sites/barak.html

Green Beat, Internet Links to Air Quality Resources: http://www.tec.org/greenbeat/may96/net.html

The Green Building Information Center: http://greenbuilding.ca/GBIC.htm

The Green Building Program Sustainable Building Sourcebook: http://www.greenbuilder.com/sourcebook/contents.html

"I Have a Dream" Foundation: http://www.ihad.org/

K-12 News Releases: www.solutions.ibm.com/k12/news/newsrelease.html

K-12 Weblinks: www.solutions.ibm.com/k12/weblink/links/html

K-12 School Resources (tech-based): www.merit.edu/k12.michigan/usf/res/resources.html

K-12 Web Sites of Interest: www.merit.edu/k12.michigan/hotlist/

Learning Disabilities Association of America: http://www.ldanatl.org/

Michigan State's Technology Plan: http://www.mde.state.mi.us/tplan/final.shtml

National Association for the Education of Young Children: naeyc@naeyc.org

National Association of Independent Schools: http://www.nais-schools.org

National Catholic Educational Association: http://www.ncea.org

National Center for Research in Vocational Education: http://nerve.berkeley.edu/

National Clearinghouse for Educational Facilities Search: www.edfacilities.org/cgi-bin/search.ogi

National Education Association: http://www.nea.org/

National Middle School Association: http://www.nmsa.org/

National School Boards Association: http://www.nsba.org/

National Renewable Energy Laboratory: http://www.nrel.gov

New American Schools: http://naschools.org/

North Central Regional Education Laboratory: http://www.nertec.org/

Northwest Educational Technology Consortium: http://www.netc.org/software/review_sources.html

Northwest Regional Educational Laboratory: http://www.nwrel.org/tech/

Periodicals Reading Room: http://lcweb.loc.gov/rr/news/pertile.html

Renewable Energy and Sustainable Energy Systems in Canada: http://www.newenergy.org/

School-Educational Sites: www.ecepl.usl.edu/thanks/school.htm

Solstice: http://solstice.crest.org/social/eerg/index.html

Sustainable: Architecture, Building, and Culture: http://www.sustainableabc.com

Technology & Learning: www.techlearning.com/resource.htm

10 Best Websites for Educational Technology: fromnowon.org/techtopten.html

Where to Find Reviews of Children's Software on the Internet: http://www2.childrenssoftware.com/childrenssoftware/links.html

INDEX

BUILDING TYPE BASICS FOR ELEMENTARY AND SECONDARY SCHOOLS:

1. Program (predesign)
What are the principal programming requirements (space types and areas)? How do you organize the client?
1–11, 13–15, 18–25, 28–32, 34, 36–41, 46–47, 51–52, 57–61, 73–74, 87, 93, 95, 109, 130, 139, 231–32

2. Circulation
What are the desirable primary and secondary spatial relationships?
36, 38–40, 63–65, 67–68, 75, 77, 79, 81–82, 105, 180, 194–96, 199

3. Unique design concerns
What special design determinants must be considered? Design process? Obsolescence? Security?
6, 7, 10, 13, 19, 28, 35–36, 52–56, 60–61, 69–71, 76, 79, 83, 92–96, 98–99, 123, 158, 161, 172–73, 186, 187–89, 196, 199

4. Site planning/parking/access
What considerations determine external access and parking?
15–16, 22, 27, 30, 38, 62–68, 82, 101–6, 112, 121, 193, 203

5. Codes/ADA
Which building codes and regulations apply, and what are the main applicable provisions? (Examples: egress; electrical; plumbing; ADA; seismic; asbestos and other hazards)
13, 29, 30, 34, 80, 107–12, 118, 123, 125, 137–38, 150, 165–66, 180, 190–92, 201, 204–5, 209

6. Energy/environmental challenges
What are the techniques to use in obtaining appropriate energy conservation and environmental sustainability?
11, 99, 113–22, 117–19, 121, 129, 151

7. Structure system
What are the appropriate structural systems to consider?
123–28, 203, 221–24

8. Mechanical systems
What are the appropriate systems for heating, ventilating, and air–conditioning (hvac) and plumbing? Vertical transportation? What factors affect preliminary selection? What are the space requirements?
113–15, 129–34, 130–33, 136, 165, 204, 213–15, 221–24

9. Electrical/communications
What are the appropriate systems for electrical, voice, and data communications? What considerations affect preliminary selection? What are the space requirements?
59, 96–98, 133, 137–42, 144, 146, 187, 204–16, 221–24